Reminiscences
of
Chief Warrant Officer Cecil S. King, Jr.
U.S. Navy (Retired)

Copyright © 1990
U.S. Naval Institute
Annapolis, Maryland

Preface

Most of the memoirs in the Naval Institute's oral history collection are from individuals who spent nearly all of their active naval careers as commissioned officers. Cecil King is an exception to that pattern, in that he was an enlisted man during most of his career. He is an intelligent, articulate man, thus able to describe the enlisted experience with the polish of one who eventually became an officer. He tells his story in a manner that reveals his patriotism and unabashed enthusiasm for the Navy. Cecil King and the U.S. Navy were a great match, each serving the other well. Throughout this memoir he displays a delightful sense of humor and a sunny outlook on life. It is a real pleasure to read.

King grew up in a series of small Texas towns and then enlisted in the Navy in 1934, shortly after graduation from high school. Following boot camp training at San Diego, he plunged enthusiastically into the life of a sailor, serving first on board the heavy cruiser <u>Portland</u> (CA-33). It was there that he began striking for yeoman and thus laid the foundation for his entire naval career. He advanced to chief petty officer in that rating and eventually became a warrant ship's clerk. King first put on the rating badge of a petty officer when he was serving at Fleet Air Base Coco Solo in Panama. He then served for a time in destroyers before volunteering for duty in the Asiatic Fleet in 1940.

Duty on the China station, as part of the flag allowance for the fleet staff, proved to be Cecil King's cup of tea. The romance and mystique of the Far East appealed greatly to him. In fact, he would gladly have stayed much longer, but the Japanese interrupted his idyllic life style. In late December 1941, following the onset of World War II, he managed to escape from the Philippines on board the four-stack destroyer Peary (DD-226). He had a number of near brushes with death. The man next to him on the bridge of the ship was killed during an airplane attack. After the Peary got to the Dutch East Indies, King was evacuated to Australia for a time before returning to duty with the fleet.

Before the war, King had long had the feeling that the Japanese would be no match for the powerful U.S. Fleet. The fall of the Philippines robbed him of those illusions. When he joined the crew of the carrier Hornet (CV-12), flagship of Rear Admiral Jocko Clark, his faith in the power of the U.S. Navy was restored. King was on board for the Battle of the Philippine Sea and other actions during the Central Pacific campaign. That duty was one of a number of billets King had in connection with naval aviation. At war's end he was in the commissioning crew of the new carrier _Princeton_ (CV-37) and later served on the staff of Commander Air Force Pacific Fleet and Chief of Naval Air Training. In the 1950s, as a warrant officer, he was in the crew of the carriers _Midway_ (CVB-41) and _Franklin D. Roosevelt_ (CVA-42).

A tribute to King's talents and his sense of loyalty to the Navy was the fact that he served in the front office of three successive Chiefs of Naval Operations in the 1950s: Admiral William M. Fechteler, Admiral Robert B. Carney, and Admiral Arleigh Burke. He provides insight into the operating style of each, particularly that of Burke. Every other day, King had to work from early in the morning until late at night to keep up with the requirements of the workaholic Burke. During the in-between days, when King had a normal working schedule, he spent his evenings selling cookware in order to support his family. Such was the lot of a Navy warrant officer trying to make ends meet while living in the Washington, D.C., area in the 1950s.

Parting from the Navy was not an easy thing to do, but King reluctantly made the break in 1957 so he could take care of his family adequately. He wound up with a second career serving as the assistant to two successive chairmen of the Atomic Energy Commission, John McCone and Glenn Seaborg. He has since done a good deal of volunteer work, particularly on behalf of the American Cancer Society. He is a past chairman of the board of the Virginia Division and was recently elected to the national board of the American Cancer Society.

Joanne Patmore of the oral history staff transcribed the interview tapes for this memoir and incorporated into the text the various corrections made on the way to the final version. Because of the inevitable vagaries of oral speech, both King and I did some editing of the transcript in the interests of smoothness, accuracy, and clarity. He has given his blessing to this final version. A copy of the original raw transcript is on file at the Naval Institute.

                                        Paul Stillwell
                                        Director of Oral History
                                        U. S. Naval Institute
                                        September 1990

CHIEF WARRANT OFFICER CECIL ST. CLAIR KING, JR.
U.S. NAVY (RETIRED)

Personal Data

Born:	11 May 1917, Alice (Jim Wells County), Texas
Parents:	Cecil St. Clair King and Ethel Jones King
Married:	1939 to Catherine Jackman; divorced 1943
	1945 to Emily Westall
Children:	Cecil St. Clair King III (23 July 1946)
	William Henry Howard King (23 July 1948)
Education:	Aransas Pass High School, Aransas Pass, Texas 1930-1934

Dates of Rank

Seaman 2/c through Yeoman 1/c	1934-1942
Chief Yeoman	1942-1950
CWO (W-1 through W-2), Ship's Clerk, and CWO	1950-1957

Decorations and Medals

Navy Presidential Unit Citation (USS Hornet [CV-12])
Army Distinguished Unit Badge (Philippines 1941)
Good Conduct Medal (2 bronze stars)
China Service Medal
American Defense (1 bronze star, Sea Clasp)
Asiatic-Pacific Theatre (1 silver, 2 bronze stars)
American Theatre
World War II Victory
Philippine Defense -1941 (1 bronze star)

Chronological Transcript of Service

17 July 1934	Enlisted
July 1934-October 1934	Naval Training Station, San Diego, California
November 1934-November 1935	USS Portland (CA-33) deck division
November 1935-April 1938	C.A. yeoman striker Fleet Air Base, Coco Solo
May 1938-June 1938	Discharge and reenlistment
July 1938-November 1938	Precommissioning detail, USS Davis (DD-395)
November 1938-March 1940	Log room, ship's office USS Davis (DD-395)
March 1940-May 1940	USS Warrington (DD-383)
May 1940-July 1940	USS Chaumont (AP-5), en route to China
July 1940-November 1940	Staff operations yeoman, USS Augusta (CA-31)
November 1940-October 1941	Staff operations yeoman USS Houston (CA-30)
October 1941-25 December 1941	Flag allowance based ashore in Marsman Building, Manila, Philippines
27 December 1941-11 January 1942	Passage from Corregidor to Port Darwin, Australia aboard USS Peary (DD-226)
11 January 1942-16 January 1942	Communications duties aboard USS Langley (AV-3) and AlusNob Port Darwin
16 January 1942-19 January 1942	Passage from Port Darwin to Surabaya, Java, aboard USS Boise (CL-47)
19 January 1942-27 February 1942	Operations and communications duties, shore based in Surabaya and Tjilatjap, Java
27 February 1942-3 March 1942	Classified publications courier, Tjilatjap, Java, to Freemantle, Australia, aboard USS Sturgeon (SS-187)

March 1942-April 1942	Communication duties ComSoWesPac, Perth, Australia
April 1942-April 1942	Chief yeoman in charge of issuing office, RP90 in Melbourne, Australia
April 1943-June 1943	En route to United States. Leave and assignment to new construction
June 1943-September 1943	Captain's office in R/S Tacoma, Washington. Precommissioning detail, USS Carnegie (CVE)
September 1943-October 1944	Executive officer's office aboard USS Hornet (CV-12)
October 1944-December 1944	En route to United States. Leave and reassignment
December 1944-March 1945	Captain's writer stationed at Minneapolis Naval Air Station
March 1945	Requested sea duty. Assigned by BuPers to precommissioning detail, USS Princeton (CV-37)
April 1945-August 1946	Captain's writer, USS Princeton (CV-37)
August 1946-February 1948	Chief in charge, central flag office, Commander Air Force, US Pacific Fleet
March 1948-October 1948	Admiral's writer, ComNavAnTra, Jacksonville, Florida
November 1948-March 1948	Admiral's writer, ComNavAnTra, Corpus Christi, Texas
March 1949-1 August 1950	Flag detail CNaTra, Pensacola, Florida
15 August 1950-July 1952	Personnel officer, appointed WO (W-1) aboard USS Midway (CVB-41)

August 1952-February 1956	Administrative assistant to Chiefs of Naval Operations (Admirals Fechteler, Carney, and Burke)
February 1956-August 1957	Personnel officer aboard USS <u>Franklin Delano Roosevelt</u> (CVB-43)
1 September 1957	Retired as Chief Warrant Officer (W-2)

Civilian Employment

4 September 1957-January 1958	GS-9 (Research Analyst) Office of the Secretariat, Atomic Energy Commission (AEC)
February 1958-January 1960	Special Services assistant to AEC Chairman John A. McCone
January 1960-June 1965	Special Services assistant to AEC Chairman Glenn T. Seaborg
June 1965-January 1972	Assistant to the AEC assistant general manager
March 1972	Retired from government service
1972-1987	Management consultant

Civic Service

1974-present	Member, Virginia State Board of the American Cancer Society (ACS)
1984-1986	Chairman of the Virginia State Board of the ACS
1990-	Member, National Board of the ACS

Authorization

The U. S. Naval Institute is hereby authorized to make available to individuals, libraries, and other repositories of its choosing the transcripts of four oral history interviews concerning the life and career of the undersigned. The interviews were recorded on 28 July 1986, 4 August 1986, 11 August 1986, and 23 October 1989 in collaboration with Paul Stillwell for the U.S. Naval Institute.

The undersigned does hereby release and assign to the U.S. Naval Institute all right, title, restrictions, and interest in the interviews. The copyright in both the oral and transcribed versions shall be the sole property of the U.S. Naval Institute. The tape recordings of the interviews are and will remain the property of the U.S. Naval Institute.

Signed and sealed this 27TH day of JULY 1990.

Chief Ship's Clerk Cecil S. King, USN (Ret.)

C. S. King #1 - 1

Interview Number 1 with Chief Warrant Officer
    Cecil S. King, Jr., U.S. Navy (Retired)

Place: U.S. Naval Institute, Annapolis, Maryland

Date: Monday, 28 July 1986

Interviewer: Paul Stillwell

Q: Mr. King, to start at the beginning, could you tell something about your boyhood, your parents, and your immediate family back in Texas?

Mr. King: Okay. My father was a railroad man, as the saying goes, and we moved about every 18 months all during my childhood--mother, father, and four boys. The four sons all wound up in the Navy. It was essentially a very happy childhood. I don't have any negative memories at all of my childhood. The Depression days, when I was going to high school, were a little lean, but we had enough money. My dad made about $100.00 a month, and in those days my mother took in boarders, schoolteachers mostly. So we had enough.

Q: How big a town did you live in?

Mr. King: Well, we lived in a series of small towns. I was born in Alice, Texas, in Jim Wells County, and lived there, I suppose, seven or eight years. Then we moved to a little town named Alanreed, a town named Bloomington, and then Wichita Falls. We then went back to Alice for a little while and then to the Rio Grande Valley. We lived in Mercedes and Mission and La Feria. Then my dad changed jobs. By that time he was working for the Humble Oil Company as a telegraph operator, the same job he had with the railroad. We lived in a little town named Whitsett, which is nonexistent now. It just sort of died. It was a very small town--one store. We lived there for a year and a half or so; it was a great place for a kid. I used to spend all my time with a .22 rifle out wandering around the mesquite thickets. I have a lot of happy memories of Whitsett.

One thing that happened at Whitsett had nothing to do with the Navy but had a tremendous impact on me. A young boy, a friend of mine named Daniel Caldwell, and I were going hunting one day. Daniel had a .22 pump, while I had a .22 single shot. We were walking down this little dusty Texas road, and a car went by. We had swapped guns because Daniel's pump was heavier. I was carrying his, and he was carrying mine. As this car went by, he said, "I think I'll hit his license plate." So he pulled up my gun and just snapped it.

I said, "Okay, I will too." I pulled up my gun and fired and hit the back of this old black Model T Ford with a man and his wife in it. The bullet hit the trunk, and I saw this blossom where it hit. I guess up till that time, that was probably the blackest moment of my life. I was really terribly upset. He stopped and came back, and he was so mad he could hardly talk. "Where do you live?"

I just pointed to our house, which was up on a hill there. So he turned around and headed for my house. I ran up the hill, and I got there before he did. I really couldn't talk. I was just making noises. I had video but no audio, and I was trying to tell my mother that I had shot this man's car. She said, "Go on upstairs."

I went upstairs, and pretty soon I saw him drive up. My mother went out, and an animated conversation took place for the longest time. My mother was great; she knew how to communicate, and she let him go on and on. He finally left. I think she told him that she would certainly take care of the discipline problems at my end. She came upstairs, and I was still in a state of complete panic, because I was thinking about what if I'd aimed for him or aimed for her. I had nightmares over that for the longest time. She sensed that my feeling was such that further punishment was not needed.

But, anyway, then from Whitsett we moved to Aransas Pass, which was as near a hometown as I have. We got there in 1930 when I was in the eighth grade. Spent four years there. Beautiful--was just a great period in my life. It was a little Texas Gulf town. We spent most of our time either on the water or around the water or in the water.

C. S. King #1 - 4

Q: Was it disruptive to your education to do all this moving around?

Mr. King: I don't recall that it was. I could pick up pretty quick, and I made friends fast. I have since read about the trauma associated with moving from town to town for children. I don't know whether I got used to it, or whether it just didn't bother me. But I didn't have any trauma; you just roll with the punches, so to speak. I was not a terribly dedicated student, not at all. I got along. That was about the best you can say.

Q: How did you measure up to your peers once you got into the Navy?

Mr. King: I always had a high IQ and for years now have belonged to Mensa.* In boot camp, or in preliminary screening, my grades were fairly high. I always got along very well with my peers.

Q: I was just wondering in terms of education, though.

Mr. King: Well, you know, in education, in Texas I always felt a high school education was equivalent of a bachelor's

---
*Mensa is an organization comprised of particularly intelligent individuals.

degree now, because it was a pretty tough curriculum in high school, as I recall. As a matter of fact, I got a dummy diploma when I graduated and had to go back to summer school and get my diploma because I flunked trigonometry, I guess it was, or algebra. Anyway, I had to go back and make that up.

But I got along, I'd say, average or a little better. I wasn't a very motivated student. I was more interested in horsing around and that sort of thing, so I just studied enough to get by. That's about the size of it.

Q: How close were you to your brothers during those growing-up years?

Mr. King: Very close. I was the oldest. I did a lot of babysitting for my mother and dad when I got old enough to take care of the other three. I mean, they just felt free to go and leave me in charge. Our ages were not that far apart. There was my brother Bobby, who's dead now, about a year and a half, two years younger, something like that; and then from Bobby to Howard was about a year, a year and a half again; and from Howard to Jimmy was maybe three or four years, something like that. So the four of us were very close-knit growing up. We used to get along very well together and were with each other a lot. Howard died since

C. S. King #1 - 6

we started this book. He had lung cancer--same as Bobby and my dad. Jimmy and I quit smoking years ago.

My mother told me later that when the war started, Dad went over to the Navy recruiting office at Corpus Christi to enlist. I guess the recruiter was being kind, and he told my dad he could not get in because he had false teeth, upper and lower. Dad came home fuming and told Mother he protested to the recruiter and said, "What I had in mind was shooting Japs, not biting them."

Q: Why all the moving around? Was this from your father's jobs?

Mr. King: Yes, he was transferred on the railroad every couple of years. That was sort of expected in those days. And then the same thing with the pipeline. I think my dad probably contributed to that. I guess the grass was always greener to him. In addition to working for the pipeline and the railroad, he was always into projects. He was going to make a fortune doing this, that, and the other thing. He raised tomatoes in Aransas Pass and lost his shirt, and raised chickens in Alice and lost his shirt. He silvered mirrors at one time. He always had these things going that he was going to make a pile, but he never did.

Q: At least you didn't feel the effects of the Depression

as some people did.

Mr. King: Oh, no. My dad was a great guy. During the Depression, we really were at rock bottom financially, but every time I asked him for a quarter, he gave me a half a dollar. If I asked him for a half, he'd give me a dollar. The guy was really great in a low-key way--very undemonstrative. But he was a very generous, good-hearted man--terribly proud of his four sons in the Navy.

Q: How much awareness did you have of the Navy during those years in Texas?

Mr. King: Very little. Well, now I always had a kind of an affinity for salt water. I spent a lot of time in and around the water in Aransas Pass, working on shrimp boats in the summertime and that kind of thing. Had a series of small boats and skiffs. When my class graduated in 1934, we received a form letter from the naval recruiter over at Corpus Christi. That just put it all together for me. I thought, "This is it; I'm going to have to do this." There was no hope of my going to college, none whatsoever. There was no work in Aransas Pass; there were no jobs to speak of. It was really a hard, grinding economic time in a small town. I mean, it wasn't a hardship, but I was pragmatic enough to know that there was nothing for me in

C. S. King #1 - 8

Aransas Pass, nor would there be.

So when I got that letter, I think I hitchhiked over to Corpus the very next day. There was a waiting list, they told us at that time, of several months. I did this on my own; I didn't consult with my folks. I just thought it was a good thing to do. That was in May, when I graduated, or June, something like that. Anyway, I was told it would be several months, but my number came up very quickly, in July.

Q: I thought you had the summer school you had to go to.

Mr. King: It was a short course. I got that finished up before my number came up. As a matter of fact, I guess they made some adjustments so I could join the Navy. But they did send my diploma to my mother, and I finally wound up with it.

Q: That speaks well for you, because the Navy was very selective during that time, because it was a small force.

Mr. King: It was, and I was terribly surprised that my number came up. But, again, I did pretty well on the test, and was a high school graduate. It wasn't a rarity, but I think high school graduates had a certain amount of prestige in that part of Texas in those days.

Q: How accurate a picture of the Navy did the recruiter give you?

Mr. King: The main point that he made in the letter was the security--that I could do 20 years and come out with $62.00 a month, or something like that. I never dreamed of such wealth in such a short period. I thought, "Twenty years! I'll be 37 years old and will have 60-some-odd dollars a month." That was enough to get along on in those days. I told my dad, and he almost fell out of his chair. He said, "Great goodness alive, 37 years old and you can retire." He was all for it. Also, I had somewhat of a patriotic--if that's the right word--term of mind. I think most kids were in those days. So there was something about serving my country that appealed to me. I liked that aspect of it. I liked the security, and it all came together; this is what I wanted to do.

Q: Were they selling the adventure and "see the world" aspect of it?

Mr. King: I think there was certain flavor of travel, see the world and that sort of thing. But this was 1934, and war was not even thought of. It was just mainly, "Join the Navy and see the world."

C. S. King #1 - 10

Q: Also, there wasn't the sense that came along later, that every person had a military obligation to fulfill.

Mr. King: No, there was nothing like that. I just wanted to join the Navy and see the world. It seemed to me the greatest opportunity that I ever had.

Q: Could you describe the beginning of this great adventure?

Mr. King: Well, I remember taking all my exams in Corpus Christi, which was a substation; Houston was the main station. The chief petty officer, the recruiter there--I just kind of felt a certain rapport with him and he with me. Whether or not that was just to get me in, I don't know. He was a great guy. I liked him very much. I remember I took my physical there at Corpus. I guess they had a pharmacist's mate. I had no marks or scars. That was unusual, because he said, "Marks or scars, don't you have any?" And I didn't have a mark or scar anywhere on me at that time. Just a bit of trivia.

But when the day came--my mother was not sold on this at all--the bird leaving the nest and all. However, she went along with it, so I went to Houston. We took a train to Houston, showing up with a draft of 30 or 40 kids. We were sworn in in Houston, signed our shipping articles, and then we were put on a train to go to San Diego.

They put one kid in charge of all of us, and the reason he was in charge was because he had been in the National Guard at one time. So he was our draft commander. We gave him a lot of respect. I thought that was really something, that the guy was in charge of all us troops. But we just had a good time on the train. I'd never been away from home before in my whole life, never been far at all from wherever we lived.

Q: Did that cause you to make any adjustments? Did you have the inevitable homesickness feelings at the outset?

Mr. King: No, I didn't. I did a little bit when I got to boot camp at San Diego. This was a Texas draft, and we got a lot of hooting and, you know, this thing about Texas. We took a lot of kidding when we checked in at boot camp. I failed my preliminary physical because my pulse was high. I guess I was excited; there were several of us, RPB--rapid pulse beat or something like that. They put us off to one side. I was scared to death that I wouldn't pass. But I settled down after a while, and my pulse was normal. And so we went through the line to get our clothes and gear. It was just a great, brand-new, wonderful world to me. I enjoyed every second of it.

I had a few pangs of homesickness after several days, when it finally dawned on me that I was away from home. It had some impact on me, but it was transient. I was so wrapped up in being in the Navy and it was great. I mean, I just loved everything about it.

Q: Could you describe the life in the barracks there in San Diego?

Mr. King: Yes. This was 1934, and I was in Company 34-23. Our company commander was a chief torpedoman named Adams. We slept in hammocks that were, oh, six feet or so above the concrete deck. There was a certain amount of trepidation in climbing up and getting to a hammock over a concrete deck. The Navy was a little cavalier about our well-being. But I detected no note of sympathy or concern about falling out of our hammocks. I mean, you just didn't fall out of your hammock.

Q: Or if you did, you suffered the consequences.

Mr. King: If you did, you suffered the consequences. And I remember about getting in the hammocks. That was kind of an adventure, but once you got the hang of it, it was fine. We trained and were out on the grinder--drill field--every day. We were unconscious the minute our heads hit the pillow at night.

Q: Why were they so high off the deck?

Mr. King: I don't know why that was. I told lots of stories about them when I got home. I mentioned about the perils of my hammock. But I don't know that it was really a physical danger. I remember that height off that concrete floor. But we got used to it fast, very fast.

Q: How did you take to the drilling and the discipline part of it?

Mr. King: Oh, I liked it. We were on the grinder every morning at 8:00 o'clock. We wore leggings, whites, and neckerchiefs. Tucked in our leggings we had little semaphore flags. We would drill with semaphore flags, through the alphabet and everything. The little Navy white hats that we wore were no protection from the California sun. We had some severe cases of sunburn. Some kids got burnt just terribly bad. I was not at the time impressed in a negative way about the Navy, but I remember the terrible cases of kids burnt to a crisp. But we stayed out on the grinder, and the sunburn eventually cleared up.

I got the impression that the Navy was a no-nonsense organization, and I'd better get along in it. It was up to me. I wasn't going to get any free rides.

Q: And you weren't offered the opportunity to ask why things were done the way they were.

Mr. King: None of us dared ask why. I wouldn't have asked why for a million dollars. I mean [laughter], I did what I was told.

Q: Did you feel a sense of intimidation by the way things were done?

Mr. King: Well, the sudden entry into military existence-- there was not any trauma connected to it, but I was so wrapped up in that transition that it never occurred to me to question anything. I just did exactly what I was told, the minute I was told to do it.

There were a couple of kids that did get in trouble because of various minor infractions. That made an impression on me. That wasn't going to happen to me.

But it was kind of a grinding routine, a rough routine. We had field day every Friday; we got up at 4:00 o'clock. We scrubbed our hammocks. We didn't have liberty for the first three weeks. First three weeks was detention--to see if we had any communicable diseases, I suppose. After that we had weekend liberty, just had to be back in by midnight.

Q: What sorts of places would you go, and what would you do on liberty?

Mr. King: Well, most of us would just go around wide-eyed at San Diego and California. It was a brand-new world to us. They had a YMCA there. I didn't hang out in the YMCA, but usually you would just go there, just because that was the kind of place where you spent a few minutes before you decided where to go in town--to go here or go there. We were strictly on our own. Oh, I drank a little beer and smoke-stacked when I got back. Smoke-stacking's when you act like you had more beer than you really had. I wanted to be a real salty sailor.

Q: Did you go any of those places along Broadway there that particularly catered to sailors?

Mr. King: Oh, yes. One was called the Pot O' Gold, where they had a 26-ounce mug of beer for ten cents.

San Diego was a 100% Navy town. It was oriented towards the Navy, so I really felt completely at home in San Diego. I enjoyed being in that atmosphere with sailors everywhere; there were no civilian clothes in those days.

C. S. King #1 - 16

Q: How were you treated by civilians?

Mr. King: Well, the kind of places I went, where civilians were, was very fine: cafes, dance halls, and that sort of thing. I didn't notice any negative feeling. We heard stories in those days about Norfolk.

Q: Yes.

Mr. King: We were told, "Boy, don't ever go to Norfolk. They have 'Dogs and sailors, keep off the grass' signs." I don't know how true that was. I liked San Diego very much. It was just an immersion in Navy atmosphere, and I just immersed myself and enjoyed it.

Q: Meet any girls there on liberty?

Mr. King: Well, not any serious affairs. You know, there were a lot of dance halls, and in the 1930s a dance hall was not a bad place to go. It was really the place to go. Music was big in those days--the big band sort of thing and I liked dancing. I liked the popular music, and I danced a lot. I don't remember any one particular girl; I didn't have any serious affairs of the heart there. As a matter of fact, none of my peers, none of us--oh, one or two guys would come back and tell these tremendous stories about how they met this girl with a Cadillac, and she had a white bearskin rug, or something like that. But we didn't really believe it.

Q: That's another version of smoke-stacking.

Mr. King: Yes. [Laughter] No, again, I just have pleasant memories of boot camp, and also, I sensed the maturing process in myself. I could feel that going on, and I thought that was good too.

I didn't write home, I was so busy being a sailor. My mother wrote to the chaplain. I was hauled up before the chaplain--which scared the bejesus out of me, because he was a commander. So I went up to see him, and he wanted to know why I hadn't written home. I didn't have any good reason. So he had me sit down in his office and write a letter home, that he mailed. He told me I'd better write home, which I did then. I wrote fairly often.

I made an allotment out to my folks of $10.00 a month. Our pay was $19.75 a month, because that was still during the pay cut era, 5% pay cut. Twenty-one dollars a month less 5% made it $19.75, which left me $9.75, which was the riches of Croesus. I was rich beyond my wildest dreams.

Q: Some of these merchants were sort of unscrupulous. They would get people involved in time-payment plans and

C. S. King #1 - 18

what have you.

Mr. King: Oh, yes, they had jewelry stores and tailor shops. They would stand out on the sidewalk and pull you right in. Now that you mention it, I recall that very vividly. A lot of my friends bought wristwatches and things like that on time payment.

Q: They were still doing that when I was there 30 years later.

Mr. King: I think that's probably the routine, and our economic life at home had been such that I was scared to death of being in debt. So I just steered clear of any kind of credit arrangement. I smoked; I started smoking when I was 13, 14 years old, so I felt as long as I had enough money for cigarettes and a dollar or two for liberty from time to time, that was all I asked out of life.

Q: Was Chief Adams a fatherly type?

Mr. King: Kind of a fatherly type. He was a no-nonsense guy, as they all were. And I recall, also, in barracks conversation at night, how we would say about these chiefs, "You know, those guys, they're 38, they're 40 years old. They're really old." I couldn't imagine a guy that old that had been in the Navy that long. They just seemed like old, wrinkled men to me. I remember this tremendous impact--how old these fellows were.

I remember we had a picture taken in boot camp, and we all lined up. It was one of these cameras where you turn it on, and it takes the whole company.

Q: Panoramic.

Mr. King: Panoramic camera, and Chief Adams stood at one end of the line. Then when the camera started, he ran around to the other end and got in line again. That was so out of character for him--to do something like that. That made quite an impact on me, to realize that he was a human being and had a sense of humor.

Q: What sort of curriculum was there as far as class work?

Mr. King: Very little formal. I think we were issued an A to N manual. But I recall very little of that kind of curriculum; it was mostly the grinder. We spent an awful lot of time on the grinder. There were some practical things. We had whaleboats, we had boat drill, and so on. It was mostly the practical aspects; there was very little academic work.

C. S. King #1 - 20

Q: Did you get introduced to <u>The Bluejackets' Manual</u>?*

Mr. King: Yes, although I think we weren't issued one. That was something that you had to buy. We were issued an A to N book, and we were aware of the virtues of <u>The Bluejackets' Manual</u>. I think I probably bought one.

Q: Was there a great emphasis on uniforms and personal appearance?

Mr. King: Great emphasis on uniforms and personal appearance. Haircut inspection much more often than it was needed, just for the effect. Bag inspection with clothes stops and all. Every day we had bag inspection--lay our bags out, roll our clothes up, and tie them up with clothes stops. We got quite a heavy dose of that.

Q: Were there lectures on health and VD in particular?

Mr. King: I don't recall any. Well, there were lectures on health, but I don't recall anything on VD. I just think that was something that they didn't expect us to get involved in. Most of us, at our age, were not really prime candidates. There was just not much said about it. I

---

*<u>The Bluejackets' Manual</u>, which has been published in 20 editions since the beginning of the century, is a basic handbook for Navy enlisted men.

C. S. King #1 - 21

mean, I was aware of the fact that there was such a thing as venereal disease, but in my part of Texas it was just something you didn't do and you didn't think about. It was just, I suppose, in the same category as leprosy or some terrible disease. You didn't fool around with that kind of thing.

Q: Did you get to visit any ships?

Mr. King: No, they didn't take us aboard any ships. My company graduated. We went in July and got out in October. We got an extra few days off of our boot leave for Navy Day--October, whenever it was.

Q: Twenty-seventh.

Mr. King: Yes, we had a few extra days off, and that was communicated to us early on. So about the last half of boot camp, we were thinking about going home and showing off our uniforms, that sort of stuff--great anticipation for going home on leave.

So my boot camp passed very quickly, and it was great. I just enjoyed it. When I did get home--I went home on a train--I felt like I was about nine feet tall. My dad was very proud of me, and my mother cried a lot. She thought I'd gotten too old, too quick. I was anxious to get back.

I wanted to get back and go to sea duty. We were allowed, in boot camp, to indicate our preference, but we really didn't know what we were asking for. Some kids asked for battleships, because they were big. But most of our education about that was just word of mouth at night. We talked about, "What're you going to get on?"

"I'm going to get on a heavy cruiser."

"How about you?"

"I'm going to get on a light cruiser."

We didn't know what a heavy cruiser or light cruiser was. I decided in favor of a heavy cruiser, because it sounded kind of glamorous to me. You know, kids would say, "Well, a heavy cruiser's not as big as a battleship, but it's bigger than a destroyer."

I didn't know what a battleship or a destroyer was, so I put in for a heavy cruiser. When we got back to San Diego, we were put at the naval base there. I think there was a ship called the _Rigel_.

Q: She was a destroyer tender and, I think, sort of a station ship.

Mr. King: Yes, on the _Rigel_. And then as we were gradually sorted out from battleships, to cruisers, to destroyers, to whatever, then the heavy cruiser bunch--I guess a couple hundred of us. Because there were several companies involved. We all were up for transfer at the same time, maybe 150, something like that. We all went aboard the USS Relief, a hospital ship, in San Diego and then went to Long Beach, where the fleet was. There was an aviator who'd been killed who was in the morgue on the Rigel, and we lined up to see that. I mean, that was such a momentous thing to us: "There's a dead aviator in the morgue."

"Really?"

"You can see him if you go down this deck there and look through the porthole."

So we lined up, and we went down this deck and looked through the porthole. There was this body on the slab and, I don't know, but I just thought, "My God, there is this dead aviator." That was a tremendous experience to me.

Q: It's interesting the things that stick in your mind.

Mr. King: Yes, and, apparently, the plane crash had broken up a lot of his bones. His body had sort of flattened out; it was just about that flat.

Q: Three or four inches.

Mr. King: Yes, and there was a pharmacist's mate in there on guard there with him. He would look up at us with a blasé look on his face. But I had dreams about that for a couple of days, about this body on the slab. That was my first experience with the real life in the Navy.

We went to Long Beach. The USS Houston was the cruiser flagship, and also the Houston was the ship that President Roosevelt was very fond of.* It had quite a name in the Navy, the USS Houston. I'd always thought it'd be kind of nice to be on the Houston, because I was from Texas. So we went aboard the Houston at night, and they lined us all up in the mess hall. The fleet athletic officer came around, and there were three or four officers that just looked at us as though we were cattle. I mean, they were looking for big fellows, because fleet athletics were big in those days--the fleet rowing teams, fleet boxing, fleet this, and fleet that. Houston had quite a name as having a lot of good athletic teams. So these officers just lined us all up: "You're on the Houston. You're on the Houston"--anybody over six feet, or that had any athletic ability.

Q: How big were you at that time?

Mr. King: Oh, I was small; I was, I guess, five-eight or five-nine, something like that. I was skinny. But this annoyed me. I felt discriminated against. It made me mad.

---
*Franklin D. Roosevelt was President of the United States from 1933 to 1945.

So then after they picked all the big jocks for the Houston, then they said, "Now who wants to be on the Houston?" They had that kind of latitude. So a lot of guys stepped out from Texas.

But I thought, "I'll be damned if I will. By God, I don't care what I get. I'm not going to be on that Houston."

So I sat back, and then they just divided up all these cruisers: the Chester, the Indianapolis, and the Portland, for instance. They each had 10 or 12, and they were alphabetical. They got to the K's, and the K's were the Portland. That's how I got the Portland. I was pleased about that. I thought, "That's great. That's the luck of the draw." So I went aboard the Portland.

Q: She was a fairly new ship at that time.

Mr. King: Yes, she and the Indianapolis were near-sister ships.* They were beautiful ships to me. They had that flared bow. The Indianapolis had two even stacks, and the Portland had a stack and a half. I thought that looked kind of rakish. I thought, "Boy, that's a good-looking ship."

---

*The USS Portland (CA-33) was commissioned in February 1933 and the USS Indianapolis (CA-35) in November 1932. Each was 610 feet long, had a beam of 66 feet, and had a main battery of nine 8-inch guns. Standard displacements: Portland, 9,950 tons; Indianapolis, 9,800 tons.

Q: They had that thing up over the bridge, too, kind of a hood.

Mr. King: Flared. Yes, I thought that was great. I really thought that the <u>Portland</u> was beautiful. When I got on there, I thought, "Now, it kind of worked out. I got the best ship in the Navy."

We went aboard the <u>Portland</u> and, again, it was a kind of a hit-or-miss thing about assignment. The chief engineer came up and tried to make a pitch to some of these kids about, "You want to be in the black gang, down below deck, no weather and wear dungarees," and this great stuff. Then the gunnery officer said, "Now think about the deck force. You're up there. You get a battle station; you get a gun; you're up on topside and see what's going on." So I chose the deck force. I thought that would be good, and I got the fourth division, had the boat deck--had 5-inch deck guns.

When you first went aboard a ship in those days as a seaman in the deck division, it was a strict pecking order. I had a leading seaman in charge of my group; he might as well have been an admiral. I really thought he was great. It was a good routine. We had the boat deck--a teak deck-- and every morning, in the morning watch, we got up and scrubbed the deck down with brushes and holystoned it on Fridays. I remember how good I felt physically those days. No dungarees--we all wore undress blues to work in. I'd get up with the rest of the guys in the morning and go up on the boat deck. They used salt water with a fire hose to wash it down. We'd roll up our blues and be barefooted. I'd stand there in that ice-cold salt water and scrub that deck down. I remember just feeling like I could whip my weight in wildcats. After morning watch, we'd have breakfast, chow down.

Q: Where did you eat?

Mr. King: We had mess tables that were on racks in the overhead--wooden mess tables that folded up.

Q: This was in your berthing compartment?

Mr. King: No, on the Portland we had berthing compartments and the mess compartments were different.

Q: I see.

Mr. King: They had red linoleum on the deck, in the mess deck. I got very familiar with that linoleum when I was mess cook. Also, in the deck force, you did your turn.

You were a mess cook for three months, and you were a side cleaner three months. And if you weren't careful, you were captain of the head for three months. You know, you get these various duties. I was somewhere in the middle. I wasn't captain of the head, but I was a side cleaner for a while. I was a mess cook for three months.

The mess cooks would take the mess tables down out of these metal overhead racks and set them up for each meal, then spread oilcloth on them. Then the guys would come down and sit at their assigned mess table and we, the mess cooks, would go up to the galley and get these metal tureens in a rack. You'd rush back down and put the tureens up on the table. Each mess had a mess captain, and the mess captain sat at the head of the table. He was the bull of the woods for that particular table, called all the shots.

The guys at each table would tip their mess cook on payday--a moderate amount, a dime or a quarter, something like that. But that was big money, so we worked our tails off for these tips that we would get.

Q: This was before the time of metal trays to eat out of, wasn't it?

Mr. King: Yes. We ate off crockery. We had white GI coffee cups and white crockery. And the mess cooks--we would set up a table, put the silverware out, and so on.

Q: How good was the food?

Mr. King: It was excellent food. There was a lot of competition amongst the mess cooks to curry favor with the galley to get good chow for your particular mess, because the better you fed your mess, the more tips you got. There was a certain amount of jockeying that went on. The cooks were aware of this, and they'd play favorites, too, you know. If you got along with the cooks, you'd probably get better steaks and so on.

Q: Was there any cumshaw involved with the cooks there?*

Mr. King: There wasn't any cumshaw involved with the cooks, but I remember what power they had over the mess cooks. You really better get along with the cooks, or your name is mud. During the time that I was mess cook, we drew a week's duty with the jack-of-the-dust. During that week you had vegetable detail. You would peel spuds, by hand. There were no mechanical spud peelers. The ship's cook striker in charge of our detail was an ugly guy whose name was Dogface Lee. He was ugly as he could be, and he had an ugly disposition. He was ugly inside and ugly outside.

---
*Cumshaw is a system of providing small, non-monetary bribes in return for favors.

One day, while peeling a potato, I carved this dog's head out of a potato, and while he wasn't looking showed it to all the other guys, and Dogface caught me. So he hailed me right up to the OOD, and put me on report for disrespect and all kinds of things.* I thought I was in a heap of trouble, but his reputation was well known, so I just got chewed out a little bit, and it all passed over. I haven't thought about that in a long time.

Q: What did the jack-of-the-dust do?

Mr. King: The jack-of-the-dust was in charge, in effect, of dry stores. I remember coffee was under jack-of-the-dust. I was wrong a while ago. This guy Lee was not a jack-of-the-dust. But you did draw a tour with the jack-of-the-dust, just loading things and carrying them around.

This guy Lee was one of the cook strikers that was in charge of the spud-peeling detail. But the jack-of-the-dust was a guy that I kind of had a little bit of a rapport with. We would sit up and drink coffee and smoke cigarettes at night after taps in the mess hall, which was kind of devilish, you know. It was all right. Nobody ever bothered anybody; a lot of kids did that.

Smoking cigarettes was not really fostered, but it was certainly not only condoned, but everybody was expected to

---

*OOD--officer of the deck.

smoke. You know, I smoked like a stove. In fact, I didn't know anybody that didn't smoke amongst my friends there on the ship.

Q: They were pretty cheap, too, to buy.

Mr. King: Oh, four cents a pack for sea stores.

One time we went to sea for a special gunnery drill. The main battery was 8-inch guns, and the <u>Portland</u> was selected as some kind of a guinea pig. We went out and fired the 8-inch, fired until the sleeves came out of the inside--it was an intentional destruct. We just fired all day long. Finally the sleeves came out and they put new ones in their place. I remember all the gunnery stuff; I really liked that. I thought that was real Navy. I could always see an enemy just over the horizon. On the 8-inch guns you could see the projectile as it left the gun, and you could see it in the air. I remember the gunner's mates telling us about battleships and 16-inch guns, where you could really see the projectile very clearly. We could just see kind of a blob going through the air. But my battle station was not the 8-inch; my battle station was a 5-inch. The 5-inch made a hell of a noise--a crack; it would just ring your head. We had a fair amount of gunnery drills and other drills.

Our skipper on the Portland was named David McDougal Le Breton. He was a friend of this famous Broadway couple, Alfred Lunt and Lynn Fontanne. Later on, on the Portland, I got to be a yeoman striker. I remember seeing personal correspondence--not personal-personal, but carbon copies of letters from him saying, "Dear Alfred," and I thought, "My God." I couldn't get over that. Here's a guy that actually knows famous people. He was a frosty old character, Le Breton was. When I had occasion to take something in to him--a dispatch or whatever--and knock on his door, he would say, "Come!" I thought that was great--first class!

One time we had a battle practice of some kind, night battle practice. The whole fleet was involved in it. There were star shells and lots of light and noise, and it was just really great. My battle station was as JV talker from the bridge to a gun station. This one night there came a very critical point in these war games, involving searchlights. We had done this before as drill, but not the real McCoy. This was a real battle practice. Captain Le Breton was on the bridge and some enemy--blue force or red force--came into view. I was all wrapped up in it, and I sort of forgot my duties as talker, so the critical

---
*Captain David M. Le Breton, USN
**Star shells are illumination rounds fired by 5-inch guns.
***JV is the designation of an intra-ship telephone circuit.

moment came, and Captain Le Breton said, "Illuminate." The OOD said, "Illuminate." And I was supposed to say, "Illuminate," but I didn't say, "Illuminate." I was watching, and Le Breton said it a second time: "Goddamn it, I said 'Illuminate.'"

Then it dawned on me. "Illuminate," I said. But we missed the opportunity. So, gee, that was terrible.

The captain said, "I want to find out who didn't pass the word." So it finally got down to me.

I said, "I sure did." I lied like a trooper. I said, "I passed it. I certainly did."

Q: Well, that was true.

Mr. King: It was true, but I thought, "I'm going to get in the firing squad here." So I swore that I said "Illuminate."

Later on, after I served my time on the deck force on the Portland, I had an opportunity to be a yeoman striker because I took shorthand and typing in high school.* The only reason I took typing and shorthand was because of all the girls in the class; I didn't take it because of any motivation. But those two courses that I took did me more good than anything else in the Navy. I wound up in the

---
*A striker is a nonrated enlisted man who undergoes training in a particular rating specialty as preparation for becoming a petty officer in that rating.

captain's office as a yeoman striker.

I remember the chief yeoman was a guy that smoked cigars. (That was an awesome thing, being a chief yeoman.) He had an eccentricity, which was that he never used carbon paper twice. Back in those days when you did an official letter, you had a lot of copies. You'd put together your carbons, your bonds, your yellows, your greens, and so on. He'd put a fresh set of carbons in his typewriter then and do the letter, yank it out, and throw the carbons in the wastepaper basket. The next batch was a brand-new set of carbons again. That's just the way he did. His basket was always full of carbon paper. He would smoke cigars and would sometimes tap his cigar. The hot ash would fall in the carbon paper, and the basket would flare up. So it was my job to always put out the carbon paper in the chief's wastepaper basket before something happened.

Q: That was a rather extravagant way of using the carbon paper.

Mr. King: It was indeed, it was indeed. But that was just the mark of the authority and responsibility of a chief petty officer. If he wanted to use fresh carbons, he could use them. I thought that was wonderful.

Q: How much association was there between the officers and

the enlisted men?

Mr. King: None. Well, I shouldn't be so final; there was a little bit, but not much. It was mainly enlisted to enlisted. Now, up above me, up in the petty officer and chiefs, I guess, there certainly was. But the only one I was much in contact with was the ship's secretary, a lieutenant. When I was in the captain's office, I reported to him. He was the first officer that I ever spoke much to or had much contact with. That also made a big impression on me. His name was Arthur D. Ayrault.* He was an aristocratic guy. I remember I would have to go to him with a requisition for anything: a pencil, piece of paper, or whatever. One day this bright idea occurred to me. I went to Lieutenant Ayrault, and I said, "You know, if I brought you several requisitions and you just signed them all, and then when I needed something I would just go ahead and fill it in and go down and get it, and I wouldn't have to bother you."

He looked at me for a moment. I mean, I'm sure he didn't think I was serious at first. He finally saw that I was serious. It never dawned on me that anyone could do that and use those requisitions for anything unorthodox, because I was such a straight arrow that I just thought that that would be a good way to do business. But he was

---
*Lieutenant Arthur D. Ayrault, Jr., USN.

so shocked when I asked him, when finally it dawned on him that I was serious or naive. So then he explained to me that maybe it's better each time that I bring them to him, so he could sign and he would know what it was all about.

We had an officer on the Portland who had a bit of a liquor problem. One day he was put in his room by the skipper, and that made a tremendous impression on me, that an officer could be disciplined. I couldn't imagine an officer doing anything wrong.

Q: That was much more common then than now, to put somebody under hack.

Mr. King: Yes. Well, this guy went into hack. At one time I had to take a piece of paper or something down to him. I remember I waited a long time for him, knocked on his door. I didn't want to look at him. I mean, I felt so bad about it.

Q: You didn't want to embarrass him probably.

Mr. King: No, I didn't want to embarrass him. But I finally knocked on his door. He came to the door, and he looked terrible. He looked awful. So I gave him the piece of paper, and he took it and closed the door. I think he deserved his time in hack; he had a serious bottle problem.

Anyway, later on, the *Portland* and the *Houston*, with President Roosevelt on board the *Houston*, went around to the East Coast. On the way there, President Roosevelt was going to go fishing down in the Galapagos Islands. That was a great fishing spot of his. There were only two ships, the *Portland* and the *Houston*, on this junket. Again, that was the big thing to me to have the President of the United States on the ship next to us.

When we got down to the Galapagos Islands, one day he went out fishing and had good luck, caught several big fish--I don't know what kind, tarpon or something. Then he had the coxswain of his boat come over to the *Portland* and circle our ship. When he circled the *Portland*, he held a big fish up as he went by. We just manned the rail and cheered and hollered and yelled like nothing you ever saw; we just thought that was great. He had that old straw hat of his on and that cigarette holder.

We finally made a stop at the Galapagos Islands, and they sounded swimming call. Everybody just leaped over the side. There was no discussion about who could swim and who couldn't swim, just swimming call. I guess it was about a quarter or half a mile in to the beach. I just started swimming, and I swam too fast. I was just like the kid in the story, Aram, running a race where he thought he was the fastest guy in the world. I mean, I thought I was the fastest swimmer. Pretty soon I got tired; I got real tired, and I opened my eyes and looked up. I was still quite a ways from the beach. I was in deep water too. For a few minutes there, I was really kind of worried, because I had just run myself out of gas. But then I just paced myself and floated until I got my second wind and swam on in to the beach. But the thought occurred to me, you know, "I'm a son of a gun. It would be easy to get into trouble here if you want to." But we went ashore and just poked around, didn't do much of anything, played baseball, and came back to the ship.

President Roosevelt came over to the Portland to go to church one Sunday. In those days you had a chaplain of one faith on one ship and one of another on another ship, so he came on board on the Portland to go to church. I had morning watch and was shining brightwork with a friend of mine named Johnson from Denver. The President was in a wheelchair, but it was not a big deal. I mean, he didn't seem disabled. He could walk with a cane or ride in a wheelchair, either one. He had a certain charisma about him that when he would look at a group of people, I guess everybody in the group felt like he was talking or looking at them. He came over to where Johnson and I were. He had this tremendous capacity for personalizing with anybody. I was standing at attention so much that I was almost paralyzed. He said, "Where are you from?"

I said, "Aransas Pass, Texas."

C. S. King #1 - 39

He said, "Oh, I know it well. Good fishing down there, great fishing. You know [somebody]?" I didn't know him.

Then he went to Johnson, and he said, "Where are you from?"

He said, "Denver."

"Oh," he said, "that's a great place. I've done [so and so] there. You remember [so and so]?"

Every person he had contact with, he could personalize it, and I felt for the longest time like that was a great encounter with the President of the United States, to say something like that.

Q: He was a remarkable politician.

Mr. King: He was a tremendous politician. He really had that gift.

But, anyway, then we went on to Panama and went through the Panama Canal. I don't remember anything spectacular, except it was great to go through the canal. We went through the canal and on to Norfolk to the Navy yard. Oh, we had been in the Navy yard in Bremerton, but we were just going in for a short time this time.* In the Navy yard everyone went over the side to scrape and clean. It was the rule. The only people that didn't go

---
*Puget Sound Navy Yard, Bremerton, Washington.

over the side were key people.

Q: You mean when you're in dry dock.

Mr. King: When you're in dry dock. Going over the side was like loading ammunition. It was all-hands evolution.

Q: Was this to scrape the bottom?

Mr. King: Yes. It was all handwork on the barnacles and marine growth. Everybody went over the side. I remember vividly in that dry dock, it was a long way to the bottom-- when a big ship's in dry dock, such as a heavy cruiser. It was in the wintertime, and it was cold. They just put us on wooden stages with no training and no safety line. Just let us over the side. I don't mind planes and stuff, but I'm not all that crazy about height for height's sake. I didn't like that a damn bit.

Q: I don't blame you.

Mr. King: My friend Johnson was on the other end of the stage--two of us to a stage. Once you got on the stage, you let yourself down. You know, you have a line going up, being tended on the deck, and it comes back. Then there's a Y-shape line at each end of the stage, and the line goes under it, so you just let yourself go down. You pass the line through the Y and then take a couple of hitches and then go ahead and scrape and let yourself down again, two guys on the stage. I didn't like that at all. That's my most vivid recollection of that trip in the Navy yard.

When we came back through the Panama Canal, an opportunity was presented for several seamen to get off and be assigned to duty at the Panama Canal. I don't know why I did it. I just thought it'd be a good thing to do. I put in for it and got it.

Q: Before we get that, there are a couple of other things. I wonder if you could describe what it was like being a side cleaner in the Portland.

Mr. King: Well, an average side cleaner was always in the water in port. Not in a dry dock--just daily routine in port. Every time that the ship hit port, the side cleaners went over the side. I didn't do a full three months of it. I forget why now. I only did it for a couple or three weeks. You went over on stages and also in small boats, worked over the side of the ship and kept it painted. It was, admittedly, not such a rough job, but the hours were such that sometimes side cleaners got special liberty when the crew didn't because of the hours.

Q: This is when the ships were that light gray color, weren't they?

Mr. King: Yes. They were kept immaculate. We just kept on painting, like painting the Golden Gate Bridge. You're always painting somewhere on it. You're always painting on the ship.

Q: Was there a lot of competition with other ships as far as appearance and so forth?

Mr. King: It was a highly competitive Navy. Yes, it was. And that was a great mark of pride, to have your ship in top-notch shape. If you passed by a train ship, like a tanker, something like that, an old, beat-up tanker, I thought, "What a terrible thing to be on a ship like that."* Early in my naval career, I thought I would never serve on a train ship. I'd always be on a warship, because they just seemed--I don't know. It was just something about them I liked.

Q: Did you get involved in any of the sports?

Mr. King: Not organized sports. We'd play catch or

---

*The fleet train comprised auxiliary ships that provided services to combatants: fuel, repair parts, medical care, and so forth.

something like that. I was not a real athlete. I was healthy and agile, but I was not that much of an athlete.

Q: What do you recall about the West Coast liberty ports?

Mr. King: Well, Long Beach was just simply great. At the Pico Street landing and up from the landing, there was a dance hall. I've forgotten the name of it now; it was very well known. I remember that money went a long way. By that time I was a seaman second, less my $10.00 a month. And we'd gotten our cut back. I was getting $26.00 a month, so I had all the money in the world that I needed. There was a kind of a midway at Long Beach, off the landing there.

Q: Amusement park.

Mr. King: Something like that, yes. And, you know, when you went ashore, just force of gravity, you got off at the Pico Street Landing. Then you slowly went on up and began to fan out into the side streets. Finally everybody would go wherever they were going to go. But no one got very far from the waterfront and the amusements, you know, that sort of thing. That's where you went, and that's where you stayed. That was the liberty.

Q: Any recollections of those boat rides back and forth?

Mr. King: Well, the motor launches, big 50-footers, were for enlisted. Going back at night, there was, you know, a certain amount of guys getting sick from too much beer and throwing up in the boat. I mean, that wasn't happy, but it was something you expected going back at night--a kind of eventful ride. They always had a boat officer to keep order.

Q: You said it was expected that people would smoke. Did the same apply to drinking?

Mr. King: I guess probably so. I don't know of anybody that didn't drink, I mean, just beer. There were not many hard whiskey drinkers or people who had problems, but when you went ashore, you drank. I don't ever recall alcohol being that much of a problem per se, that people got staggering drunk. Oh, there'd be fistfights sometimes. The drinking was the center of gravity of a liberty. You wouldn't go ashore unless you had some beers, but it never did seem to be the kind of thing where it was a real problem. Just fun on the beach.

Q: You talked about competition between ships. Was there competition between the various divisions on board the

Portland?

Mr. King: Yes, there was. The first division had the quarterdeck, and the fourth division had the boat deck, although that was not a clear line of demarcation. There were elite groups on there like the fire controlmen and so on.* They were just kind of a cut above. I don't know whether it was because of the equipment they used. The quartermasters, the people up on the bridge, were kind of an elite group too.

Q: Well, this is more head work than back work.

Mr. King: Yes. The deck apes--and I was a full-fledged deck ape for most of my time on the Portland--we just worked. They'd pass the word from time to time, "Now send one hand from the first, second, third, and fourth divisions. Report to the boatswain's mate of the watch for a working party."

I used to say that they'd pass the word for one hand, first, second, third, and King from the fourth division report to the boatswain's mate of the watch. I drew every working party that came along, it seemed like. But we did have a great respect for petty officers, and particularly for elite petty officers like fire control and

───────────
*Fire controlmen were the enlisted men who operated the equipment that aimed the ship's guns.

quartermasters and signalmen.

Q: How about radiomen?

Mr. King: Radiomen, communicators.

Q: You've talked about the sense of adventure that you felt. What was it like to be in a fleet problem and to see the battleships, the destroyers, and what have you?

Mr. King: Oh, I felt like it was Hollywood. I mean, those battleships with big clocks on the after mast. I remember one time the USS <u>Macon</u>, the dirigible, was taking part in the fleet maneuvers, and the <u>Macon</u> had planes on board. During the course of this particular fleet maneuver, the <u>Macon</u> was very close to the <u>Portland</u>, and she launched her planes. The way they launched them, they had kind of a V-shaped metal rack came down; the planes had a hook that hooked on to the rack. They were just dropped down and fired off, and then off they'd go. The name of the squadron was the High Hat Squadron because of the flying trapeze. That meant a lot to me, too, to actually see that.

Later on, when I was in the captain's office, the postal clerk on there was a great collector of first day covers and cachets and whatnot. One day the Macon went down, crashed off Point Sur.* This guy came down and got me out of my bunk and took me up to the captain's office, and he made a quick rubber stamp that said, "USS Macon down off Point Sur." He asked me to stamp it with the ship's date-and-time-stamp machine in the captain's office. I hesitated at first, but then it seemed legitimate, so I went ahead and did it. So I did 25 or 50 of them. He gave me some of the covers--I still have a couple of them at home somewhere.

These people like him that collect these first-day covers and cachets, that was almost an obsession with him. I remember being impressed at the time with how wrapped up he was in this tremendous thing he was doing to get the USS Macon memento.

Q: Did you get out to Hawaii at all?

Mr. King: Yes. We went out to Hawaii, and that was my first "foreign" liberty. It was a magical moment for me to be in Hawaii. You know, they had the usual thing on the dock, girls and hula skirts and the ukuleles and all. I went ashore every chance I got. A friend of mine had a camera, and we went up on some mountain there--I don't know whether it was Diamond Head or what--took some pictures. I

---

*The USS Macon (ZRS-5) crashed and sank off the California coast on 12 February 1935.

C. S. King #1 - 48

was very much impressed with being in a foreign port.

Q: This must have been before Panama.

Mr. King: Yes, it was before Panama. In fact, it was not too long after I went aboard the Portland when we got to Honolulu. I thought that was great.

Q: That was the sort of thing you hadn't even dreamed of when you were in Texas.

Mr. King: Never dreamed of. We also went to Alaska at one time, and that was a great adventure for me. We went to Nome and Juneau and Unalaska. The captain took the ship up very close to the Columbia glacier, and we fired the ship's signal guns. Great big chunks of ice would fall off the glacier. I thought that was great stuff too. We went ashore in Alaska. There was not much liberty there. It was really a sort of primitive place at that time, very primitive. Of course, I wrote letters home, "Dear Folks. I'm now in Alaska." But those were the only two foreign ports that we hit. We did one three-month session in the Bremerton Navy Yard. We didn't go over the side that time. I remember being not negatively impressed by the civilian workmen, but I was conscious of the gap, the chasm, between the military and civilians.

Q: There's usually a contempt for the so-called yard birds.

Mr. King: We felt that to some extent.

Q: What do you recall about being ashore there?

Mr. King: Bremerton, in those days, was not much of a liberty port. Yet they had a streamlined ferry--the upper deck was sort of rounded off.

Q: The *Kalakala*.

Mr. King: Was that what it was? I thought that was great to have a streamlined ferry. Had to take the ferry to go from Bremerton over to Seattle. I didn't go to Seattle but once or twice, because it was expensive, and I didn't think it was that much of a liberty port. Bremerton was really a compression of San Diego. It was 100% military. I didn't go ashore much in Bremerton either, because it was cold and wet all the time, it seemed to me, when we were there.

Q: Kind of a drab place.

C. S. King #1 - 50

Mr. King: It was a very drab place, and I just stayed aboard most of the time.

Q: Did you get to San Francisco?

Mr. King: Yes, got to San Francisco and I remember very well passing Alcatraz. At that time it was an active prison. I remember I thought of all the Alcatraz movies I'd seen and the poor devils on Alcatraz. It was cold in San Francisco. My God, it was cold. It was in the summertime, but, boy, when the sun went down it was really bitter cold. I wasn't dressed for it the first time; I almost froze to death. But San Francisco is kind of a glamorous place, had a lot going on in there--night life and the restaurants. In fact, I thought it was more glamorous to me, by Aransas Pass standards, than Honolulu was. I thought that was a great city, San Francisco. And it was not at all like it is now: I mean, the impression you have about the homosexual community and stuff like that. There was no flavor of that in those days.

Q: Well, it just wasn't open at all in the society then.

Mr. King: No. There were two places in San Francisco that were talked about in the Navy. One was called Pinocchio's that had a reputation of being a homosexual place. And another place used to be where women who were lesbians hung out. It had some crazy name like "Where Girls Will Be Boys." These things were talked about aboard ship, but it was really talked about in terms of San Francisco's overall cosmopolitan air, such an international city, just had everything.

Q: Well, and sailors do love to talk.

Mr. King: Oh, I mean, that's where you make your real liberty. If you make a liberty ashore then you go back and you make it again on the ship.

Q: You have the real liberty and then the enhanced liberty.

Mr. King: Then the enhanced liberty.

Q: Was the <u>Our Navy</u> magazine popular with the crew?

Mr. King: It was indeed. That was a great event once a month, when the <u>Our Navy</u> magazine came on board. We all got our copies.

Q: That was twice a month, actually.

Mr. King: Yes. I guess it was. I had some connection with Our Navy on the ship. I think one guy was the agent, and I carried it for him or something like that. Made a few nickels. Also, I used to write a lot. I think I sent them something and they didn't use it. But I sent another magazine--a cheap imitation of Our Navy--a little story of some kind, and they printed it. But Our Navy magazine was an event to look forward to when it came out.

Q: What do you recall about the medical care on board ship?

Mr. King: I doubt that I went to sick bay any time while I was aboard. I really don't think I had an encounter with the medics or the dental clinic, either one, on the Portland. I may have. We got shots. We got those in the mess hall. We had short-arm inspection.* But I don't remember going down and saying, "I'm sick," not on the Portland.

Q: How frequent were the short-arm inspections?

Mr. King: For mess cooks, it was fairly often. And for the crew, it would be, I guess, once every several months, something like that.

---

*A "short-arm" inspection was an examination of a sailor's penis for evidence of venereal disease.

C. S. King #1 - 53

Q: By then were you getting any indoctrination on VD?

Mr. King: Not a word. There was plenty of conversation, you know, in sailor talk.

Q: Unofficial.

Mr. King: There were horror stories about this guy and that guy. Also, when any members of the crew did have a venereal disease, and it was a very rare thing, they went on the venereal restricted list. They couldn't go ashore. That was like having the scarlet letter. Some poor guy would be on the VD list; he would be known all over the ship.

It was not very common, and I don't know who could take the credit for it. I don't know whether it was just peer word of mouth about precautions or whatever, or whether or not, contrary to everything you'd been told, or people are told, that, among my group, in the <u>Portland</u>, there was not that active a sex life. I mean, there was a lot of talk. There was a lot more talk than actual happenstance. Mostly, kids came back and told sea stories about what a great liberty they made, but I don't think there was ever that much real activity. In fact, the guys that were on the venereal list were usually one-hash markers or something like that, very few of the younger element.*

Q: So they'd been in and were on their second enlistment.

Mr. King: Yes.

Q: What do you remember about disciplinary treatment of the crew?

Mr. King: Well, the discipline, that wasn't a big problem. I had a run-in with a boatswain's mate named Szymanski.** He was in charge of the mess cooks and he was rough; he was very rough. When he had reveille, he was physical. He'd slam you out of your bunk and everything. I didn't much care for that. He would give you extra duty. He had that power. The chemistry wasn't very good between us, and he gave me a lot of extra duty. One time he was holding reveille, and we had a kind of a--not a physical encounter, but I just got kind of tired of it. So he put me on report for late hammocks. But I didn't go to mast. I was sent to my division officer. He chewed me out, for the system. I shouldn't have sassed Szymanski. But I didn't go to mast.

---
*A hash mark is a diagonal stripe on an enlisted man's sleeve to indicate four years of service.
**Boatswain's Mate F. J. Szymanski, USN, master-at-arms.

On the <u>Portland</u>, at least, there was not much of a disciplinary problem, as I recall. I never went to mast, and I don't remember any of my friends that ever went to mast.

Talking about Szymanski reminds me of another master-at-arms. One morning he was making reveille rounds and taking names of late sleepers. He stopped at one bunk, shook the guy, and said, "What's your name?"

The guy said, "Smith."

The MAA wrote it down and said, "Smith, you're on report."

Same with the next guy, "Okay, Jones, you're on report."

The MAA came to the next guy and said, ""What's your name?"

The guy said "Przystovski."

The MAA put his pencil back and said, "Watch it, Ski. Don't let this happen again."

Q: So you slept in hammocks rather than in bunks in that ship?

Mr. King: No, on the <u>Portland</u> we had bunks, folding bunks. It was quite crowded. We had our one GI issue white blanket. You know, you made up your bunk in the morning when you got up, with a strap over the pillow and a strap over the blanket, and then folded up the bunk. We'd have air bedding once or twice a month when we were out at sea.

Q: Anything else you recall about that ship?

Mr. King: Oh, I guess not right off the bat. Since we talked the other day, a few scattered things came to mind, but I guess that's probably about the size of it. It was just a typical first-duty ship for a younger sailor, and I guess I went through all the chairs, different jobs that you'd have.

Q: Did you get the satisfaction from that that you thought you would when you asked for a heavy cruiser?

Mr. King: Yes, because, you know, there's a great sense of loyalty in the Navy, generally speaking--ship loyalty. Every ship I was ever on I thought was about the best ship I was ever on. I liked the Portland very much. I really was very proud to be on there.

Q: Anything to say about your yeoman work after you made that transition?

Mr. King: Well, no, the routine was not as tough as it was being in the deck force. But it was not that great. As a matter of fact, in my own mind, I don't recall what portion of my time on the Portland I was a yeoman and when I was a seaman. I could probably reconstruct it. But when I got off the Portland, I went to Panama. I went there as a yeoman striker. My job in Panama was as a yeoman striker in the admin office.

Q: Well, could you tell me all about what you did in Panama? Where specifically were you stationed?

Mr. King: The fleet air base was adjacent to the submarine base--Fleet Air Base, Coco Solo. Our daily working routine there was 7:00 A.M. to 1:00 P.M., and after 1:00 o'clock you were through for the day. There was a little, green frame wooden building at one end of the base, the administration building. In this administration building were the radiomen, the captain's office, and the base administration office. That was my duty station. Our barracks there were cement barracks, and the entire sides were screened. They weren't solid sides. There were a lot of bedbugs, I remember, in the bunks. You would borrow a blowtorch, fire it off, and you would burn your bedsprings. At the end of the bunk where the spring ends--the spring is about six inches long--you'd run your flame on that, and it would be just alive with bedbugs in those springs.

Q: You did this every night with a torch?

Mr. King: Not every night. Just from time to time, whenever you noticed you had a little bit of a problem, you'd take off your mattress and burn your bunk.

Q: Fried bedbugs.

Mr. King: It was awful. The routine there was great, because you had these 7:00 to 1:00 working hours, and you'd break at 10:00 for a soup and a sandwich. And then at 1:00, you were off for the day.

Q: Was that because of the heat?

Mr. King: The heat, tropical hours. Ships would come through and would marvel at this.

The base routine was such that a lot of guys just spent most of their time on the base, because it had a big swimming pool, and there were a lot of activities on the base. We had our beer parties out in the jungle and the liberty was unusual. It was Panamanian liberty. But you had to be off the streets in uniform at 11:00 P.M. You had to wear sliders, had to wear civilian clothes after 11:00 o'clock. They had rental places down there that would rent clothes. Most sailors couldn't afford civilian clothes.

Those that could would have a locker on the beach. Those of us that couldn't would pay 50 cents to rent an aloha shirt and a pair of pants. (We called the garb "sliders.") So at 11:00 P.M. if you're going to stay over for a while, you go down to Sam's Locker Club and put your clothes in a locker--put on your aloha shirt, your pants and Navy shoes. Then you were okay.

The base itself was really old. It was in bad shape. There were no new buildings on the base except for the barracks. They had three seaplane squadrons--VP-2, VP-3, and VP-5.* When I got there in '35, VP-2 had these old P2Ds with pontoons.** They had fabric fuselages and aviation carpenter's mates down there that did aviation woodwork. One squadron had PM-2s, Martins.*** They called them "motor boats," because they had trouble taking off. We had the first PBYs down there.**** And there was another kind of plane--I've forgotten now--that was a kind of a forerunner of the PBY.

Q: P2Y probably.

---

*The abbreviations stand for Patrol Squadron Two, Patrol Squadron Three, and Patrol Squadron Five.
**Developed from the Douglas T2D torpedo plane, the P2D was a patrol plane with two pontoon floats suspended beneath the wings. The P2Ds in VP-3 were replaced in 1937 by PBYs.
***Built by the Glenn L. Martin Company, the PM-2 was a flying boat rather than a pontoon plane.
****The PBY Catalina, built by Consolidated Aircraft Company, first entered fleet squadrons in late 1936. It was the Navy's standard patrol bomber through World War II.

Mr. King: P2Y.* I used to spend a lot of time bumming rides down there. They were very good about it. I flew in all those old planes they had. As a matter of fact, they had a daily guard mail plane trip from Coco Solo over to Balboa. My boss, Lieutenant L. H. Hunte, was an aviator, and I would go with him from time to time.** It was an O2U.*** It had a handcrank inertia starter, and as hot as it was down there, the guy in the other seat--which would be me, of course--would crank it. I would take this inertia starter and engage it and stand up on the wing, with one foot on a foothole there, and one on the edge of the wing, and you'd crank the starter very slow at first because it was stiff, and then it would pick up momentum. You'd go faster and faster, and then you disengaged it, ran back and got in the rear seat, and he would fire the thing off and take off. Our VJ squadron was a utility squadron; they had every kind of plane you ever heard of.

But I remember those flights from Coco Solo to Balboa very well, because he sometime would get a fair amount of altitude. One time the conditions were such that we could see both the Atlantic and Pacific oceans at one time. So I wrote a letter home that night, "Dear Folks: Today I saw the Atlantic and Pacific at the same time."

---

*The P2Y was a Consolidated flying boat that entered fleet service in the early 1930s.
**Lieutenant (junior grade) Louis H. Hunte, USN.
***The Vought O2U was a biplane observation aircraft that was catapulted from battleships and cruisers to spot the fall of shot from ships' guns.

Q: Do you remember any of the individual aviators that you met?

Mr. King: Gosh, I remember a lot of them. One of them just died the other day--E. A. Junghans.* We had some aviation cadets down there. Several of them made names for themselves in World War II. Their names don't come to me right off the bat, but I remember several of them. One was a famous explorer and went to the North Pole several times. He was in one of our squadrons down there. Chick Hayward was there.** Commander Frank Fake was in charge of O&R-- overhaul and repair.***

Commander Fake was a naval aviator, and, also, his hobby was glider planes. I believe he built one himself, more or less. Being in charge of overhaul and repair was not really a hindrance to the project. Anyway, one time he was doing some glider flying on a weekend when no other planes were in the air. Our landing strip was just grass, I believe--we were primarily a seaplane base--and on

---
*Lieutenant (junior grade) Earl A. Junghans, USN, Patrol Squadron Three. Junghans eventually retired as a captain; he died 17 July 1986.
**Lieutenant (junior grade) John T. Hayward, USN, Patrol Squadron Two. Hayward retired as a vice admiral and has been interviewed as part of the Naval Institute's oral history program.
***Lieutenant Commander Frank C. Fake, USN, was assigned to the fleet air base.

takeoffs you had to clear an old balloon hangar at one end of the strip. Anyway, Commander Fake was coming in for a glider landing and with the control tower not manned he had to clear himself. Well, just at the last moment he was about to touch down and some officer, with his family out for a Sunday stroll, was walking across the strip. The glider was completely silent, of course, and the wind was in the wrong direction for the group to hear Commander Fake yelling, so he tried to pull over and spun in, which just about demolished the glider, but nothing was hurt on Commander Fake except his disposition. I believe the officer involved with his family was a lieutenant (j.g.), and I think he suffered some mental anguish over the incident from Commander Fake.

Q: What do you recall about Chick Hayward?

Mr. King: Not much about him down there except the name. My direct boss was a lieutenant named J. C. S. McKillip.* He was a meteorologist. Another boss of mine was L. H. Hunte, and still another was W. J. Richter.** The exec was Commander Samuel Ginder, who used to give me a dollar for baby-sitting his young son.***

---
*Lieutenant John C. S. McKillip, USN, aerological officer at the fleet air base.
**Lieutenant (junior grade) William J. Richter, USN.
***Commander Samuel P. Ginder, USN. As a rear admiral during World War II, Ginder commanded a fast carrier task group under Vice Admiral Marc A. Mitscher.

C. S. King #1 - 63

Q: Were you tempted to go into an aviation rating at all?

Mr. King: I put in for flight school down there and flunked--my eyes. I also put in for the Naval Academy down there. And in both cases, my eyes--I didn't have bad eyes, I didn't wear glasses, but I was flunked out because of my eyes. I liked to fly, and I thought at that time I'd like to be a pilot. We had enlisted aviators down there.

Q: APs.

Mr. King: APs. I thought that was kind of nice to be an AP.

Q: So evidently that dead pilot you'd seen in the <u>Relief</u> didn't make all that lasting an impression.

Mr. King: No. I liked to fly. One time there was a Pan American Grace "Panagra" plane crash that killed several people. The pilot of that plane was a former naval aviator; he had some connection with the Naval Reserve or something. Anyway, they had a naval court of inquiry into this crash. I was the Navy court reporter in Panama. A chief yeoman and I took this court of inquiry for this plane crash. It lasted, I guess, three weeks. The chief would take the morning, and I would take the afternoon or vice versa. And the other guy would transcribe what we took in the morning. At one time Sikorsky himself came down--it was a Sikorsky plane--and testified.* I remember being very impressed by him. He had a thick Russian accent. At one time during that court, something happened that was unusual. Sikorsky apparently gave the chief and me each a $20.00 bill, something like that, and the chief gave me my $20.00. I remember I started to say something about it. He said, "Shut up, we're not supposed to do that." Sikorsky, I think, was impressed by this chief and I doing all the shorthand work for this inquiry.

Another time down there, there was a general court-martial. The regular court reporter, Reynolds, was a first class yeoman who had a bottle problem. I was asked to be ready to take this general court-martial. I had never taken a general. So Reynolds said to me, "Now, the first day I'll take it. You just watch me and get the routine. Then, if you feel up to it, you take it in the afternoon."

So in the morning session I tried. I watched him, and I tried to take everything I could. The thing wound up in half a day. It was all over. So I went back and threw my notebook in my desk and went about my business. A Marine

---
*Igor I. Sikorsky was a Russian-born aeronautical engineer who built and flew the first multi-engine plane in the early 1910s. He was later instrumental in helicopter development in the United States.

first lieutenant was the judge advocate of that court-martial. The next day he called me up and said, "Have you got your notes?"

I said, "I got some notes."

He said, "Well, Reynolds is back in the hospital, in sick bay with the delirium tremens or something." He didn't take any notes at all. He just didn't take anything. So I got my notes and resurrected them. That lieutenant and I, for the next two days, just kind of reconstructed the court-martial. I had it pretty well, but we just wrote the whole darn thing. I think the guy changed his plea and pled guilty. It was a postal theft, something like that, some nickel-and-dime thing. It wasn't all that big a deal.

Q: Are there any of the aviators that you specifically have some recollections about?

Mr. King: No, I just recall some of the names there. We would, on a given time, go down and bum a ride, just to fool around for a half hour or so.

At one point I was trying to make third class any way I could, and I took the exam for radioman and yeoman. And at that time I was in VP-5 for purposes of studying at night for radioman and taking the exam. When my yeoman rating came back, I went back on the ship's company at the base.

Q: How tough was it to make petty officer in that era?

Mr. King: It was really tough. For example, they used to post the pay list every payday in seniority order. I was number one seaman at the airbase for quite some little time, because I'd been seaman for such a long time in those days before I made third class. My pay number was S-1, which made me the bull seaman first class on the base.*
It was awfully tough. In fact, when it finally opened up a little bit in '37 and '38, they had fleet-wide exams, even for third class. You'd take the exam and wait, and wait, and wait until the results came out. You didn't expect to make third class on your first cruise.

Q: Well, it was probably possible to pass but still not be advanced.

Mr. King: Oh, yes, you could pass and still not make it. It's however high you score on the test that would determine whether or not. For example, if they had ten third class yeomen rates at a given time and 100 guys took the exam, then the top ten would make the crow, and the

---

*In this case, "bull" indicates that King was the senior man in his pay grade at the time.

rest of them wouldn't.*

Q: What sort of study materials did you have to prepare for the exams?

Mr. King: Well, for each rate there was a manual. There was a manual for third class yeoman; and then, also, there was in existence a book of answers to the questions that you would get on the qualifying exams for that particular manual. The answer books had red stripes down the side; they were kept in safes, but they were not all that sacrosanct. I was aware of the fact that they existed before I took third class exams, but they really were of no help in the exam. What was necessary was that you had to get in your record that you were qualified. You studied that manual and were examined on it until you were qualified. Then after that you would take the regular fleet-wide, or whatever exam for that rate.

Q: What was the format of the fleet-wide exam--multiple choice?

Mr. King: I think it was all multiple choice or true and false. There were no essay-type questions that I can

---

*A eagle is included in the rating badge for petty officer. On the white enlisted uniform, the eagle is black and thus known as a "crow" in sailor vernacular.

recall.

Q: Well, since it was so tough to make rate, there were probably some very capable seamen.

Mr. King: Oh, heck, yes. There certainly were. I can recall on the Portland, for example, the scuttlebutt being that So-and-so in whatever division was either a college graduate, or had college courses to his credit. I remember a guy named Carrico, who became a quartermaster on the Portland, was quite well educated.*

Then high school graduates were subject to some derision from the old-timers. They called us wristwatch sailors and things like that. You know, "Oh, well, he's a high school graduate. My goodness, he's got a wristwatch." We had some scorn heaped on us by some of the old-timers.

Q: Well, it must have been considerable satisfaction when you did make third class.

Mr. King: It was indeed. I was very set up about that.

Q: How did you celebrate that one?

Mr. King: Oh, I think we had a wetting-down party of some kind, and I went around with my left arm paralyzed. You

---

*Quartermaster Third Class Peter Carrico, USN.

know, they had left-arm rates and right-arm rates.

Q: So people could see the new crow on your sleeve.

Mr. King: So they could see the new crow.

Q: What were your duties there with the patrol wings?

Mr. King: My work with VP-5 was mainly in connection with my trying to make third class radioman, at the same time I was trying to make yeoman. Now, my primary job was as a yeoman, but I just wanted to get a crow of some kind. My duties at the base were varied. I was editor of the ship's paper down there. I was also in communications, so-called. There was no newspaper. We had daily press news. The radiomen would copy press. They were so good that they could copy it right on the stencil. Then part of my job was to run the stencils off and staple them together, and that was our newspaper.

We had a kid down there named Almour; his father was a Navy chief warrant officer. Almour was a little strange. He was not dense; he was just sort of eccentric. Almour loved anything connected with the possibility of war. Anything that had to do with war he got very excited about, so much so that a radioman named Stevens, who was a good friend of mine--Steve and I cooked this up. Almour was a messenger and had a bicycle, went around the whole base every hour or so. It'd take him some little time.

One time, while he was out on his bike, I wrote these phony press items, and Steve sandwiched them in between regular items. The first one said, "Flash, flash, Japanese Bomb Hits U.S. Embassy in Shanghai." Then "Stock market" items, then three or four more. "Death Toll High In Embassy Bombing," then some more stuff. We embellished it with "British Ambassador Missing." And then "U.S. Declares State of Alert." We had the whole thing on this one stencil, or a couple of stencils. When Almour came back, he would always look over Steve's shoulders to see what the hot news was. When he saw this, he went absolutely bonkers. He was trying to pull it out of the typewriter. But Steve played the game and said, "Go on, Almour, leave us alone. We've got stuff to do that's important."

So we had as much fun as we thought we should, and then Steve and I were going to lunch. So Steve just tore the stencils up and threw the pieces in this one great big barrel for used stencils and stencil ink. It was an awful-looking thing--full of soggy, inky used stencils.

Q: Not intending them to go any farther.

Mr. King: Of course not. They were torn up too. Well, we

went to lunch and took our time. After about an hour, we came back. As we got close to the ad building, something told me that things weren't right.* I mean, I had this terrible premonition that something bad's going to happen. In fact, I looked up, and there was a big black limousine in front of the ad building. I went in the building, and it was high excitement, people running around. What had happened was Almour had retrieved those stencils, had taken them out, pieced them together, and had run off a copy of it.

Captain J. S. McCain was our skipper then.** He was trying to get at the bottom of this foolishness. I looked up, and there was Lieutenant McKillip, my boss, dashing up and down the hall looking all unglued. So I went up, and tried to catch him. He said, "Don't bother me now, don't bother me."

I said, "I've got to. I think there's something wrong with this press news." That brought him to a halt, so I told him the whole thing then.

He said, "I'm not going to tell the skipper. You're going to tell him. You're going to go in there."

So he went in and closed the door. After a while he said, "Okay."

So I went in. McCain was a little, wizened guy,

---
*Ad--administration.
**Captain John S. McCain, USN, Commander Aircraft Squadrons and Attending Craft, Fleet Air Base Coco Solo; commanding officer, Fleet Air Base Coco Solo.

physically, but such a great man. He smoked Bull Durham cigarettes and didn't wear shoes at all at the office. He was walking around in his stocking feet, rolling Bull Durham cigarettes. So I walked in. He had the story, I guess, from Lieutenant McKillip. He said, "I'm not going to do anything right now. I'm too mad." He said, "I'm really mad. That was dumb." He said, "What you guys did--you're in trouble. You're really in bad trouble." Then he said, "Just get out of here. I want to think about this for a while. I don't know what I'm going to do to you--general court-martial or what."

Oh, my God, I walked out of there, and I was really shaken. I considered desertion, the French Foreign Legion, anything you could think of. I knew I was in the worst trouble I'd ever been in my whole life. I don't believe I slept that night. The next day I went back to the ad building and saw McKillip, who said, "The captain wants to see you."

I went in and McCain--by that time, I guess, perspective had set in. So he just chewed me out, and I mean he chewed me out. He said, "I hope you've learned your lesson." When he said that, I thought I might be home free. He said, "You can cause terrible trouble by things like that. Don't ever fool with official dispatches." He just gave me a hell of a lecture.

C. S. King #1 - 73

The sequel to that story was that I was on Manus in New Guinea when I got rotated off the Hornet in 1944. I was a chief then, and a bunch of us were at the receiving unit there at Manus, waiting for a ride home to the U.S. They had fleet liberty and base liberty. The fleet liberty for the chiefs was from 1:00 P.M. until 5:00 P.M., or something, and base liberty from 5:00 P.M. till 8:00 P.M., or whatever. Three or four of us chiefs were walking down a very muddy road, going back to our barracks. Up toward us came three or four officers. This is the height of the war, and everybody was in khaki. Rank was really not very distinguishable from outward appearances. They got closer, and one of them had all sorts of stars on his collar. So one of us said, "Admiral!" So we all lined up, and as he came down the road, we gave him a real tremendous salute. It was McCain. At that time he was Commander Task Force 38.* They went right on by and went walking down the road. We started walking this way, and then I heard this, "Hey!" And I looked around, and it was Admiral McCain here.

Q: He was pointing his finger at you.

Mr. King: Yes. I went back and he said, "You're the son-of-a-bitch that almost started World War II all by

---
*Task Force 38 was the fast carrier task force in Admiral William F. Halsey's Third Fleet.

yourself." He laughed and said, "I've told that story many a time since then."

So I laughed and he laughed, and he went on down the road. And I thought, "What a memory."

Q: Indeed. What else do you recall about him from the time in Panama?

Mr. King: Well, every skipper's a legend to his people. He was a legend to us. The fact that he smoked Bull Durham cigarettes, rolled them himself; the fact that he didn't wear shoes; the fact that he was just really a hell of a sailor. I mean, he just was a giant of a guy. Everything he did was first class. He was a high-class guy. Look where he wound up in World War II: as a major task force commander.

Q: Do you have some examples of things that he did?

Mr. King: Not right off the top of my head. I just remember that it was the unanimous opinion of the people down there that he was a hell of a skipper. And the aviators thought awfully highly of him.

There was one of the aviators that belonged to the utility squadron, VJ-1, that crashed and killed himself. I don't know. I think there was a question of some booze in his room or something. Anyway, McCain covered the whole situation. I just mean he did a class act. He took care of the guy for the sake of his next of kin. I was so struck by his compassion and understanding. It was that kind of thing, where he just was really someone that you respected. The common conception was that he would go the last mile and some more too.

Q: Did he get out and fly?

Mr. King: Yes. He was a four-striper, too, then.

Q: Yes, and he had qualified as an aviator late in his career.

Mr. King: He was a late aviator, yes. He didn't fly an awful lot. It was said the base prayed for his safe return each time he flew. But he did put in his time. I think he used one of the VJ planes. They had a utility unit that had all kinds of planes in it.

I don't recall much about his aviation experience. Also, the gap between a seaman like myself and him was so wide that it was just the conception I had that we had a damn good skipper. We had Captain McWhorter, and we had

McCain, and we had E. L. Gunther.*

Q: What do you remember about the other two?

Mr. King: I didn't have very much exposure to them as skippers. I mean, the guys that I had my most exposure with were McKillip, my division officer, and Lieutenant Hunte, who was over McKillip. I flew a lot with Hunte, because he would take me anywhere when he was getting his time in.

Q: Did you type a lot of correspondence? How did you spend your time?

Mr. King: A lot of time working with the press news and general yeoman work. I did a lot of courts-martial work. A lot of time as editor of the paper that came out, I think maybe once a month. It was called the Coco Solo Contact. I still have some old copies. Some of my duties were connected with classified material or what passed for it then. We had an old, beat-up safe that was really a sad excuse for a safe. It had some old classified correspondence in it that we had to inventory every so often. I guess the truth of the matter is that the working hours that we had from 7:00 to 1:00 resulted in a very

---
*Captain Ernest D. McWhorter, USN; Captain Ernest L. Gunther, USN.

relaxed pace. I don't mean we did nothing, but I don't recall any arduous duties.

Q: Any unusual or interesting cases you recall?

Mr. King: No, not right off the bat. Most of our cases didn't involve murders or anything like that. I think most of it was run-of-the-mill stuff, AWOL, and things like that.*

Q: Did you actively take radioman training along with your yeoman work?

Mr. King: Well, I guess I spent so much time with the radiomen and my duties in the communications office that I had a pretty good knowledge and feel for that activity. Then I really was upset because I hadn't made third class yet. That's when it came to me, and I checked into it that I could take the exam for radioman or yeoman at the same time. McKillip said I could go ahead and get qualified down at VP-5. He worked it out that I could go down there and spend some time in the evening, and the guys would work with me. I really wasn't very good at it, because I didn't know the code too well. I was just trying to qualify from a paperwork standpoint so I could take the exam. But

---

*AWOL--Absent without leave.

yeoman, I had that down pretty well.

Q: There was a real war in progress then. Well, there were two: there was the Chinese-Japanese War, and then there was the Spanish Civil War. How much did you keep up with those?

Mr. King: Well, the Chinese-Japanese War, that kind of seemed closer to home, because, I guess, of the naval involvement--the Panay and so on.* I was a great Hemingway fan.** I loved Hemingway. And I read everything he ever wrote. To that extent, I was interested in the Spanish War, but not to the extent I was in the Chinese-Japanese War. That was closer home to me. I just had the feeling--that seemed to be more of something that would mean involvement by me, if anything ever happened.

Q: Then you had an idea that the United States might be getting into that one?

Mr. King: Yes. We talked about that a lot--the sailors

---

*On 12 December 1937, the Yangtze River gunboat Panay (PR-5) was sunk by low-flying Japanese aircraft near Nanking, China, despite prominent U.S. markings. Two men were killed and 43 wounded. Japan claimed it was a case of mistaken identity, apologized, and paid indemnities.
**Correspondent/author Ernest M. Hemingway went to Spain and wrote of the Spanish Civil War. The war was the subject of what is considered by some his greatest novel, For Whom the Bell Tolls, published in 1940.

did. We drew these scenarios, probably something happening someday, but not very specific. See, this is still back a couple years before Pearl Harbor. But there was an atmosphere about that conflict that just seemed to be growing stronger. I think all of us saw it as something that we'd hear more about before we heard less.

Q: Well, that did bring it close to home when the Panay got sunk.

Mr. King: Yes. You know, there was a guy called the pantless gunner of Panay. His name was Swede Mahlmann.* There was a poem written about him.

Q: I don't know that one.

Mr. King: Well, there was a guy named Mahlmann who was on the Panay when it was sunk. He was in his bunk and came up in his skivvy pants and manned this machine gun. A poem was written about him which was in Time magazine.** He was nationally known, "The pantless gunner of Panay." About a year later, after I left Coco Solo, I was in New

---
*Chief Boatswain's Mate Ernest R. Mahlmann, USN.
**Kansas City poet Vaun Al Arnold wrote a poem about Chief Mahlmann's courageous manning of a gun on board the Panay. It was distributed by the Associated Press and widely published. A copy of the poem appears in Hamilton Darby Perry, The Panay Incident: Prelude to Pearl Harbor (New York: The Macmillan Company, 1969), pages 102-103.

York, and he was at the receiving station there. To me he was a legendary figure. I spent some time around him, just to sort of say I shook the hand of the pantless gunner of Panay. That was quite a feeling, you know. That one incident really brought it home to the U.S. Navy, when the Panay was sunk.

Q: How much contact did you have with the USS Wright, the flagship for the patrol wings?

Mr. King: I rode her from Panama back to San Diego, and that was two or three weeks, I guess.

Q: What was the purpose of that trip?

Mr. King: I was going on leave. I got one leave from Panama in the three years I was there. I know when I left there for good, I was on a tanker, the Salinas. But the Wright was just a ride from Panama to San Diego. That was the flagship of ComAirBaseFor, E. J. King.*

Q: What do you recall about him?

Mr. King: Oh, he was a stormy, controversial figure. He

---

*Rear Admiral Ernest J. King, USN, Commander Aircraft Base Force. During World War II, King served as Chief of Naval Operations and Commander in Chief U.S. Fleet.

was the guy that crashed in the XP3D.*

Q: Well, you haven't told that story on tape, so let's get that one.

Mr. King: He was going on an early morning flight. We'd had some kind of an exercise with the Wright. When I say "we," I was just a passenger. Admiral King was supposed to take off the next morning in an experimental four-engine seaplane. The pilot was a boatswain, a flying boatswain named Baker, who was a kind of legendary figure in naval aviation.** Boatswain Baker had done it all. Admiral King gave Baker the conn when they were taking off. I was looking out a porthole of the Wright that morning, from the head, and the plane took off and headed away from the Wright, towards the mouth of the channel. There was no wind at all; the water was just like a mirror. Apparently he couldn't get it up on the step. When the plane hit the entrance to the channel, the wind was coming down the coast, so he turned around a little bit, and somehow the right wingtip--I think it had a pontoon on it--hit the water. The plane spun around a couple times and pancaked. Panic, pandemonium, the admiral's in and everything.

---
*The incident occurred in early 1937 during an attempted takeoff from Acapulco Bay, Mexico. For details see Gerard T. Morton, "Sixty Seconds to Live," U.S. Naval Institute Proceedings, September 1985, pages 70-72.
**Chief Boatswain Albert E. Baker, USN, attached to Utility Squadron One in the Wright (AV-1).

The only boat that wouldn't start was the crash boat. The coxswain flooded the engine in his haste, so they finally had to chug-chug out in a motorboat or motor launch to pick up the people from the plane. The plane hadn't sunk. It was in the water, and they were in the water hanging on. The boat came back with Admiral King, and Admiral King came up the gangway. When Admiral King came up the gangway, the OOD was a young jaygee or ensign. He just said something like, "Oh, Admiral, I'm so glad you're alive," or whatever. The admiral just roasted him, just ate him alive, on how to properly bring an admiral aboard ship. He just ate him up, to the amusement of quite a few people who were gathered around.

Q: But not to the ensign.

Mr. King: But not to the ensign, no. Oh, he ate him up. You know, he was a very stern, forbidding, formidable figure. He had a volcanic temper.

The other recollection I have is that King had this thing about uniforms. During the time I was on there, at different times, he would prescribe these variations on the standard uniform. For example, white tops and blue bottoms; white jumpers and blue trousers one day, and the next day it'd be blue jumpers and white trousers for officers and crew. It just looked so funny. We were all saying, "Well, the next thing will be mattress covers and peacoats." But he didn't get around to that. There were some strange-looking uniforms, and that was his idea. As a matter of fact, I believe that during World War II when they had that off-color, that sort of a blue, slate blue color, that he . . .

Q: Well, he was the father of the gray uniform.

Mr. King: Yes, that was another indication of his obsession with uniforms and colors and so on. The slate blue uniform was his.

Q: There must have been some odd-looking combinations, especially since the two weren't designed to go together.

Mr. King: They weren't designed to go together. As I said, to see a guy with a potbelly with about four inches of skin between the top of his pants and the bottom of his jumper walking around the ship trying to pull them down--it was ludicrous, it really was.

I don't think King had much of a sense of humor.

Q: Not that I've heard of. What did you do on liberty in Panama itself?

Mr. King: Oh, to a young kid like me, Panama was sort of glamorous. There were no laws to speak of. I mean, the barrooms and cabarets didn't close up. They had no doors. They were all open 24 hours a day. There was a chief petty officer, about 80 years old, who wore canvas uniforms. He was a legendary figure and was a chief shore patrol in Panama. I remember he would come out when there'd be some fellow in trouble, and I'd be going to mast with the captain, take notes and all, and this old guy would come in that canvas uniform of his. Had a bushy white beard and was fluent in Spanish.

The town of Colon was our liberty port. There wasn't any organized entertainment in Panama; it was just kind of a cabaret town. We did a lot of things out in the jungle. We would have a jungle party: get a keg of beer, go out in the jungle somewhere, and shoot iguanas and drink beer. We had fishing expeditions, but most of the activity was base-oriented. It was a hell of a nice base for creature comfort. It had a big swimming pool. With tropical working hours, your time is generally your own. There were free movies every night. I guess the average sailor went to the movies, as much as he did anything else. Might go ashore only once a week, something like that, because it was expensive.

Q: Did you get to know any of the Panamanian people?

Mr. King: Not real well, no. Looking back, I probably should have, but I didn't. There was quite a gap between the Panamanian people and the military and civil service. They had gold quarters and silver quarters in the housing, for example. The gold for Caucasian and silver for the Panamanian people. The Panamanians would come aboard the station there and do our laundry once a week. But a lot of the bartenders in all the gin mills and cabarets were retired Navy. There weren't many Panamanians in that line of work. There were some foreigners. There was a guy named Chris that ran the Lighthouse Bar, one of the most popular places down there. I think he was German or Czechoslovakian.

Q: Did you get the idea that the Navy provided these creature comforts on the base to discourage people from going into the town?

Mr. King: Probably so. It worked very well, because there was never any inexorable pull to go ashore. As a matter of fact, we didn't go ashore at all when a Navy ship was in. Every time a ship came, we wouldn't go near the beach. Pandemonium.

Q: I remember seeing this movie, Hell Divers, with Clark Gable and Wallace Beery as Navy men going ashore in Panama. I always wondered how true to life that was.

Mr. King: I do recall one incident down there that may or may not be true. We had some aviation tenders; the Teal, Lapwing were two of them. There was a submarine rescue ship down there whose skipper was named Hawes.* His nickname was "Spitting Dick" because he had this habit when he got excited and talked, he would spray a little bit-- very excited, volcanic. This is all secondhand; I didn't know the guy. But the story was that a fleet battleship came down one time, and Spitting Dick Hawes's ship was to tow the target, which was SOP.** When a battleship was going to fire at a target, it was tremendously important that the proper speed was observed. Hawes got very excited about keeping the exact speed.

I think the pit log broke.*** So he told the quartermaster to throw an orange crate or something over the side, and follow it down with a stopwatch and take a reading on the ship's speed so he would maintain his exact speed. Otherwise, this four-striper on the battleship would eat him up. So the quartermaster, it is said, threw

---
*Lieutenant (junior grade) Richard E. Hawes, USN, was commanding officer of the USS Falcon (ASR-2).
**SOP--standard operating procedure.
***Pit log--the pitometer log is a device for indicating the speed of a ship and distance run by measuring water pressure on a pitot tube projected outside the ship's hull.

the orange crate over the side, and then tried to follow it back down the deck with a stopwatch. A lot of guys were on deck watching what was going on, and he lost track of the orange crate. So the skipper up on the bridge saw him, and lost his temper, and came down and said, "All right, now we'll do it, and then you follow me."

So they went up the bow, threw an orange crate or something over the side, and Hawes got in front of the quartermaster, and was yelling and hollering and waving his arms running down the deck, "Gangway, gangway." The ship's cook in the galley heard the commotion, looked out, and saw the skipper running down the deck with this quartermaster chasing him with something his hand. He thought that the quartermaster had gone Asiatic and was chasing the skipper with a knife or something. So when the quartermaster went by, he stuck a skillet out the port and whacked the quartermaster on the head. I don't know how true it was, but that was a story that was widely told in Panama.

Q: Dick Hawes was skipper of a ship called the Pigeon when Cavite was bombed and was quite heroic.* One of the new frigates was named for him.**

---

*For details on Hawes's command of the USS Pigeon (ASR-6), see Anthony C. Santore, "The Mustang and the Pigeon," U.S. Naval Institute Proceedings, April 1985, pages 154-156.
**USS Hawes (FFG-53).

C. S. King #1 - 88

Mr. King: I'll be darned. Well, that very well could have been the same guy.

Q: Well, you really wound up your enlistment there in Panama, didn't you?

Mr. King: Yes, I was on what they called a kiddie cruise, a minority cruise, until the day before I was 21. I rode the tanker Salinas back to Houston. Anyway, I got off at the receiving station in Norfolk and went home on leave. I didn't know what I wanted to do really. I guess in the back of my mind I knew that I was staying in the Navy, but it was something we talked about: to do your time and go home. So I went home, and I looked around for a job a little bit. My heart wasn't really in it. I spent some time there just hanging around town.

All of a sudden, it began to really eat on me about shipping over.* In those days, if you didn't ship over inside of 90 days, you'd had it. You couldn't get back in. I began to get very worried about that 90-day period. So I anticipated a little bit, I guess, and I decided that I'd better get back where I knew I should be. I hitchhiked to Houston and went in to ship over. In fact, I was a third class yeoman then, and they said, "Well, you can ship yourself over," and they just handed me the forms. So I

---
*Ship over--to reenlist.

shipped myself over.

I think I mentioned to you that when I came to the shipping articles, it has a line in there for "Occupation." I asked this first class yeoman what to put on there, and he said, "Put down 'mariner'." So I did, and that was one of the proudest moments of my life when I put that in, "Goddamn, I'm a mariner." That was great. So I shipped over, to my great relief.

Q: How had you spent the time in the meantime, the three months?

Mr. King: Oh, nothing constructive. I just renewed my acquaintance in Aransas Pass with all my high school friends. I took up with a girl from my high school class and just had a real good time.

Q: But you evidently missed the Navy during this period.

Mr. King: Yes, I did. I was really highly conscious of the fact that I was on a ticking time bomb, and if I didn't get back in, I was going to be out of luck. So I guess in my heart I knew I was going to ship over.

Q: Well, they might have taken you back, but you wouldn't have had your crow, would you?

Mr. King: No, and I wasn't about to let that happen. So I shipped over. While I was out, I sent a telegram to the Navy Department. There was a squadron called Squadron 40T over in Europe, and I thought that'd be the greatest thing in the world, to be in Europe. So I sent a telegram asking for duty in Squadron 40T if I shipped over. I got a reply that said "No, no luck." So I just shipped over and asked for a destroyer, because I'd never been on one, and I got the Davis.*

Q: What do you remember about her?

Mr. King: A lot. The Davis was a colorful ship. We had a skipper who was a real Captain Queeg.** In his blessed memory, I don't want to say anything on tape that would diminish his memory, but he was an eccentric guy. For example, the smoking lamp was out during working hours on the Davis, and he would give a court-martial for being one minute over leave. One minute would be a court-martial, if there were circumstances that he didn't approve of. It was

---

*The USS Davis (DD-395) was commissioned 9 November 1938, one of the so-called "gold-platers," as new destroyers of the era were known to contrast them with the World War I four-stack types. The Davis was 391 feet long, had a beam of 37 feet, and a standard displacement of 1,850 tons.
**Lieutenant Commander Philip Francis Queeg was the fictitious commanding officer of the destroyer minesweeper USS Caine in Herman Wouk's celebrated novel The Caine Mutiny (Garden City, New York: Doubleday and Company, Inc., 1951). As created by Wouk, Queeg was a cowardly martinet.

common scuttlebutt around the ship that this couldn't happen, that BuNav would kick it back.* They never did.

It was quite a disciplinary ship--red hot, as they say.

Q: What was this man's name?

Mr. King: T. De Witt Carr.** He was athletic officer on a battleship before he came to the <u>Davis</u>. The guy meant well, he really did. He was a perfectionist. For example, he brought evangelists aboard ship to hold services and things like that; the smoking lamp out during working hours and so on.

During my duty aboard the <u>Davis</u>, one time the first class storekeeper went on a couple of weeks' leave, and I took over his office to relieve him of various and assorted duties, mainly paperwork, during his leave.

One of the forms that I had to fill out for him was called the quarterly inventory of dry stores, or something like that. It was a hellish form to complete, as it was not standard width, being narrower and about twice standard length. This meant trimming the carbons and filling in the blanks by typewriter on this lengthy, single-spaced form.

Another one of Captain Carr's rules was that any

---
*BuNav--Bureau of Navigation, which controlled personnel matters.
**Commander T. De Witt Carr, USN.

typing had to be court-martial quality, that is, no typos, erasures, or corrections. As was the case in most of his rules, there were no deviations.

After a very lengthy time, I finally got the form finished, checked, and rechecked it, added a paper clip, and took it up to the captain's cabin. Captain Carr took the form and began carefully reading every entry. He completed his review and started over again and finally threw it on his desk in front of me and said, "What's wrong?" I could have sworn it was perfect, but I carefully went over it again and, finding no errors, I said so.

He grabbed the form, stood up, and almost shouted, "The paper clip. The paper clip."

I was really baffled now, and he said, "The small side out. The small side out." He then gave me a graphic display on how to slide on a paper clip with the large side out that took one motion instead of the small side out, which required two.

Believe me, there was no humor in the situation. To this day, I slide paper clips on with the large side out instead of vice versa.

It was an uncomfortable ship from the standpoint of the crew. But we had a hell of a good crew on there, great crew. The _Davis_ went into commission in Boston. She was built in Bath, Maine. I went to Boston for the commissioning detail and was there about three months. In fact, I was there during that big East Coast hurricane in 1938. I made second class while I was in the pre-commissioning detail of the Davis, which was a source of great satisfaction to me.

Boston was a good liberty town, A-number one liberty port.

Q: What was so attractive about it?

Mr. King: Oh, I don't know, it was just a combination of things. It was a place that all the sailors agreed was a good liberty town. It's like the difference between San Diego and Bremerton or Long Beach and Bremerton. It was just a good liberty town.

I got married the first time in Boston. I've been married twice. When I was on the Davis, we went to Bermuda on our shakedown cruise. Bermuda in those days was not a liberty port, not at all. It was a high-dollar place. On our first liberty, the word got back that it was no liberty port. There was a ship's cook on the Davis named Buck Ogle. Buck and I were kind of running mates on the beach. We made a bet. We bet some guys on the ship that we could go ashore, pick up a couple of good-looking girls, and bring them back out to the ship. I don't know why you make a foolish bet--we just did it.

So we went ashore, and we tried and failed miserably. We went to an English bobby, a policeman, and told him our story. He thought that was the greatest thing in the world. So he said, "I know a couple of Yank girls here. I'll see that you all win your bet."

I forget the details, but he came back with two nice-looking girls. They lived in New England and worked at the Hamilton Hotel in Bermuda in the summertime. They thought this bet was the funniest thing they ever heard of. So they said, "Sure, we'll go out and help you win your bet."

So we pooled our money, and we found enough for a boat ride. They had a great big, mahogany speedboat there that took people for a ride out on the bay. We took every cent we had and talked this speedboat operator into taking us out to the ship, to circle the ship, and then come back. He said he'd do that for however much money we had, $10.00 or whatever. We got in the back with these two girls and put our arms around them. We went out to the Davis, and this guy went around the Davis and we waved. We made sure that everybody on the ship saw us, caused a commotion. That was about the end of it. They said they had a good time, we had a good time, and that was all. We went back and collected our bet.

Later on, while I was still on the Davis, my appendix ruptured. I was in Boston in the hospital for about three months. While I was in the hospital, the guy in the bunk next to me for a while was a reporter for a tabloid paper in Boston in those days, the Boston Globe or the Boston Mirror, something like that. He was a Navy vet and was in for some chronic medical problem. I corresponded with this girl, Cathy Jackman, that was my date on the speedboat. We had picked up a correspondence by mail, and when I was in the hospital, she came down to see me.

Q: Since she was from that area.

Mr. King: We began to get closer and closer. This reporter thought that was great. You know, in a hospital you have no secrets. I told him all this about the speedboat, and he thought that was terrific.

Q: Didn't have anything else to do.

Mr. King: No. So we finally agreed to get married, Kathy and I did. I thought I was in love, but it wasn't really a carefully thought-out process. Anyway, we got married. We stayed at a large hotel there in Boston over a weekend. We got married by some well-known judge in Boston. The last person he'd married before us--and this newspaper reporter arranged that--was Charles Winninger, who was the central character on a well-known radio show called "Showboat"--he married an actress, Blanche Ring. Anyway, we were the next couple he married.

The next morning, I thought about this reporter, and I went down to get a newspaper. I looked at one paper to see if there was anything in it. Nothing. I looked at this one here, and I just picked it up and turned it over to the front page. The whole front page--I've still got it--is a picture of Kathy and me standing before this judge to get married. The headline says "Lonely Texas Bluejacket Weds Heiress." She wasn't an heiress, you know. I wasn't a lonely Texas bluejacket.

Q: Other than that . . .

Mr. King: Other than that, but it read well. But, anyway, that's what happened to the case of the marriage.

Q: So how long did that one last?

Mr. King: Until I went to China. We got divorced after I got back from China. We were only together a fairly short time. Both of our intentions were good, but it was not a marriage destined for enduring. We parted amicably.

Anyway, back to the *Davis*. It was a memorable ship, because we spent all our time talking about the captain. The whole crew did. I mean, he was such a martinet and we just never knew what was going to happen next.

Let's see, that was in '39, and in '39 the Navy set up something called the Grand Banks Patrol. Captain Louis Denfeld was ComGrandBanPat.* There was the <u>Davis</u> and the <u>Jouett</u>, and two or three destroyers and the <u>Alexander Hamilton</u>, I believe, was the Coast Guard cutter. We were doing patrol duty off the Grand Banks, antisubmarine patrol. Supposed to be 11 days out and 11 days in, but it took longer than 11 days in to fix up the damage that you'd take in 11 days out, because it was rough; it was really rough water. The <u>Davis</u> was not a seaworthy ship. She rolled excessively. She was top-heavy. That was really an adventurous time.

Q: How did you take that? Did you get seasick?

Mr. King: No, I never did get very seasick, but it was awfully hard. We couldn't eat regular meals. We had to eat sandwiches and soup, and stuff like that. It was really miserable weather. But it was kind of exciting. You know, all of a sudden, there's dirty submarines out there and all that sort of stuff.

After the Grand Banks Patrol, we went down to Texas, where we were going to be assigned to the Gulf of Mexico. There was a well-known case, at that time, of a ship, a German ship that we were to take station on and not let out

---
*Captain Louis E. Denfeld, USN. Denfeld later served as Chief of Naval Operations from 1947 to 1949.

of our sight.

Q: The <u>Columbus</u>?

Mr. King: It was a merchant ship. She scuttled herself off the East Coast of the United States.

Q: I think there was one called the <u>Columbus</u> that the British had some ships after.*

Mr. King: That might have been, because we were involved with that ship. This was in the Gulf of Mexico, and we didn't have radar. But one night she anchored on one side of a small island, and we anchored on the other side. During the night these people had gone ashore and had put up some scaffolding, and some lights on the scaffolding to look like lights on a ship. The next morning she was gone, and we had egg all over our face. But that was kind of an exciting thing--for us, at least.

We went around to the West Coast. On the West Coast, there was a newspaper in San Diego called <u>The Keyhole</u>. We had acquired the name the "Dipsy Doodle <u>Davis</u>" because of all this funny stuff on board.

---

*On 12 December 1939, the 32,581-ton German luxury liner <u>Columbus</u> was scuttled by her own crew 450 miles off the U.S. East Coast when intercepted by a British destroyer. Prior to that she had been shadowed by U.S. destroyers and the cruiser USS <u>Tuscaloosa</u> (CA-37).

Q: Well, how did people outside the ship learn about your problems?

Mr. King: It was a well-known fact in the Navy in those days. Everybody knew what a hot ship was and which one was a home and a feeder. They found out, particularly when we'd be nested with some other destroyers, and the boatswain's mate on the <u>Davis</u> would pass the word the smoking lamp was out at 8:00. This kind of thing doesn't go unnoticed. So the <u>Keyhole</u>, which was <u>National Enquirer</u> style, came out with the headline when we got to San Diego, the "Dipsy Doodle Arrives in San Diego." That didn't please the skipper at all.

About that time, to my great relief, I went from the <u>Davis</u> to the <u>Warrington</u>, the DD-383.* She was really a great ship, just a wonderful ship. I liked her. The skipper was F. G. Fahrion, and the exec was D. C. Varian.** I had a battle station up in the fire control.

Q: Director?

---

*The USS <u>Warrington</u> (DD-383) had been commissioned 9 February 1938. She was 381 feet long, 37 feet in the beam, standard displacement of 1,850 tons and main battery of eight 5-inch guns.
**Commander Frank G. Fahrion, USN; Lieutenant Donald C. Varian, USN.

Mr. King: Gun director, yes. I got $5.00 extra a month for being gun pointer on the director.

About that time, we were in San Diego, and the Asiatic draft came out. In those days for the Asiatic Fleet, a draft came out twice a year listing the ratings that were needed. Anybody that had 30 months' obligated service was fair game. If you were a married man with a home and family and you had 30 months' obligated service, and your rating came up on the list, it was bad news, principally because dependents were no longer allowed on the Asiatic Station.

I began to get copies of mimeographed notes in the guard mail from different destroyers in San Diego saying in effect, "My name is Jones, yeoman first. I'm on the 'Neversail.' I have a wife and three kids, and I've got 30 months' obligated service. If you'll take my draft, I'll give you $300.00 or my Model A." Anyway, it was serious business. These people were not anxious to leave home without their families, and I couldn't blame them a bit. All of a sudden, it dawned on me: this was my great opportunity to go to China.

Q: Had you already had a falling-out with your wife, so it didn't bother you to leave her?

Mr. King: We had sort of come to an understanding.

Q: Before you get to that, maybe you could talk some more about the Warrington and mention some of these individuals and what you recall about them.

Mr. King: Well, I was impressed with the gunnery officer, because he had a good sense of humor, but he also was no nonsense. He took some extra pains with me in getting my qualifications for gun director and the $5.00 a month. I liked that. The skipper and the exec were so different from anything we'd seen on the Davis that it was kind of refreshing to me. Both the skipper and the exec were hard-driving, no-nonsense type of individuals. I had a very positive feeling towards both of them, but I was only on the Warrington for about three months. So I didn't get to know that many people that well. The Warrington was later sunk with almost all hands off the East Coast, around Cape Hatteras, in a hurricane. She was another one of those top-heavy tin cans. She wasn't in the exact same class as the Davis. But, I think a lot of those destroyers at that time were a little top-heavy for heavy weather.

Q: What kind of jobs did you have in these two destroyers?

Mr. King: Well, on the _Davis_, when I first went aboard, I was logroom yeoman. They had a chief yeoman, Gus Wren, and a first class in the ship's office. At that time I was second class and had the logroom, engineering office. I also had the gedunk stand, which wasn't bad.

Q: How did that go with the other duty? Was it just collateral?

Mr. King: It was collateral. I think I got $5.00 a month extra to run the gedunk stand. It was really very small, about the size of an average closet, and we just had cigarettes, razors, and that sort of business on a destroyer.

Q: So it wasn't a soda fountain type thing?

Mr. King: No, far from it. Just a little wire-screen cage receptacle. I opened it whenever the mood struck me and closed it when the mood struck me.

Q: Sounds like you just had mostly necessities.

Mr. King: Bare necessities. One thing I recall now is our shakedown cruise, when we went to Rio, to Buenos Aires, and to Puerto Belgrano, down in South America. In one of those places--I think it was Buenos Aires--I bought some miscellaneous candies for the gedunk stand, a case of this and a case of that. Well, one of the cases of candies that I got were little chocolate jugs that had liqueur in them. It was the real McCoy, which I didn't know about. But the word got around very, very fast. And so the first time we went to sea, after a weekend liberty wherever it was, I began to have a run on that candy, from the various guys on board ship after the word got out. I guess maybe it was the chief engineer got wind of it, and he disposed of those candy liqueur jugs.

Later on, I was transferred from the logroom. I was on the Davis a year and a half, maybe. I finally wound up in the ship's office with Chief Yeoman Gus Wren. As logroom yeoman, I was keeping all the paperwork associated with the engineering department. In fact, I had a getting-under-way station down in the main engine room. And then later on I wound up in the ship's office. The ship's office--you just do all the paperwork that happens on a destroyer other than logroom, personnel, and so on. By that time I was first class.

Q: Was there a separate rating for personnelman then?

Mr. King: No, yeoman was everything. I was always kind of

gung-ho about my job. I liked being a yeoman. I thought it was a good rating, and I took a lot of pride in it. I went the extra mile in keeping records and doing things a little fancy, that kind of thing. I was just a round peg in a round hole.

The chief on a destroyer can retire to chiefs' quarters if he's got a good first class, and that's what Chief Wren did. He just moved into the chiefs' quarters, and I became *de facto* chief, which was fine with both of us. It suited me, and it suited him.

Q: Any specific recollections about working with the service records? You really have a control over a guy's career there. If you make a mistake, you can really mess him up.

Mr. King: I took that very, very seriously. In those days we had the small brown foldover service records. They were about that wide and about this high and opened out.

Q: About six by eight, six by ten?

Mr. King: Yes, and they had small pages, about eight inches by three inches, something like that. It was really quite a trick to get everything typed on these pages. Every time you typed on a page, or made an entry on a page, you sent a copy to BuNav, so there were duplicate copies of everything. There were these horror stories about guys that would not send in a copy to BuNav. That was like smoking in a magazine; you didn't do something like that. I took a great deal of pride in the records that I kept. A man's record was him. That's him on the piece of paper. So whatever happens, for better or worse, goes on his record. Then in those days we had a CSC--a continuous service certificate--that opens out to about that long.

Q: Two or three feet?

Mr. King: Yes, and these CSCs kept track of everything. See, your service record, when you shipped over, went back to BuNav, and you got a new one. But the CSC goes on forever. Very nice thing; it's got a green hard binder on it. Also the pages have geographical entries. Wherever you are, you put down that entry in the CSC. I used to sit up at night, reading CSCs, to see all the names in there, Shanghai and Cairo. Some of the old hands had been all over everywhere. I thought how neat that would be if I ever had stuff like that in my CSC.

Q: How would you compare destroyer life with what you'd known in the cruiser?

Mr. King: Oh, it's as different as night is from day. In a cruiser, your division is your world. On a destroyer, the ship is the world, and you get to know everybody on the ship. The black gang and the deck force--they're all part of one unit. It's very closely knit. It always seemed kind of funny to me how when sailors would spend all day long on a ship working side by side, then they'd go ashore at night and run into each other, and you'd think they hadn't seen each other in six months: "Goddamn, you old son . . ."--that kind of spirit was more pronounced on a destroyer. When you went ashore, you would feel a lot more pride in your own ship when two destroyers were in the same port. They're kind of like two alley cats: "You're okay, but that's the *Somers*, and this is the *Davis* over here." That kind of business. I liked the destroyer Navy.

Q: I imagine the edge was taken off some of that enjoyment by having to endure Carr's weird behavior.

Mr. King: Yes, I think that brought the crew closer together. Everybody wanted to get off, and people would have various schemes. They'd tell me, "Now, my dad knows this congressman," or something like that. But it wouldn't work. You couldn't do that. I was almost like a chaplain, because so many guys wanted to get off. In fact, they were ready to fake anything to get off there, but there just wasn't much you could do.

Q: Do you have any other examples of the things that he would pull?

Mr. King: Well, this business about the evangelists. We had a radioman by the name of Ryan on there one time. Ryan was the most no-good guy that ever came down the pike. He was as immoral as an alley cat. A kind of likable guy, but he made his own rules. When Ryan came aboard the Davis, all he had in the world was the uniform he had on his back and a seabag that just had junk in it. He had a very bad record, and everybody said, "Carr is going to eat him up." Well, Ryan hadn't been aboard ship more than a week before he was over leave several hours. So we all said, "Boy, he's going to get it." Ryan sensed something in Carr maybe from his bringing the evangelists aboard. So Ryan asked for permission to see Carr before he held mast.* So Ryan went to the skipper and said, "Captain, I'm going to mast today. I want you to throw the book at me. I'm no good. I'm no good at all. I got no business in the Navy. I'm rotten to the core."

And Carr said, "Now wait a minute. There's some good in all of us."

---

*Captain's mast is a procedure by which the commanding officer hears cases and imposes nonjudicial punishment. It is a lesser step than a court-martial.

Ryan said, "No, no sympathy, Captain. I want you to throw the book at me. I don't deserve it. I've let you down, I've let the Navy down. I just don't deserve it."

Q: Reverse psychology.

Mr. King: So Ryan went to mast and got a warning or some damn thing. We all said, "God, almighty, how can that happen?" It happened again and again. Every time Ryan got in trouble, he would go up and would con Carr. He would say, "Captain, I told you I was no good."

The captain would say, "Now, Ryan, now, Ryan." I don't know how--that guy just had his number. But anybody else, I mean, one minute over leave or late hammocks, was bad news. We had another guy that had a deck court for late hammocks.

Q: What do you mean late hammocks?

Mr. King: Late reveille. I mean, just not getting up exactly at the right time. You got a deck court for sleeping in. I kept saying, "This can't happen. They're going to throw this out when it gets to Washington," but it never did get thrown out.

Carr wanted very much to be liked. I felt, in some cases, a little bit of sympathy for the guy. Because I saw some letters he wrote in trying to get an assignment off the Davis. He mentioned how he was athletic officer of the West Virginia. He had done this and he had done that on the West Virginia, and he really had an opinion of himself that didn't square with the Davis.

When we were flagship of ComGranBanPat, Grand Banks Patrol, and Louis Denfeld was the commodore, I spent some time on the bridge when both of them were up there. Carr would paint this picture of himself to Denfeld that was not factually wrong. But it seemed to me a kind of desperate attempt for approbation by Denfeld. I never did really dislike the guy personally that much. I thought he was wrong in some of the things he did, but I always had an undercurrent way down deep, a kind of, I don't know, a sympathy, or I had a feeling for the guy.

Q: Well, you know, Herman Wouk made an interesting point about Queeg in The Caine Mutiny. He said that the guy was kind of a martinet in his ship. He didn't do all that well under pressure, but he and his peers were the guys that held the Navy together before the war so there was a nucleus to build around.

Mr. King: Yes. That's very apropos in Carr's case, and I don't want to paint too bad a picture of him. I mean, the things he did were bad, but maybe not for bad reasons.

C. S. King #1 - 110

Q: His intentions were good.

Mr. King: His intentions were very good. He always thought of himself as someone who would one day go on to be CNO or something like that.* He really had this vision of himself.

Q: Well, what impressions did you form of Denfeld in that capacity?

Mr. King: I was terribly impressed with the guy, because Denfeld approached this job as Commander Grand Banks Patrol in such a confident, easygoing, low-key manner. When he was on the bridge, no doubt about who was in charge. But it was a very low-key thing. I mean, he was smooth and understated. There was no question about his competence or confidence. He just struck me as a guy who was really a very competent man, but in a low-key undemonstrative way.

Q: Did you have any contacts at all, or was it just patrolling and getting bashed about?

Mr. King: That was about the size of it, because Captain Denfeld would leave the ship when we got into port and set up somewhere, come back to the ship for the next go-around.

---
*CNO--Chief of Naval Operations.

The whole thing was in a state of flux. For example, I remember that task force we had off of Boston, but when we went down to the Gulf of Mexico and were chasing that merchant ship, we were by ourselves then. It was the kind of atmosphere that made all of us feel that we were on the edge of something. Things were going along in the big world. I couldn't say that I saw war coming, but at the same time, it was being brought home, the war in Europe, for example. I knew something was going to happen.

Q: I would think that would be a great burden on the exec in having a skipper like that and in trying to moderate some of his influence for the benefit of the wardroom and the crew.

Mr. King: Well, he was hard on his officers. We had a guy, G. P. Enright, who was gunnery officer.* And Carr reduced him almost to nothing. I mean, Enright was ineffective at his job because Carr was so hard on him.

There was a young ensign on there who was always in trouble, and Carr would say, "Up or down." And the guy'd say "Down." Carr was awfully hard on his officers. I think harder than he was on the crew. He was a tough guy.

Q: What led to the Davis getting transferred then to the

---
*Lieutenant George P. Enright, USN.

Pacific?

Mr. King: I don't really know what caused that. It was just a shift. I don't have any background on that.

Q: What kind of skipper was Fahrion in the Warrington?

Mr. King: Well, Fahrion on the Warrington, the three months that I was on there, I didn't have much personal exposure to him. I didn't have a bridge battle station, but was in the director, and I was ship's writer. There was a chief yeoman on there, but when I came aboard as ship's writer--and I was competent because of the work on the Davis--the chief yeoman just really sort of turned it over to me. I had more time with the exec. I can't give any specific personality things about the guys. I remember that Varian, the exec, was terribly upset when I came back with my orders from the Argonne, but he got philosophical pretty quick on that. I think down deep inside, he couldn't really fault me for what I wanted to do. He faulted me for doing it the way that I did.

Q: You told me that story the other day.

Mr. King: We didn't part enemies or anything.

C. S. King #1 - 113

Q: Why don't you put that story on tape then?

Mr. King: Anyway, on the Warrington, when I got these notes from other yeomen, I saw how really serious it was about someone going to China. All this came together in my mind that now was the time for me to go. The Argonne was the flagship of Commander Base Force, the command that ran the personnel matters of the whole Pacific Fleet. The Argonne was a former transport and former submarine tender that hadn't been to sea for some years. There were kind of jokes about being on shore duty on the Argonne. I went over to the Argonne in one of the Warrington's boats. In the Argonne there was an enormous office space down below decks, like a whole mess hall had been converted into one big office. They had a fence outside and about 30 or 40 desks behind the fence for the yeomen that handled all these different phases of personnel. One guy worried about yeomen, storekeepers; someone else, engineers.

So I went up and waited at the gate for the longest time, but they aren't anxious to see people. I mean, everybody wants something. So finally some bored seaman came over and said, "What do you want?"

I said, "I want to see about going to China."

A hush fell over the place. You could have heard a pin drop in that whole office space. Not one key hit a typewriter; there was just dead silence.

Q: That wasn't the sort of thing people volunteered for.

Mr. King: I guess I was the first one that ever did that, I don't know. And that guy says, "Come in."

He opened the gate and took me over to this chief, who said, "Sit down."

So I sat down. And, without saying anything, he started putting a paper in his typewriter and he said, "You want to go to China?"

And I said, "Yeah." So he started typing. Then I said, "Wait a minute. I need to talk about a relief. I'm on the Warrington."

He said, "Oh, we'll take care of that," and kept on typing. And he said, "Have you got obligated service?"

I think I did have obligated service. I don't think I had to extend. Anyway, it didn't make any difference. If I wanted to go, I went. So I saw the deed was done. All of a sudden, I got kind of a funny feeling. I said, "Now, wait a minute." I said, "Let me get back to the ship before you send the dispatch, because I'll be in a heap of trouble."

He said, "Not to worry."

I was riding the boat back to the Warrington, and I looked up and I saw this signalman transmitting from the bridge of the Argonne. I knew damn well what it was about, because he was aiming that signal at the Warrington. So I got back, and Commander Varian was at the gangway. He had the yellow copy of the signalman's message. He was hot, and I don't blame him a damn bit. That was a rotten thing for me to do, not to say anything to him. But I really had gone over only to explore the possibility. I had no idea I'd get into what I did. My intentions were good. I gave him the facts, and he said something like, "You should have known better than that." He was really ticked off, but he very quickly assumed a kind of philosophical attitude.

I think they did get a relief for me, and so I went to the Chaumont in about a week.

Q: That was the slow boat to China.

Mr. King: Yes, the Chaumont was another colorful ship. In those days there were only two transports in the whole Navy--the Chaumont and the Henderson. The Chaumont had a bad name about carrying Marines. The old story goes that at one time a Marine was on the Chaumont and was on one of these perpetual working parties. They had him over the side, and his job was to touch up the paint around the Chaumont's name on the stern. So he wrote under each letter. Under C, he wrote "Christ." Under H, he wrote "Help." Under A, he wrote "All." "Christ, Help All U.S. Marines On Naval Transports." He left it there, and it wasn't detected for a day or so. But the ships in the vicinity had a laugh. That may or may not be true; I don't know.

The <u>Chaumont</u> was a colorful ship in that it had this hodgepodge on it all the time of every conceivable type-- all the way from prisoners and nuts to, and from, the Asiatic station and drafts.

Q: Dependents.

Mr. King: I don't think she carried dependents when I was on there.

Yeomen were kind of welcome on transports, because they were able to be of help in keeping up all the personnel records and everything. There was a chief on the <u>Chaumont</u> named Ralston, who was a legend in the Navy. He really effectively ran the whole business of drafts to and from the Asiatic Fleet and their assignments, the whole thing. He was really the man.

Q: Well, BuNav didn't assign people to a specific ship. It just assigned you to Asiatic Fleet, then the fleet assigned you within.

Mr. King: The way it worked was that the Asiatic Fleet would send the numbers it needed in to BuNav. BuNav would divide it up by fleets and put out the numbers, heavily West Coast oriented for transportation cost.

Then when the Chaumont or the Henderson was on the way out, they would send in a radio dispatch--the passenger list, names and rates. Then the Asiatic Fleet flagship would put names and rates on a dispatch assignment. Smith, Jones, and Brown to the Augusta, that kind of thing. So that before you left the Chaumont, you were assigned. In a lot of cases, there were reassignments. If you went to the tender Black Hawk, you might wind up on any one of the Black Hawk destroyers. If you went to the Augusta, you might wind up ship's company or flag allowance. I went to the Augusta, and was reassigned to the flag.

Q: Well, why don't we take the Augusta first. What do you recall about her? Where was she geographically?

Mr. King: Geographically she was in Shanghai. I had this feeling--almost a mystic feeling--about the Asiatic Fleet. By that time, I had seen so many Asiatic sailors and heard so many tales and everything that I could hardly realize I was finally in the Asiatic Fleet. I remember on the Chaumont when we went by the island of Formosa. We were fairly close to it one night. There were many cooking fires. You could smell smoke from them, and it just struck me as incredibly romantic to be there in that part of the world and smell these strange smells.

When I went aboard the Augusta, it was the same type of feeling. There was a bronze plaque on the quarterdeck, where a sailor was killed when a Japanese shell struck the Augusta. On board the Augusta were all these legends--guys I'd heard so much about--Danny Wahlmer, the dental technician who had been at Peking for a number of years and had an imaginary dog. You know, there were real Asiatic sailors. You've probably heard a thousand stories.

Q: I'd like to hear yours. Tell me about the imaginary dog, for example.

Mr. King: Well, Danny Wahlmer was a first class dental technician, who had spent a lot of time in the Far East and at one time was at the Peking Embassy as a naval dental tech. Danny and the Asiatic Fleet were made for each other. He took on all the coloration.

I can give you one example of Danny--the print shop on the Augusta was the place. That's where the insiders met-- the yeomen, the printers, an occasional cook. That's where they had the coffee pot, and they had a windup record player. That was the elite place to meet. I mean, if you could hang out in the print shop, you were in. I hung out in the print shop. We did all sorts of things in the print shop.

One time a guy named Squirrel Worrels, one of the printers, wanted to get a gold dragon in his ear. So he asked Danny to pierce his ear. Danny said, "Of course." So the next night Danny brought up this kit from the sick bay, and he had a needle. I don't know what kind of a needle it was. But I remember it was curved and had three sides. So Danny put Squirrel on a little stool, sat him there, and he grabbed his ear. He punched that needle into his ear. When he got it halfway through, he said to Squirrel--and his voice sounded very funny--"Are you all right?"

Squirrel said, "Yeah."

Danny fainted, just fell right over. So none of us knew what to do. Hell, I wasn't going to pull that needle out of some guy's ear, that big, three-cornered needle. So somebody went to the sick bay, and the doctor came up. I guess he saw as much humor in it as anything else, so he went over to Squirrel, and pulled it on through, and stuffed some cotton or something in there. By that time Danny was sitting up. And Danny was wailing. The doctor said to Squirrel, "If you people want to get your ears pierced, if you're that stupid, come down to sick bay and we'll talk about it. But don't sit up here in the print shop poking holes in somebody's ears with [whatever kind of needle it was]."

Everything Danny did was kind of colorful. He just

went from story to story.

Q: Well, what was the dog?

Mr. King: For some reason he had this imaginary dog. And everybody went along with it, you know. He would go down the ship calling the dog along with him as if it were really there--just another indication of Danny's being Asiatic.

It was that kind of thing and those kinds of people that I thought were the real Asiatics.

Q: Do you have more examples?

Mr. King: Well, more began to be evident after I'd been there for a while. A lot of these bamboo Americans, so-called, left the Navy and retired out there. Most of them settled in the Philippines, but some of them were in China and various places. A lot of these stories probably are not factual at all. One guy on the _Augusta_ was supposed to have bought a horse in Shanghai and rode the horse out in the Whangpoo River, back out to the ship. He tied the horse up to the gangway, and came on board, and left this horse, which drowned at the gangway. That may or may not be true. That's the kind of thing that you hear about Asiatic sailors. I mean, I just wanted to know more about them, and I wanted to be one.

I got aboard the Augusta, and on my first liberty there I was, going ashore in Shanghai, China. I just couldn't get over it. In those days, the mess attendants in the officers' mess on the flag were all Chinese, but they were not really U.S. Navy. They changed from ship to ship. When the Houston came out to relieve the Augusta, all these Chinese mess boys shifted to the Houston.* I don't really know to this day what the paperwork was on those people, how they did it. But to be a naval mess boy was for a Chinese man a position of great privilege and wealth. They were very, very proud. All of them just wore apprentice seaman stripes. None of them had hash marks or crows.

I was sitting in the motor launch across from this one Chinese who was going ashore. I guess he was married and had all his family and children on the beach--a real honest-to-god local Chinese mess-boy type. Older man--I guess he was 50 years old. He knew that I was a new arrival, so he said to me in a very imperious tone of voice, "Which name belong to you?"

He knew I was fresh on the "Augie." I was as respectful as if he were an admiral. I said, "My name is

---

*The USS Houston (CA-30) relieved the USS Augusta (CA-31) as the flagship of Commander in Chief Asiatic Fleet on 19 November 1940. Each ship was 600 feet long, had a beam of 66 feet, a standard displacement of 9,050 tons, and a main battery of nine 8-inch guns. The Houston was commissioned in June 1930 and the Augusta in January 1931.

King."

And he said, "It's a good Chinese name. You take care. You be good boy."

I said, "Right. Right." I mean, I was going to do what he told me to. I was real impressed with the guy. I cultivated these guys, because I love Chinese food and enjoyed being around them. They had the commuted ration system. They didn't have a regular mess for the Chinese guys. Their rations were commuted into cash and credited to the officers' mess. They cooked their own meals, their own style, their own fashion, in the galley, and they ate after the officers ate, and they all ate in the galley. If you got to know them well enough, and got to be in, you could eat with them. So I finally got in with them. That was wonderful food, because they took just leftovers from the officers' food, mixed it with rice, seasoned it up, and it was just wonderful food. I ate as many meals up there in the galley as I did back in the mess, because it was such good food and I just liked those guys.

Later on, there was a fellow named Jimmy Ho who worked for the Secretary of the Navy, when I was in the Pentagon working for Arleigh Burke.* Jimmy Ho was also on the _Augusta_ and the _Houston_. He at that time had made the transition and went from Chinese mess boy to a regular U.S. Navy type. He was chief commissary steward. He had charge

---
*Admiral Arleigh A. Burke, USN, was Chief of Naval Operations from August 1955 to August 1961.

of the SecNav mess.* I would go down and chat with him from time to time about the "good old days."

Q: Did any of these bamboo-Americans, as you call them, have Chinese wives?

Mr. King: Yes, a lot of them did.

Q: Even before they retired?

Mr. King: Yes. That was not too uncommon.

There was a guy named Cal Coolidge that ran a bar in Manila; he was a retired chief water tender. He was not married, but had a household in Manila. When the Japs took over, he was captured, and he had put his uniform back on. Cal was a guy I got to know pretty well. Before the war he was in one of the prison camps in the Philippines and later, during the war, was being transferred by a Japanese ship from the Philippines to Japan. His ship was attacked by American planes, and he was killed when it went down. There were a lot of cases like that of these poor guys that got picked up when the Japanese took over the Philippines.

Q: What was your job in the flag allowance?

---
*SecNav--Secretary of the Navy.

C. S. King #1 - 124

Mr. King: I was operations yeoman. There was a fleet operations officer, whose name was Commander H. B. Slocum.* I was his yeoman. The flag office on the <u>Augusta</u>, and also on the <u>Houston</u>, was a large office, midships, second deck. There was a big outer office with maybe 15 or 20 desks for the various yeoman. Then behind it was kind of an elongated office with about six desks where the officers sat: the fleet gunnery officer, the fleet operations officer, the fleet maintenance officer, and so on. When we were at our desks in the office, and, say, Commander Slocum wanted me, he would buzz dit-da-dit for K on the buzzer. Then I would go in the back, stand there with my shorthand pad, and take dictation. Then I'd go back out and type it. But each of us yeoman had our call sign on the buzzer.

Q: I take it you were a pretty good typist.

Mr. King: I was. If I am immodest enough to say so, I was an excellent typist. I was a good shorthand man too. I forget my speed exactly. I guess I got pretty close to 70-80 words a minute on the typewriter. I was very fast, accurate. I could take shorthand at 100 words a minute. I took great pride in being a good typist and a good shorthand man. Those were all manual typewriters, too, in

---
*Commander Harry B. Slocum, USN.

those days.

Q: Sure. What sort of things do you remember about Slocum and the work you did for him?

Mr. King: Well, this was in the days where we were getting closer and closer to having a problem with the Japanese. One of the biggest jobs that I had for Slocum was the fleet movement reports which were all encrypted. I maintained a master list of all the geographical ports in the Far East. Then we would put out dispatches that listed all the ships, their whereabouts, and so on.

Slocum was a good man, but he was no-nonsense; he had very little sense of humor. He was just a good man, a full commander. Now when I was on the Houston, the USS Gold Star was going into Hong Kong on a certain day. It was part of my job to type up a dispatch which would then go out to customs, etcetera, requesting medical pratique on arrival and so forth for the USS Gold Star into Hong Kong on so-and-so day. The dispatch had to get there three days before the arrival. It was a routine thing. I did it for all the ships in the fleet.

Q: The Gold Star was the station ship for Guam.

Mr. King: Right. The <u>Houston</u> had been down towards Mindanao somewhere for a short-range battle practice, and we had done very well. We came back, and I was at my desk doing various things, when the announcement came over the system that because of the excellent short-range battle practice, all hands not in the duty section were given a 72-hour liberty. Well, I had the dispatch for the <u>Gold Star</u> all made up, ready to be signed. When they passed that word about the liberty, I put that dispatch in the lock drawer of my desk. I meant to go down, put on my liberty uniform, come back up, take it up and get it released, leave it with the CWO, and go ashore.* Worked out just fine, except I didn't go back up to the office. I went ashore and was ashore for the weekend.

Monday I came back, and all of a sudden it was like that time at Coco Solo. I felt this terrible premonition come on me. I opened my lock drawer, and there was that dispatch. This was Monday, and the <u>Gold Star</u> was due into Hong Kong on Monday. So I just took the dispatch and went on up to the radio shack to the CWO. When I showed it to him he was as filled with alarm as I was. I said, "Is there any way in the world you can get this off right now?"

He said, "I'll try, but this is bad. This is real, real, real bad."

So I gave it to him. He was the same guy that was

---

*CWO--communication watch officer.

later aboard the Peary during that fateful run who put in to stay on the Peary and was killed. His name was Ensign Hirst.*

Anyway, I went back to my desk and was told, "Commander Slocum wants to see you."

I knew that I was in bad trouble. God, he ate me out. He emphasized the gravity, because Hong Kong was an international port and the Gold Star could have been kept out of the harbor if the British had wanted to. After the preliminaries, I said, "Well, Commander Slocum, all I can say is that I've worked for you a year and a half, and I've never made a mistake like this before."

He said, "You don't make a mistake like this the first time. You don't _ever_ make a mistake like this." Oh, he gave me hell. He should have. There was no reason in the world why he shouldn't. I deserved every damn thing that he said.

But he didn't hold a grudge, because I worked for him some little time after that, and he saved my neck, literally, a couple times in all the maneuvering in who went where after the war started. I'd be a dead duck today if it wasn't for him.

Q: How do you mean that?

---

*Ensign William B. Hirst, Jr., USNR.

Mr. King: Well, in deciding who would go with Admiral Hart, for example, on that plane that time. He put me on that list. And in Java, he got me on the Sturgeon.* I don't mean out of a sense of being a teacher's pet or something, but because decisions were made, and I just feel that because I was his direct yeoman such a long time that--I don't mean this in a toadying sense, but I really feel that he was practicing loyalty up and loyalty down in its finest sense.

Q: Bet you didn't ever make a mistake even remotely similar to that one after that.

Mr. King: Never, ever, never. In fact, from the time of Coco Solo, I never made up a fake communications item. And after that time with the dispatch, I never again put something in my desk in a lock drawer that was action. Never hid an action thing from that time to this.

Q: What impressions do you have of Admiral Hart from that period?**

Mr. King: I got to see a fair amount of him. I was very

---

*The submarine USS Sturgeon (SS-187) evacuated a number of people, including King, from the Dutch East Indies, in early 1942.
**Admiral Thomas C. Hart, USN, Commander in Chief U.S. Asiatic Fleet, 1939-42.

much aware of his seniority. His signal number as admiral was number one in the U.S. Navy. I was also very much aware of the burden of command that was on him, being in that place at that time. I was really filled with admiration and respect for the burden that he carried. Although he carried it in such a manner--he was a guy, I guess, who never had the slightest doubt about his own competency. He was a small man physically. He was an extremely heavy cigarette smoker. He had an ego. Concealed somewhat, but I mean nonetheless, he had no doubts about his own competency. I read a book recently, a book was written about him that I got through the Proceedings.* That pretty well sums up Admiral Hart. I didn't have that much exposure to him in a very personal nature.

Now, his assigned yeoman, I did some work for. From time to time, like you would on a flag, you rotate and fill in for each other taking minutes, that sort of thing. His personal yeoman was a guy named Harold Boaz, who knew him much better than I did. Boaz was with me on the Peary. I don't have any human-relations sort of thing to shed on Hart except that, as I say, he was a guy at a particular point in time that met his destiny. And I'm not sure he made all the decisions, after reading that book, that he

---
*James Leutze, A Different Kind of Victory: A Biography of Admiral Thomas C. Hart (Annapolis: Naval Institute Press, 1981).

should have made. But, nonetheless, at the time, he was our commander in chief.

Q: I don't think he had as much freedom of action as he should have either. I mean, his hands were tied in a lot of things, especially having to go along with the Dutch, and so on.

Mr. King: I think that pretty well broke his heart, that ABDACom thing.* I think that he had a much less sanguine view of the future at all times out there than MacArthur did, for example.** The fact that he took us all off the Houston when he did. I think there was no doubt in his mind whatsoever about the outcome.

Q: Well, we're right at the end of the tape, so we'll get the rest of that story the next time.

Mr. King: All right.

---

*ABDA Com--American-British-Dutch-Australian Command, an international command that proved notoriously ineffective in prosecuting the war effort against the Japanese in late 1941-early 1942.
**Lieutenant General Douglas MacArthur was commander of U.S. Army forces in the Far East. His headquarters was in the Philippines.

C. S. King #2 - 131

Interview Number 2 with Chief Warrant Officer
   Cecil S. King, Jr., U.S. Navy (Retired)

Place: U. S. Naval Institute, Annapolis, Maryland

Date: Monday, 4 August 1986

Interviewer: Paul Stillwell

Q: Mr. King, the last time we got you to the USS Augusta, as part of the flag allowance.

Mr. King: Yes.

Q: I wonder if you could talk about your experiences with the ship per se: where you lived, where you worked, and interacting with the ship's company.

Mr. King: Well, there's a certain amount of insulation between a flag allowance and a ship's company, such as there is on a transport like the Chaumont. You know, "Gangway, ship's company!" I don't mean there was hostility, but there was not a lot of interchange. We had our own berthing compartment and so on. The Augusta, generally speaking, was, by Navy criteria, a happy ship. It was a good ship. It had been on the Asiatic station a number of years.*

There was a good deal of evidence of this in the ship's interior. The flag office, for example, had a Chinese

---
*The Augusta served as Asiatic Fleet flagship from November 1933 to November 1940.

motif, you might say. There were not decorations all over the place, but it was obvious when you walked into the place, to me, that this was a China station ship. They had overhead fans, spinning fans, in the flag office. One of my first acquaintances was a guy named Taylor, G. W. Taylor, second class yeoman. We were rushing to go ashore about the second or third night I was on there. Taylor's nickname was Ah Koo. He was putting on his jumper in the office--he was a big, tall fellow--and he stuck both hands into this fan. It wasn't a serious injury, but it made a lot of noise, so we called him Ah Koo Fan Taylor from that point on.

Q: I take it the overhead was rather low in the flag office.

Mr. King: It was indeed. I was surprised to see these overhead fans on a Navy ship. Because my experience up to that time had been pretty well with the U.S. Fleet ships, and, as you know, they didn't go in for much extraneous equipment, but "the flag is the flag is the flag."

Q: Was there more spit and polish in her than in the rest of the Asiatic Fleet ships?

Mr. King: Yes, there was. I didn't spend that much time on

other Asiatic Fleet ships, as a matter of fact. But, let's see, the Marblehead and the Augusta were the two cruisers. Then there was DesRon 5, 13 destroyers; a couple of squadrons of submarines; two tenders, Black Hawk and Canopus; a tanker, the Pecos; and some gunboats that stayed in China waters.* It was a fairly small fleet.

The Augusta, of course, being the flagship and having a four-star admiral on board--his signal number was number one--you know, you didn't overlook that or forget it. There was not any overt, terribly hard-nosed, "we're-the-flagship" kind of thing. It was good duty. There was nothing about it that stuck out as being anything other than just a good, happy ship. Food was good, and I think I told you those Chinese messboys that were on there--it always paid to know them; I got awfully good food.

Q: How did she compare with the Portland?

Mr. King: Well, the Portland was, of course, very much a Pacific Fleet cruiser. There was more spit and polish on the Portland than there was on the Augusta. The Augusta was a comfortable ship, and there was not the real "gung-ho" military type of atmosphere. It was more of an easygoing ship than the Portland.

---

*DesRon 5--Destroyer Squadron Five, which comprised Destroyer Divisions 13, 14, and 15.

Q: Do you think that reflects the pace of the Asiatic Fleet in general?

Mr. King: I think it did, yes, more than anything else. On most of the ships in the Asiatic Fleet, there was a definite air of pride in being an Asiatic sailor. That really permeated the whole ship. This manifested itself in certain ways that were not real overt. I think on the ships, by and large, everyone was aware that this was the Asiatic Fleet, the "bamboo navy," and there really was pride in that. It was like a French Foreign Legion type thing.

Q: That's interesting. You talked about the reluctance of people on the West Coast to go out there, and yet, once people got there, they seemed to fall in with it.

Mr. King: Yes, the reluctance, I think, was really confined mostly to the higher grades. I'd say it was limited almost 100% to married people, because at that time you couldn't take your families out there. It was a 30-month tour. Not many married men want to spend 30 months away from their families. But there were a lot of younger kids in the Navy who were dying to go to the Asiatic Fleet. My younger brother Howard was on the _Davis_ with me. When he found out I was going, he wangled himself a set of orders and got on the <u>Chaumont</u>, and we went out together. He was crazy to go to China. So I think the distinction was that family men, generally, didn't want to spend 30 months away from their families. There was a mixture amongst other people. Either you were kind of oriented towards the Asiatic Fleet or you weren't.

Q: Some men stayed out there for years and years.

Mr. King: Oh, my goodness, alive. If it hadn't been for World War II, I would never have come back. I was at the peak of my life then. I had already extended once or put in my papers to extend once, because you could extend one year at a time. The reason for that was that if you got too "Asiatic," you'd be sent back. But as long as you maintained a reasonable military atmosphere and so on, well, then you could ship over a year at a time. Of course, the smaller the ship you were on, the more lax they were about the criteria for the one-year extensions. I knew a lot of guys out there who'd been there for 10, 15, 20 years and had no idea of ever going back.

Q: Was there a prohibition against their marrying, say, Chinese or Filipinos?

Mr. King: When I got out there, there was a prohibition.

C. S. King #2 - 136

But there were a number of Asiatic Fleet sailors that I knew that had Chinese wives; some had Russian wives. I guess all of them went back a few years. There was a prohibition at the time I was there of marrying other than U.S. citizens.

Q: And there were probably some who were married in fact, if not in law.

Mr. King: Oh, by all means, yes. That was not rare, I would say.

Q: I've heard that there was a practice in which senior petty officers would essentially take these new young sailors under their wings, and be very protective of them. Did you see this?

Mr. King: Well, I guess an example of that was, when I mentioned the other day about this Chinese mess attendant, this older fellow who really nailed me when he saw me, "Which name belong to you?" He knew I was new. And when I said "King," he said, "That's a good Chinese name. You be a good boy." He was deadly serious, and I was impressed by it. But your general point, I think, is well taken, because--again, this goes back to the sort of pride that there was in being "Asiatic." Generally, there was a lot of pride in being in the Asiatic Fleet. Newcomers were looked

C. S. King #2 - 137

after to that extent and sort of indoctrinated.

As a matter of fact, in the latter days of 1941--maybe even before that, I've forgotten exactly now--there were one or two stateside ships that came out to the Asiatic Fleet, bringing troops. This annoyed us no end. We didn't like that at all. We called them Hollywood sailors and that sort of business. We didn't go out and get in serious trouble, but there was a feeling of resentment. Here we had volunteered to go out there and had our 30 months' obligated service, and these guys came out and enjoyed our privileges without paying their dues. So we didn't like that.

My brother Howard, the eccentric one of our family, and I were ashore one night when the USS Cincinnati was in Manila. We went ashore, and we saw a few of them here and there. The more we thought about it, the madder we got. Finally Howard said, "Let's chase a couple of them back to their ship." So under the influence of, I guess, some rum and Cokes, we thought we'd do that. So we went to a place called Whitey Smith's Metro Garden, a very popular watering hole. Howard and I went into Whitey Smith's and sat down. It was very dark inside. Howard finally decided it was time to declare himself. He was a skinny kid--not a very formidable adversary, I must say. But he stood up and said, "Are there any Cincinnati sailors in the house?"

Right behind me, and sort of to his right, were these four big, gargantuan firemen off the Cincinnati. I guess they knew that Howard was not friendly. So they stood up, and one of them said, "Yeah, we're on the Cincinnati. So what?"

Howard said, "How does she feed--pretty good?" and then he sat back down. Boy, I was scared. I thought we were going to get murdered. But that was the kind of thing that took place. I mean, it was to some extent good-natured. There was a definite air of, "They shouldn't be out here fouling up our liberty."

Q: Did you get any impression of how they viewed you? Did they look down on Asiatic sailors?

Mr. King: I never had a personal chance to get an observation there. You know, the Navy is sort of funny. I suspect that there was probably some chip-on-the-shoulder attitude from these folks because the Asiatic Fleet was different from what they were used to. There's just a kind of thing that when any ship goes into an area or a new environment that they haven't been in before, a certain amount of adjustment goes on. That's just the Navy life. I always was accustomed to that.

Q: You talked about the Asiatic sailor as a type. Did that affect the officers as well?

C. S. King #2 - 139

Mr. King: Well, in the social sense, of course, we didn't mix and mingle. My distinct impression was that the officers in the Asiatic Fleet, to some extent, had this same feeling of being mission-oriented and pride in the Asiatic Fleet. I had a different feeling about the officers out there than I had about stateside officers. I just felt like they were one of us--at their level, of course. And, yes, I guess there was a difference.

Q: That would be reinforced by the fact that you had mostly small ships, and there's a greater degree of camaraderie there in general.

Mr. King: There is indeed. There was not only the ordinary camaraderie that you get on a small ship, out there, but that was then reinforced and emphasized by the Asiatic aspect of it: "Not only are we on this small ship but we're in the Asiatic Fleet." It was a very close-knit outfit; I was impressed by that. I saw many evidences of that on the beach and other places.

Q: How much contact did you have with the Chinese, the famous cumshaw for getting things done on board ship?

Mr. King: Oh, we had a fair amount of that, because in the first days when I was out there, particularly in the

Augusta, we went up and down the Chinese coast. We went as far north as Chingwantao and stopped in Tsingtao. Tsingtao was a real liberty port in those days. In all those ports--Chingwantao, Tsingtao, and Shanghai, too--the bumboats were just clustered around the Navy ships. On the bumboats was every variety of merchandise in the world, either for sale or barter. There were tailors in these bumboats and there were laundry people.

There were metalsmiths, and, you know, the old Navy bucket--the big, thick bucket. Gosh, it must have weighed about 20 pounds. You could take a bucket and just toss it to one of the guys on a bumboat. He would scurry off and bring it back in a couple of days, and it'd be all engraved and inlaid with dragons on it. They were just really works of art.

I was impressed also by the shoe people. They would take a long strip of brown paper, and just go around your foot, tear a little piece, around here, and tear a little piece, and have a strip like confetti. Then they'd just put it in their pocket and go on off. They'd bring you back a pair of shoes that would fit like a glove, by means of this little strip of paper. That impressed me. I thought, "That's real craftsmanship.

But we bought a lot of things from them--underwear, socks, some uniforms.

Q: Did you get tailor-made uniforms?

Mr. King: Oh, tailor-made uniforms. First thing you had to do was take your blues over and have them decorated. You know, the flap in front, on the inside of that embroidered dragons, and so on.

Q: Inside of the cuffs too.

Mr. King: Inside of the cuffs, yes. That was great stuff. I had to have that right away; that was my badge. I wish to hell I still had some of those.

We wore dress whites out there to some extent, too, which I had never worn before.

Q: These are the ones with the blue cuffs and the blue flap?

Mr. King: Yes. I thought that was a good-looking uniform. We bought most of that kind of thing on the beach. You could buy it in small stores, but you got so much better quality and fit, and a lot cheaper, on the beach.

Q: Any other liberty experiences besides this encounter with the Cincinnati men?

Mr. King: Oh, my gosh, I was quite a liberty hound in those days. A friend of mine, another first class yeoman named Eddie Gaghen, and I were running mates on the beach. When we went ashore in the first few months there, my brother Howard--the poor kid--was only a seaman. There was some foulup on his pay records and his service record. He hit there with no pay record and was getting $5.00 a month, health and comfort, plus what Eddie and I could spare for him out of our exchequer. He was really sort of up against it.

When Eddie and I were ashore--particularly in Tsingtao--we'd really see a lot while we waited for our boat to go back out to the ship. There were just hundreds of merchants down there, selling everything under the sun; mahjongg sets, real tortoise combs, anything. If you didn't believe it was real tortoise shell, they'd cut a little shaving off and light it, and it would smell like hair burning. Okay, that's the real tortoise shell.

They sold various kinds of food, a lot of peanuts and snacks. They sold fried chicken in a sort of a shoe box thing. I know I had an underlying suspicion that some of these chickens died natural deaths. But at 11:00 at night, after a liberty, you'd eat most anything. So we would take a box of chicken for Howard. He still, to this day, just raises hell, because he said we'd come in there, wake him out of a sound sleep, stick a piece of dusty chicken at him, and make him eat it.

The liberty out there was unusual in that there was no organized shore patrol type of situation. There were shore patrols, but for the most part, there were no hard and fast rules and regulations. You did pretty much, within normal limits, what you wanted to.

Q: As long as you didn't hurt people or destroy property.

Mr. King: Exactly. Yes, and there was a strict code of honor about that. For example, on drugs. Now in those days we were aware that if you wanted to buy something like that--opium or whatever--you could. There were no laws out there, but that was frowned on. I mean, the Navy just didn't do that. I don't know of any actual incidents. I might have heard scuttlebutt about some guy on the Peary or the John D. Ford who had smoked a marijuana cigarette. That was viewed with a great deal of alarm, such as, "What's wrong with that guy?" We weren't just perpetual drunks, but that was a part of a liberty, having a few drinks while you were ashore. It was done in moderation, and if you got too far out of line, another Asiatic Fleet guy would probably say something to you.

Q: Not as a shore patrolman, but just as a senior petty officer.

Mr. King: Just somebody would say, "If you can't handle it, don't drink it. Get on back to the ship, or I'll take you back." There was a certain amount of just general pride in being an Asiatic sailor, and there was not any general public to speak of out there. I mean, there was no need to impress anybody in a shallow sense.

You wore a nice-looking uniform when you went ashore. But aside from that, it was just a great place for liberty; it just seemed to suit me. I just thought I had died and gone to heaven. I couldn't get enough of it.

Q: What do you recall about the Chinese people and the Filipino people that you encountered?

Mr. King: Not much about the Chinese. The social contacts, you might say, in Shanghai, were mostly with a large colony of White Russians there. These were people that I felt so damn sorry for. They didn't have passports. But they were proud people; they were the aristocracy. And, gosh, they were nice people. We enjoyed their company. A general observation was that the girls were just beautiful. Some of them were honest-to-god royalty.

Q: Admiral Zumwalt married one of them.*

---

*Admiral Elmo R. Zumwalt, Jr., USN, was Chief of Naval Operations from 1970 to 1974. Shortly after World War II,

Mr. King: Yes, he sure did. He wasn't the only one either. It was not a great number, but I can recall some Russian-American marriages.

In Tsingtao I guess there were a good many Korean people. We had a Navy club there in Tsingtao, where they had dances in the afternoon and that sort of thing. I've got some pictures of it here.

In Chinwangtao there was not much liberty. That was mostly a coal port. I do recall Chinwangtao made an impression on me when we tied up the first time, because it was a coal port and there was a layer of coal dust that was several inches thick.

It was considered the thing to do to stand at the ship's rail and throw coins over. The Chinese would prepare for this. The coolies and all would use fire hoses and put water on that so it was just sort of a mud consistency. We would throw coins, and they would dive down in this coal dust. That was such an enormous amount of money to them; an American 25-cent piece was a substantial amount of money. Now, I guess, looking back on it, it was a callous thing to do. On the other hand, they wanted those coins. They lined up way from the dock just to get a chance to get in line and do that.

---
while in China, he met and married a White Russian woman. He recounts the tale in his book <u>On Watch: A Memoir</u> (New York: Quadrangle/The New York Times Book Company, 1976).

Q: Sounds like mud wrestling.

Mr. King: It was very much like mud wrestling. I wasn't really crazy about it, but at the same time I thought it was kind of an unusual thing to see happen.

I don't think I went ashore much in Chinwangtao; it was kind of a forbidding place. We did have a rifle range there, but I never used it. I did go ashore in Tsingtao several times. I guess most of the liberties I made in China were in Shanghai. At that time, Shanghai had the international settlement in the center of it with a French concession, a British concession, and so on. The Japanese controlled Shanghai. Inside the international settlement--the Japanese had free entry--there was not a great deal of overt hostility. But, at the same time, it was not a good situation. There was an underlying, very definite hostility. We went our way, and the Japanese went theirs. But it was not a happy situation at all.

The fleet meteorological officer was Lieutenant Knoll.* I don't know what his wife was doing there, but his wife was in Tsingtao. Maybe one of the last ones. Anyway, the Japanese set up arbitrary lines for cholera

---

*Lieutenant Denys W. Knoll, USN. Knoll's Naval Institute oral history includes his recollections of his wife's difficulties with the Japanese concerning cholera shots.

vaccination. If you crossed that line going this way, you got a cholera shot. When you came back out, you got a cholera shot. You might get six or eight cholera shots right through your jumper. Knoll's wife had had her shot, but she didn't have her chit with her to prove it, so the Japanese wanted to give her another one. You got it whether you wanted to take it or not. It worried me, because I wasn't sure how sanitary these needles were. But that was the sort of thing that went on.

In Shanghai, the policemen, the ones that we saw, were Sikhs, great big, tall guys. Most of them were extremely tall. I guess they pick out the tallest ones to be police. Their only badge of authority was a leaded cane. The beggars in Shanghai were just awful. I'd read about them. I didn't like that at all. Because, apparently, they'd mutilate children, all sorts of things. Begging is a profession there. When an American sailor comes down the street, well, these beggars just came out, and the only way to get rid of them was to call a Sikh policeman. You'd give him a couple of clackers, and boy, he'd take a cane and chase the beggars off. If you didn't get a Sikh policeman, it was hard to get away from them.

Q: How much evidence did you see of the Sino-Japanese war then in progress?

Mr. King: I don't guess I saw anything direct. One time I was in a rickshaw, and a commotion developed ahead of me. Shanghai was the kind of a place where the slightest crowd would gather if somebody snapped his fingers. A crowd gathered, and I was told that some civilian in a rickshaw up ahead of me had had a problem with a Japanese. But by the time my rickshaw got up, there was no evidence of it going on.

This guy Eddie Gaghen I mentioned a while ago--he and I took a little place in Shanghai in the French concession. We were going to be there for a couple of weeks, and that was kind of the thing to do. There was a British firm named Gandy Price that had, I believe, a franchise for almost every bit of alcoholic beverages sold in the entire Far East. They had a showroom on the waterfront--a big luxurious place with shelves all around. On those shelves were every kind of alcoholic beverages the world has ever known, every kind. It had big easy chairs, kind of a club atmosphere. You would go in and sit down. A couple of Chinese would come over and bring whatever in the world you wanted to drink. You couldn't stump them. That was all on the house. That's while you were deciding what you wanted to get. So finally you'd say, "Well, I'll take two bottles of Johnnie Walker Red," maybe 50 cents a bottle, some ridiculous price. And a bottle of this, that, and the other thing.

Eddie and I stopped in there when we took this little apartment out in the French concession. We thought we'd get a few things to take out there, so we ordered a bottle of scotch, a bottle of this, a bottle of that. We decided to get a case of beer. On this chit was supposed to be a case of beer. They were going to deliver it that afternoon. That afternoon, a big commotion developed out in the street, and we looked out. It turned out that a case of beer was not a wooden case of 12 or 24 bottles. A case was 36 quart bottles of beer, each one wrapped in straw. The Chinese way of life is that any time there's work available, 300 will line up for it. They had these yo-ho poles, and they'd have one bottle in the front basket, and one bottle in the second basket. They would come up the stairs, deliver it to the place, and get a clacker or something.

Q: What's a clacker?

Mr. King: Chinese coins. I don't know how many Chinese delivered those 36 bottles of beer, but it was a lot. We had straw-wrapped bottles of beer in the kitchen, in the bedroom, the bathroom, and all over the place.

It was just that kind of thing that made me realize that the Asiatic Fleet was unique, and I was sorry I hadn't gone out there years before. I really was crazy about it.

Q: Were there warnings against talking too freely ashore because of the Japanese?

Mr. King: There were indeed. When we got aboard the <u>Augusta</u>, a chief yeoman named Whitey Hartwick was the bull chief of the flag allowance. Whitey would take new arrivals up and see Lieutenant Nilon, who was Admiral Hart's flag lieutenant.* We called him Leo the Lion. He was kind of a colorful guy, a redheaded guy.

On my indoctrination lecture from him, which was short and sweet, the point to me was, "If you get in trouble on the beach, there goes your liberty for the rest of the time you're in China. No matter who's at fault, no matter what happens, if you get in trouble ashore, then you spend the rest of the time on the ship." I took him at his word.

One time in Shanghai I was in a restaurant. I know they were playing a lot of mahjongg in the back room. Anyway, a hassle developed, where some Japanese soldiers came in. Of course, the instant reaction was to mind your own business and hunker down. I guess I was sitting close to where they were going down this one side of the room. For some reason, all of a sudden, the attention focused on me. The Japanese pushed me back in my chair pretty roughly. It wasn't a friendly thing at all. As a matter of fact, I

---
*Lieutenant Leo W. Nilon, USN.

wouldn't even be surprised if they'd have pulled out a bayonet or something. That kind of underlined the feeling about it.

Q: And you weren't in any position to make an issue of it.

Mr. King: No, but when I got back to the ship, I thought, "Now that's a hell of a way to treat a sailor." I made the mistake of going to Lieutenant Nilon and telling him about it.

He said, "You weren't listening when I talked to you earlier," or words to that effect. He said, "We can't pursue that. We can't do it. You're just lucky you didn't get in any serious trouble. Next time don't tell me about it." Well, I understood that. That was the situation out there. It was a very uneasy situation. It didn't interfere with our liberty, not at all, because Shanghai was a paradise if there ever was one. But, at the same time, there was a very, very uneasy air.

Q: Why would you call it a paradise? What qualities made it so?

Mr. King: Just everything in the world you can think of. The cost of living was almost nothing. The first time you went ashore, you were taken over by a certain rickshaw driver. He was your rickshaw driver the rest of the time you ever went ashore. And don't ever worry about him finding you. When you went ashore, there he was. It was that sort of thing. I just had never been treated like that in my whole life, and I enjoyed it. There was something romantic about it in a town like Shanghai. I never saw anything like it, and I guess I'll never see it again. But I thought that was as near as I'll ever come to being in heaven.

Q: Where did you get your pig and chicken tattoos on your feet?

Mr. King: That was back in Panama. You know, it just seemed to be the thing to do.

Q: What made it the thing to do?

Mr. King: Well, it was a fairly uncommon tattoo. I guess tattoos might have been very popular back many years ago. But in my time in the Navy, it was frowned upon a little bit. You were told in boot camp, "Don't be dumb and get tattooed all over. If you've got to get tattooed, don't get tattooed below the elbows." So I took that pretty seriously. I have a couple of tattoos on my arms, above the elbows. But there was something about that pig and rooster on people that I saw that had it. It just seemed to be a kind of a badge of honor.

Q: It was also considered a good luck talisman.

Mr. King: Oh, by all means. The idea was that if you had a pig and rooster, you'd never get lost at sea. It worked on me. I can't complain at all.

Q: Wasn't that a painful thing to undergo?

Mr. King: It was one of the most painful things I ever had in my life. About halfway through, I wasn't at all sure I wanted to go through with it.

Q: There's no turning back at that point.

Mr. King: No turning back. No, no. But I was kind of glad to get it done, and I never have been really sorry about it because it's not noticeable. I consider that a badge of honor of the Asiatic Fleet.

Q: It's certainly a souvenir.

Mr. King: It's an unusual one.

C. S. King #2 - 154

Q: What comparisons might you draw between the Augusta and her successor, the Houston?

Mr. King: Well, when we first went aboard the Houston, she still looked like part of the U.S. Fleet. There was quite a difference. Now, the Houston had been out to China before, years before.* There may have been some in the ship's company that remembered those days; I don't know. But there was a definite difference at first. But we quickly settled into our routine. Also, I remember for some reason, there was more interaction and more socializing between the flag allowance and the ship's company on the Houston than there was on the Augusta. I don't know why that was. There was just more interchange.

Q: Did you indoctrinate them into the ways of the Asiatic Fleet then?

Mr. King: Well, I think I told you about that foolishness when we went aboard. We nested alongside the Houston in Manila Harbor to transfer over all our flag allowance gear. Somebody had the idea about getting a couple of those yo-ho poles with the basket in front and back and the Chinese conical hats. Some of us put those on and put gear in it to go aboard the Houston. We were stopped rather quickly the

---
*The USS Houston was flagship of the Asiatic Fleet from 1931 to 1933.

first time we went aboard the Houston.

The accommodations on the Houston were not as comfortable as they were aboard the Augusta, for a lot of reasons. The Houston had not had that period of indoctrination, you might say, that the Augusta had. But we quickly settled into a good routine.

When the Houston came out, also, there was getting to be a different atmosphere about the Asiatic Fleet. The war was getting awfully imminent. I mean, it was just really a fact of life. Everybody was aware of it. A lot of us were not too sanguine about the prospects of being on the Houston if war started.

Q: I think especially because your forces were so sparse.

Mr. King: We didn't have doodly-squat out there. We knew it, the Japs knew it, and everybody knew it. However, there was not any fear about it. I guess there was a bit of real sincere bravado; by God, we were the Asiatic Fleet, and there was probably going to be some trouble, but we'd give a good account of ourselves. There really was that kind of air about it. I don't know that I ever detected the slightest qualms on anybody's part.

Q: Did the operating patterns change when you went to the

new flagship?

Mr. King: Yes, they did. We were getting more and more into this atmosphere of impending problems. As a matter of fact, now that you mention it, the flag allowance did not have a battle station on the Augusta. But on the Houston, we had battle stations, and we didn't much care for this sudden change to our routine. The musicians especially--oh, they were really sore about it. They never had a battle station in their life. They put us on the 5-inch guns. I was a hot shell man.

Q: What does a hot shell man do?

Mr. King: You wrap rags around your arms, if you can imagine such a thing. Let's see, there's a first loader, and, I think, a second loader. These 5-inch shells weren't like the 8-inch. They're not powder bags and projectiles; they were fixed ammunition. There was an assembly line: second loader, first loader, into the gun. Then, when it fired, the shell bounced back out. It really bounced out, sort of, and one of the two hot shell men caught it. Boy, it was red hot. He caught it, and just kind of bounced it back to the next guy, and he bounced it back, and we stacked it on deck. There were a lot more people than I suppose they should have had. I guess there were five or six people to each 5-inch gun.

Q: Were these open mounts?

Mr. King: Open mounts, yes.

Q: Was it necessary to do that with every ejected shell?

Mr. King: It was all hand operated.

Q: How much firing did you do?

Mr. King: We didn't do much when I first went aboard, but as soon as we got our battle stations, we did quite a bit.

Q: Just against towed sleeves by aircraft?

Mr. King: Some aircraft, mostly towed sleeves, my memory is. We had night drills with star shells. The 5-inch made a hell of a noise, a cracking noise; it just tore the inside of your ears out. Hell, we didn't put cotton in our ears; I don't know why.

Q: The Navy was not as safety conscious then.

Mr. King: No, they weren't.

C. S. King #2 - 158

Q: Maybe it wasn't considered the manly thing to do either.

Mr. King: I think probably so. I've had some loss of hearing in the higher ranges in recent years. One of the Navy medics recently told me that probably that's not too uncommon to have loss of higher range from that kind of experience early on. But it's not a serious thing with me. I recall very vividly that the musicians just raised holy hell about their battle stations.

Q: They could file unfair labor practice.

Mr. King: Oh, my God, musicians said they couldn't do that kind of work. The flag band was a very elite group. Sid Zeramby was the bandmaster and was a colorful guy. He was a chief musician, chief bandmaster, kind of a legend in the Asiatic Fleet. His band played for the afternoon dances at the Navy club in Tsingtao. The first liberty I made there, Sid left the bandstand and decided to show the group some step of his. He was cavorting down the side of the dance floor, and someone had dropped a piece of a sandwich that had mayonnaise in it. Sid hit that mayonnaise with his foot, and he fell for about 15 minutes. That caused a great deal of amusement that was reviewed and reviewed many times over.

Sid had a very pronounced sense of humor. In the flag

office, we had a hand-wound victrola which we would play in the morning before working hours. There was a record on there by Rudy Vallee.* I think the front side was the Maine Stein Song. But the reverse side was "When the Mush Begins to Rush Down Father's Vest"--a comic record. So one time I got Sid into the office and played it for him. He thought that was great. He asked me to take down the words in shorthand, and he would write up some music for his band, because every noontime we had a band concert on the quarterdeck. They would play, not military music, but orchestra music. I took down the words in shorthand, and Sid made an arrangement. That was one of the most popular songs that they had. They'd say, "Play 'When the Mush Begins to Rush,'" and old Sid would play it. He would sing the words to it. He always had a cigar like a prop. Even on the quarterdeck, he had this cigar.

Q: What do you recall about your professional duties during that period?

Mr. King: Well, as we got into the 1941 days, when we began really to have this feeling of problems ahead, classification became more widely used, and we were more security conscious. One of the things that I did for

---
*Rudy Vallee was an entertainer who started as a saxophonist and band leader in the 1920s. He remained popular for many years as a singer and actor.

C. S. King #2 - 160

Commander Slocum was the so-called movement report. The movement report was a daily listing of every ship in the Asiatic Fleet--where they were, where they were going, and so on. We had code words for all the locations, and I would do that. He pretty well let me do that by myself. I was very proud of that, that I just did the whole damn thing. He would sign off on it, and I would take it up to the CWO and Slocum would never even see it. I'd take a great deal of pride in that. It was a complicated job.

Q: What was involved?

Mr. King: It just involved having the data there of all the ships.

Q: Where did you get the information?

Mr. King: Mostly from the op orders, previous movement reports, and things like that. Most of it, I guess, was traffic movement reports, incoming, and Commander Slocum, of course--that was his job as operations officer. Some of it was traffic, but you had several sources to make out the master movement report of the Asiatic Fleet. I've forgotten now how many days back and how many days ahead it projected. It was considered pretty highly classified.

C. S. King #2 - 161

Q: What was the hierarchy of classifications? Was that the same as we know today?

Mr. King: I don't recall ever seeing anything top secret. I think we had restricted and confidential and secret, maybe, something like that. I'm not real sure about the secret. I just don't recall for sure.

Q: Was there a process for clearing people to provide access to this type of information?

Mr. King: No. You just got it by virtue of your job. I didn't get any kind of a formal clearance until later on.

Q: You say there was a greater concern for security. How was that manifested, that enhanced sense of it?

Mr. King: Well, I guess the most noticeable thing to me was that all of a sudden we began to shift things that had been unclassified into classified categories, ship movements and things like that. There were more CWOs that we had to work with up in communications shack. And there was just a general awareness and a general upgrading of communications of all sorts. I think it was just real obvious to everybody that I knew out there in the middle of 1941 that we were awful close to a real big problem.

C. S. King #2 - 162

Q: You had spent some time with the radiomen back in Panama. Did you get involved with communications at all on this staff?

Mr. King: Not very much. I was a first class yeoman. My communications experience was a help to me. I spoke the language to some extent, so when I went up to the radio shack, it was always helpful that I had some common denominators. I could sometimes get my traffic in ahead of somebody else's, that sort of thing, just the usual business. But I was not into any real technical end of it, as far as using equipment and like that.

Q: But you were familiar with message formats, for example.

Mr. King: Oh, yes. Very familiar with that. And the officers on board, the flag officers, below the admiral's level, like Commander Slocum as operations officer; and Commander J. M. Robinson was fleet gunnery officer; Commander Roy W. Bruner was fleet maintenance officer/engineering.* You know, these were the people that we interchanged with, that we worked with, that all the yeomen worked with. It just became obvious that there was a higher level of sensitivity up and down the line.

---
*Lieutenant Commander James M. Robinson, USN; Commander Roy W. Bruner, USN.

Q: Any specific recollections of any of these officers that you want to recall?

Mr. King: Yes, I remember Lieutenant Commander Robinson was very gung-ho, very military, 100% business. I remember that, as part of just his ordinary way of life, Commander Slocum was a little more easygoing than Robinson was. Robinson was over in Cavite Navy Yard the day it was hit.* He came back, and he was just drenched with blood. But he made an immediate report of his day's activities. I was around when he was dictating to his yeoman, and I was very much impressed by his orderly account and the way he laid everything out. He said, "I identified myself as Lieutenant Commander Robinson." It was a very formal, but nonetheless quite a colorful account of the day's activities, of what happened that day.

Commander Bruner looked a little bit like Ed Wynn.** He was just kind of a grandfatherly old guy, who ate, slept, and drank engineering. He was one of the most dedicated technical people I had ever run into.

Then we had a Marine colonel, Colonel Clement, who was nominally in charge of all the Marine Corps activities in

---
*The large initial Japanese air attack on the Cavite Navy Yard was on 10 December 1941.
**Ed Wynn was a radio entertainer of the period, perhaps best described as looking like an elderly clown.

the Asiatic Fleet.* Before, he had served with the Fourth Marines in Shanghai. He was a classic picture of a Marine colonel. By God, it was not respect; it was almost awe when you were around him, and in a positive way--just a great guy. Those were the people that I worked with, that I was exposed to more. Up above them were the admiral and the chief of staff--Purnell.** Below them were all the CWOs and the junior officers up in the radio shack. Then we had a fleet communications officer, Commander Bull Fernald, a mustang.***

Another officer was Lieutenant Commander Rosie Mason, a very well-known guy in the intelligence field.**** He was a colorful guy and very competent man. He had a lot of experience in the intelligence field.

A. S. McDill was the flag secretary and, as such, the skipper of the flag allowance--great guy.***** Linaweaver was the communications officer.****** Denys Knoll was also, to some extent, in intelligence; so was Lieutenant Roeder.******* Now Roeder was a guy that I confused with Austin in those books in your library out there. Roeder was later on in Australia with us. Jesse Oldendorf was the skipper of the

---
*Colonel William T. Clement, USMC.
**Captain William R. Purnell, USN, was chief of staff to Commander in Chief Asiatic Fleet, Admiral Thomas C. Hart, USN.
***Commander James M. Fernald, USN.
****Lieutenant Commander Redfield Mason, USN.
*****Lieutenant Commander Alexander S. McDill, USN.
******Lieutenant Commander Walter E. Linaweaver, USN.
*******Lieutenant Bernard F. Roeder, USN.

C. S. King #2 - 165

Houston.*

Q: Any memories of him?

Mr. King: No, not any memories other than the fact that he was highly regarded on the Houston. He was the kind of skipper that really had the loyalty of the crew. I remember later on, he was in charge of the battleships that "crossed the T" in the Pacific.**

Q: Did you have any contact with Admiral Hart or Purnell at all?

Mr. King: I remember when Purnell made rear admiral. Admiral Hart called all the flag allowance to muster, and he praised him up and down. We all cheered and clapped and yelled--very popular guy, Purnell was. I had some exposure to Hart but not a great deal. He had his own yeoman, Harold Boaz.*** Boaz was the guy that wrote a narrative report on the Peary and was on the Peary with me. Boaz and I were supposed to be on the PBY that was to take Hart out of the Philippines and got shot up. Well, Hart was the first four-star admiral that I'd ever seen. To me he was God and Jesus

---
*Captain Jesse B. Oldendorf, USN.
**As a rear admiral in October 1944, Oldendorf was the tactical commander when U.S. ships scored a decisive victory in a night action at Surigao Strait in the Philippines, part of the overall Battle of Leyte Gulf.
***Chief Yeoman Harold B. Boaz, USN.

Christ and everything else. He was diminutive--a small man. I never saw him without a cigarette.

Later on, a couple years before he died, after he'd served as a senator from Connecticut, my wife and I were up in New England on an antiquing trip, and I called him up on just an impulse.* We chatted on the phone for a while, and he said, "Why don't you come over and chew the fat for a while?" Those were his exact words.

I thanked him very much, and I debated the rest of that trip whether or not to do it. I finally decided against it. I don't know why I decided against it. I didn't have any good reason. I just felt like, to some extent, it would not be proper, so I just didn't do it. But he was a man who exuded authority. He could have been in his skivvies, and you'd know he was a four-star admiral. He was that kind of a guy--not cold, but terribly competent.

Q: An air of dignity about him.

Mr. King: Dignity. He reminded me a little bit of Admiral Reeves, you know the guy that had the goatee, was Commander in Chief Pacific Fleet when I first shipped in the Navy.** I never saw Reeves, but I had the feeling about Hart that I had about Reeves.

---

*Hart served as a U.S. senator from 1945 to 1947. He died 4 July 1971.
**Admiral Joseph M. Reeves, USN, was Commander in Chief U.S. Fleet from June 1934 to June 1936.

C. S. King #2 - 167

Q: Did you ever encounter Hart during your daily business?

Mr. King: From time to time. You know, on a fairly small flag allowance, sometimes we yeomen covered for each other. There were meetings from time to time. I think I told you about that meeting he had with Admiral Sir Tom Phillips.*

Q: I don't think we've got that on tape, in any event.

Mr. King: Well, that was when the Prince of Wales and the Renown and the Repulse came out to the Far East. Admiral Sir Tom Phillips, Admiral Hart, and General MacArthur were the principals. I think they had three opposite points of view about where we were and what was going to happen. I think that Hart was the most pragmatic of the three.

Q: What was this, war planning type strategy sessions?

Mr. King: Yea, it was a kind of how-goes-it, where-are-we thing with Phillips just coming out there and sort of a strategy session, I guess. They may have more than one, but that was the one that I think was either the first one or one that was kind of a crunch meeting when they really made

---

*Vice Admiral Sir Tom S. V. Phillips, RN, was British commander at Singapore. He visited Manila on 5-6 December 1941 to confer with Hart and MacArthur.

some tough decisions as to strategy and deploying the different ships and everything.

It was several months before that when we moved off of the Houston into the Marsman Building.*

Q: Which is in Manila.

Mr. King: Which is in Manila at the foot of pier seven.

Q: How did things change when you made that move, other than the obvious, that you weren't on board ship anymore?

Mr. King: As a practical matter, we all felt like the deed was done. It was just a matter of time. There was a lot of talk amongst the sailors, the flag allowance sailors. In a time like that, one would speculate what's going to happen to Houston, Marblehead. Also, there was a lot of talk, I recall, about Japanese spies and agents in Manila keeping track of us. The flag allowance lived in a Chinese apartment house off the Luneta.** We felt pretty sure that during the day that our stuff was rummaged through. I mean, guys would put a hair over their drawer or something like that and find it moved or missing. We felt like we were under pretty close observation.

---

*The move of the fleet headquarters ashore took place in June 1941.
**The Luneta is a large park in downtown Manila.

It was not uncommon also in those days to have your picture taken by a Japanese when you were either coming out of the Marsman Building, walking down the street, or something like that. We made macabre jokes about it, "Well, that'll get on the wall of some Jap office." There was really not an air of false bravado, but there was an air of confidence. None of us really had any idea what actually was going to happen.

Q: I don't think anybody did--at least on our side.

Mr. King: The day it happened I thought, "Boy, the Pacific Fleet's going to come up over the horizon in about a week, and they're going to blow these guys out of the water." I really felt that in my bones.

Q: There had been the view all along that the Japanese people were an inferior people that didn't have the ability to do this--nearsighted, buck-toothed, and all of that sort of thing.

Mr. King: That was exactly it. You really hit the nail on the head. Now, one time in Tsingtao, I was walking from point A to point B, just about sundown, and a long file of Japanese soldiers came marching by. They were about six or eight abreast--not four, about six or eight abreast--and several hundred of them. And they looked like a giant caterpillar--these little legs with leggings on, you know. All of a sudden it just dawned on me--you know, it was kind of awesome. I thought, "There's just so many of them," and it was not like an American group walking down there. I mean, they were 100% business, and the officers were gung-ho. I just had a funny feeling; that kind of gave me a turn to see those guys. They were in full war footing right then, right that very minute. I thought about them many times after the war started in Manila.

Q: Did you have much contact with U. S. Army people there in the Philippines?

Mr. King: No, not direct. There was some mixing and mingling on the beach after the Army began to make its presence known in late '41. I remember seeing the enormous number of American soldiers that were arriving out there on these various troopships. They just seemed to be all over the place.

    I had mixed emotions about that. On the one hand, I was glad to see all the help coming out there, but on the other hand, I was unsure about how they would react in that short a time, that they probably had to get organized. I felt like they were just to some extent cannon fodder. They

C. S. King #2 - 171

didn't give me a great feeling of confidence.

Q: You felt it was up to the Navy, not the Army, to save the situation.

Mr. King: Hundred percent. I really thought of the Japs as a naval power. That was the impression I had.

Q: As indeed they were.

Mr. King: All my thoughts were on Navy versus Navy.

Q: As a senior petty officer, how much supervisory responsibility did you have, as opposed to just doing these one-man type projects?

Mr. King: I didn't have any direct supervisory capacity at all when I worked for Slocum. There were third class yeomen on the flag allowance--kind of a pool situation, you might say. But I didn't have anybody directly reporting to me, no.

Q: Was it unusual for a petty officer not to have juniors working for him?

Mr. King: Yes, because each of those principals that I

mentioned--Slocum, Bruner, Robinson, and Clement--they each had a yeoman. It was like Hart had a yeoman, a writer. That was a status thing. I was very proud to be the fleet operations yeoman.

Q: It was probably a status thing for them as well as for you.

Mr. King: Oh, I guess so. I remember some of the kids in the office. We had a good relationship on the flag allowance; we were a close-knit group. We had several third class, and one was named McCambridge--a big, awkward kid. We called him Feets McCambridge. I thought a whole lot of him. He was a great kid. They would sort of fill in for whatever needed to be done in the flag allowance. They would give us a hand if we got swamped, with some kind of a big job.

But day to day we were the writers for the principals.

Q: You were essentially male secretaries then.

Mr. King: It was something like that. My whole memory of the time in the Asiatic Fleet and the job that I had was one really of ongoing satisfaction and pride in terms of job.

Q: Well, I think it also connotes that there was a great

deal of trust in you--not only in your capability, but your reliability.

Mr. King: I suppose that's true. I told you the last time I was here about that one fracas--the one and only--I had with Slocum over that delayed dispatch. But actually he and I really got along very well indeed, as well as a full commander and his yeoman in those days got along. We didn't go ashore together, but there was a great deal of mutual rapport between us. I would have done anything for old Slocum, and, as I said, I'm sure, in retrospect, if it wasn't for him, I would have been in some other category in all the operations getting out of the Philippines.

Q: Describe the onset of the war then, as you experienced it.

Mr. King: The atmosphere and all these different indicators of impending problems just intensified. About the fifth of December, I became sick with what the pharmacist's mate diagnosed as dengue fever. I guess that's what I had. He put me in the apartment for a couple days. It might not have been that long. I hadn't been sick long when the big balloon went up--when the war started. It was the eighth, I guess, out there. It was, I think, pretty early in the morning. It was obvious, so I got well quick. I had an

C. S. King #2 - 174

instantaneous cure. I hotfooted it down to the Marsman Building.

The first day was just sort of pandemonium, in the sense of not knowing what in the hell was going on. On the tenth of December, Cavite was really beat up pretty badly, a lot of casualties. Lieutenant Commander Robinson was over there when it happened. I heard that afternoon and evening boats kept coming across the bay from Cavite with wounded and dead from the attack. Obviously, there was a lot of trauma going on but not to the extent that anyone was paralyzed. The main feeling I remember having was just trying to find out what in the heck was happening. We knew that we had been attacked. Trying to get a line on what had happened to the Air Force, and what had happened to the Army, and so on and so on. We had no knowledge at all of Pearl Harbor.

Q: When did you find that out?

Mr. King: It was, I guess, the next day. I guess the attacks were maybe somewhat simultaneous, but we didn't get much information. Maybe Hart knew, but, I mean, as far as the flag allowance people in general, we found out about it the next day. I still did not believe, in the face of what I heard, the damage as extensive as it was at Pearl Harbor. I could not make myself believe that. I just knew that the

U.S. Fleet was going to come up over the horizon in about a week and we'd be out of trouble.

Q: You probably weren't particularly surprised when it did start?

Mr. King: No, I don't think any of us were surprised at all. We were surprised at the surface aspects of it: the blood, the casualties, and so on. I think there were a couple printers off of the flag allowance that were over in Cavite that same day at the print shop. One of them was killed--Worrels, I believe--the one who had his ear pierced.

These kinds of things were brought home to us. So the first day was the eighth, and from then on until the 25th, there was not a great deal of daily destruction or attacks in the city of Manila where we were. We got bad reports on a lot of areas. I guess the Japs were, to some extent, preserving Manila, as an integral city, for that period of time. We had a lot of air raids on the waterfront, but they were not terribly destructive. They seemed to be to me, for the most part, anti-personnel bombs, that sort of thing. We had a row of sandbags all around the base of the Marsman Building. Every time they'd sound the siren, we'd go down and get in behind these sandbags, and they'd drop bombs up and down pier seven and around, but there was not any heavy destruction that I saw. I remember wondering about that at the time. I thought, "War is war; they ought to blow everything sky-high."

Q: They did some real damage at Cavite.

Mr. King: Oh, they effectively put Cavite out and the Air Force field out there.

Q: Clark Field.

Mr. King: That was right off the bat. That was, I guess, part of the plan--put them out of commission and then go on to other things.

Q: How did your duties change with the start of the war?

Mr. King: All of a sudden, everything that we had felt and thought and expected sort of came true. We just shifted right into it. It became a wartime operation; there were blackouts at night. We worked from "can till can't." I mean, we sometimes spent the whole night at the Marsman Building, working around the clock, doing all the things connected with that kind of a situation.

Q: What kinds of things were you doing?

C. S. King #2 - 177

Mr. King: We were, of course, getting out the movement report and these activities, sorting out the various units of the Asiatic Fleet. The submarines were one situation, and destroyers were another. We were taking stock of damages and making plans for eventualities. Hell, we didn't have that many ships to worry about, as a matter of fact. The submarines, as I recall, were going off on war patrols right away. We heard some scuttlebutt about some problems with torpedoes that was kind of upsetting.

I had gone aboard one of the submarines out there in 1941. I toyed with getting a transfer to a submarine. I don't know why I wanted to do that. I just went aboard and looked it over; it seemed pretty good. There was the Seadragon, the Searaven, the Sealion, and the Seawolf. Then there was a division of older S-boats. The Seadragon, I think, was the one I went aboard. I was impressed. I thought that was a great ship. I saw that I couldn't just transfer to a submarine without any training or anything else. But, anyway, I digress. The submarines went off on war patrol. My clearest recollections are just being on a wartime footing with no thought of hours or anything else.

Q: Were you keeping track of Allied ships as well as U.S.?

Mr. King: No, the British ships were not in the Philippines. I think they were down in Singapore somewhere.

And, of course, they had Admiral Phillips.

Q: And, of course, they were soon sunk.*

Mr. King: Boy, that really made an impression on me and a lot of us. We thought they were absolutely invincible. When they were both just sunk--wham, wham--that brought me up kind of short.

Q: It probably dispelled your notions about the U.S. Fleet, too.

Mr. King: Yes, well, but by that time the facts had begun to trickle in and, I think, I was more aware of the extent of Pearl Harbor. That was one of the reasons why I was so anxious to get off of Corregidor when I had the chance to volunteer for the Peary, because I saw a bleak outlook for the people on Corregidor and in the Philippines.

Q: What was the process by which you got from Manila to Corregidor?

Mr. King: Manila was declared an open city on December 25, Christmas Day, I guess it was in 1941.

---

*The British battleship Prince of Wales and battle cruiser Repulse were sunk off Malaya by Japanese aircraft on 10 December 1941.

Q: Yes, it was by MacArthur.

Mr. King: Yes. Commander Slocum told me that I was going to be going out on the plane with Hart and Slocum. I guess there were maybe 12 of us. We were to get on one of Bulkeley's PT boats down at pier seven and go out to Cavite and get on board this PBY, one of PatWing 10's planes, and fly down to our destination--I guess, Java.*

So I went back to the Luneta to get my clothes, what I was going to take with me. I just took a little bag. Another thing that struck me then, as I was walking back from the Luneta to the Marsman Building. Manila was an open city then, and the streets were full of the locals. It's hard to generalize, but the Filipinos were kind of childlike, trusting. They were sort of childlike in their attitude towards the Americans, and towards MacArthur, in particular. When they saw me walking down the street with my suitcase--I was all by myself--I picked up a pretty good size crowd. Not hostile. On the contrary: "Where are you going, sir? Where's the Navy, sir? What's going to happen to us, sir?" And all that sort of stuff.

I really felt terrible about it. I just really felt

---

*Lieutenant John D. Bulkeley, USN, Commander Motor Torpedo Boat Squadron Three. Bulkeley was later awarded the Medal of Honor for successfully evacuating General Douglas MacArthur from Corregidor to Australia. PatWing 10--Patrol Wing Ten.

awful. I hated to just lie. In fact, I didn't. I just said, "I'm going back down to the Marsman Building." I tried to be as factual as I could and as non-alarming. But that was a bad situation; I just really felt awful about that. I really felt like I was abandoning them myself. I took a personal responsibility, which, of course, wasn't the case.

But, anyway, I got down to the Marsman Building, and I went out to the end of pier seven, where we were going to pick up the PT boat. The PT boat had come in and gone back out, because there were Japanese planes all over the place. They were strafing our boat. The skipper was a tall Texan who had been under attack a couple of times and had pulled out and evaded them. He finally came back in and picked us up, and we headed out at high speed to Cavite. I thought that was really great.

We were not directly attacked on the way out. But there were planes in the air, and there was smoke here and smoke there and a lot going on. We didn't feel any particular trepidation about ourselves, because I just felt like he could outmaneuver anything that came along. I mean, he could really handle that boat. We got about halfway across the bay to Cavite, and we saw a lot of smoke coming out of the water--oil, black smoke. We got there, and that was where our plane had been. I think the skipper of this PT boat had actually seen it happen. I didn't see it happen. I was sitting back on the fantail of this boat, just hanging on at the high speed and radical maneuvering.

We got there, and that was it. The plane was gone. I think most of the crew had gotten off the plane before it was destroyed. There were no casualties that I knew of. So a decision was made to go on out to Corregidor.* That was about 20 miles or so. We got to Corregidor in the middle of the afternoon. It was sort of confusing then--okay, what the hell's going to happen now? So we got to Corregidor and set up some kind of shop in one of the tunnels there. I think Admiral Hart left that very night on a submarine.** That broke the umbilical. Slocum went off with him.

We enlisted people just sort of took stock. The Army, of course, ran the place, and so we became Army for all practical purposes. I don't know how we kept track of what was going on, but somehow I became aware that the Peary was going to leave, and I wanted to get on the Peary.*** My brother Howard, by that time, had been transferred from the crew of the Peary. He was in that communications unit on Corregidor. He and I had a chance to get together, and he showed me his hideout that he thought was great, a small cave off to one side, and he was proud of that. He had a

---
*Corregidor was an island fortress in Manila Bay.
**Admiral Hart and part of his staff were evacuated from the Philippines 26 December in the submarine Shark (SS-174).
***The USS Peary (DD-226) was a four-stack destroyer commissioned in October 1920. She was 314 feet long, had a beam of 32 feet, and standard displacement of 1,190 tons. She was armed with four 4-inch guns.

C. S. King #2 - 182

.45 on his hip. He was going to be all right, but he was worried about me. I knew damn well he didn't have a dog's chance; I was worried about him.

It finally turned out that I was going to be allowed to go on the Peary. We drew straws or something. My number came up to go on the Peary. I was so happy. Man, I was glad. So we went down and got on the Peary. Right away, I got involved in trying to type out some kind of a passenger list, because the Peary had been damaged pretty badly over in Cavite, and had lost some of her crew, lost her skipper. They had some pickup crew and us as passengers. It was pandemonium trying to get some kind of passenger list up. I remember being very busy with that, figuring out who the hell was going to be on the Peary. We finally made up a passenger list and dumped it off. That was the last thing we had to do. Then we just got under way in the early part of the evening.*

While we were doing that, a lot of the crew were busy painting the topside green, tying palm leaves to the lifelines, putting up canvas between the stacks, and all that stuff to make the Peary look like an island. The Peary and the Pillsbury had had a collision at sea two or three weeks before the war started. The Peary lost about 20 feet off her bow. The Peary was in dry dock when the war started, and that's why she got damaged so badly. They

---
*The Peary left Corregidor the evening of 26 December 1941.

quickly put on a little stubby jury bow, so she was seaworthy. She was all beat up on the topside, but the engines were sound. So we got under way that night, and I remember slipping around on that green paint, because it wasn't dry by any matter or means. We didn't have any organized place to sleep or eat.

My brother Bobby was on the <u>Peary</u>, a radioman in ship's company then. So I went up to the radio shack, and he made a bunk for me on the steel tool chest of some kind. I slept on the tool chest. It was hotter than hell in there, because they had the lights on and all the gear on. It was blackened ship at night, and there wasn't a breath of air in that place. I guess there were, I don't know, 15 or 20 people, counting all the radiomen on duty, and a couple of us passengers on deck, in one compartment. Also, everybody was smoking all at the same time. Gosh it was hot--I remember waking up at night lying on my back, and when I opened my eyes, they were pools of sweat.

Q: Still better than the alternative.

Mr. King: Oh, I was so happy I didn't complain about anything. The idea was to tie up during the day to look like part of an island, then go like hell at night. Towards the middle of the night, we fell in with some Japanese ships.

Q: How soon was this after you left Corregidor?

Mr. King: I believe it was the first night, and I believe that we must have gotten under way as soon as it got dark. We fell in with these ships sometime after midnight. They were going towards the Philippines, obviously, and we were going out. We were by ourselves, and there were several of them--I don't know how many. Right away it got pretty tense. You know, here we were in a busted-up old four-piper with no armament to speak of. Lieutenant Commander Bermingham, the skipper, just decided to go ahead and go right on down the road, not answering any signals.* Maybe they'd think we were some dumb stepchild of theirs, some ship that was off course or something. And that's essentially what happened.

Q: They just ignored you?

Mr. King: The Japs had a blinker in a long tube. We could see these orange blinkers, but, of course, we didn't respond. So I assume that they thought, "Who is that dumb Lieutenant Kokamoto over there and whatever ship he's on?" Nothing happened, but it was very hairy, because we did that for a long time--couple hours, I guess. And that's covered

---

*Lieutenant Commander John M. Bermingham, USN.

in that narrative from the Boise. Finally, it dawned on me--and I'm sure everybody else--that it was going to get light before too long. But just like in the movies, when it got light, they were over the horizon, and we were clear.

Q: I guess your tattoos were helping you there too.

Mr. King: I was glad I had my tattoos. It got light, and we pulled alongside Cebu, I think it was. I'm not real sure; it was one of the islands there. We hadn't been there more than a couple of hours--not everybody had gotten anything to eat--when some Japanese planes came over. So that was decision time--whether to stay there and hope for the best or leave. The first batch of planes left, and I guess it was not clear whether they had identified us as a ship or not. The skipper decided to go. So we headed out, and a damn, big black puff of smoke came out of our stack. I'll bet he could have killed the chief engineer. But apparently that didn't cause any problems.

So we headed on down south and pulled in at Mindanao, I believe it was. Some banquos came out and told us that there were some Japanese ships on the other side of the island. So we headed out again, away from the island, in the general direction of Borneo. I was assigned to duty as a lookout. We had no binoculars. The big concern was dive-bombers coming out of the sun, like they did on the Prince of Wales and Repulse. So some genius got the ship's cook in the galley to break up some bottles and to smoke the pieces of glass. So we were each given a piece of smoked glass. I think there were three lookouts. I was up on the flying bridge, on top of the regular bridge. There was just room for the three of us to lie down--one this way, one that way, and one that way. So we each got our little piece of smoked glass and looked up at the sun. I don't know if I'd have seen anything, but that's the way we passed our time.

Then later on--and I'm not 100% sure of my timing here, but I think in mid-afternoon, an Emily came out, an unmistakable Emily--large seaplane--and circled around three or four times. We could just imagine the contact report being made and the Japanese dive-bombers saying, "Right. Be right over." The Emily made two torpedo attacks on us, each time dropping one torpedo and each time missing badly. Hell, a battleship could have avoided them. In a four-piper we just headed into it, and they missed by about 50 or 100 yards.

But at that time a decision was made to dump our classified gear. We had several mailbags full of classified gear, some metal, some paper. There were holes and grommets already in the bags so they would sink quicker. I don't know whether they had any proper charts or not. We were supposed to be in deep water, so we dumped the bags. That finished up our mission on board.

Then the decision was being made up on the bridge--you know, you get wind of these things--whether or not to ground the _Peary_ on the island of Borneo. We were going down parallel to Borneo, and the question was whether to ground the _Peary_ on Borneo and take to the hills, or whether to go onto Ambon. We headed for Celebes. At Celebes there's one channel to the right, the Makassar Strait goes off to the right; the other straits go off to the left. We received a contact report to the effect that there was a large Japanese task force in the Makassar Strait. And that's exactly where we were going. So the skipper turned around and headed in toward Celebes, to go around the other side of the island of Celebes.

As we were going into Celebes, Lieutenant Tom Moorer was out in a PBY and sighted us.* He made a contact report that a Japanese ship--unidentified type because of the stubby bow and everything--was going into Celebes to land troops. I think he'd also seen the Emily, and my memory is now that there was also something made of the fact that we were assumed to be escorted by Japanese planes.

We got into Menado, a seaport on Celebes. It had been attacked very heavily. The whole town seemed to be on fire--smoke and fire everywhere. We were getting very low on fuel. At one time, we had planned to fuel in Menado.

---
*Lieutenant Thomas H. Moorer, Patrol Squadron 22. Moorer eventually became a four-star admiral and served as Chief of Naval Operations, 1967-70, and Chairman of the Joint Chiefs of Staff, 1970-74.

But obviously, we couldn't. We were getting very close to land, and there was a kind of a channel that goes to the left there, towards the other side of the island. We were in this channel, and it was just about sundown. It was still light, but we were losing light pretty fast. Those of us up on the flying bridge were kind of taking stock.

All of a sudden these three planes, twin-engine dive-bombers, Lockheed Hudsons, came over, made a sweep around us, and went on off. Hell, we could see the red, white, and blue circles under their wings. Everybody cheered, and, "Yay, there are Allied people left in the world." Damned if they didn't come back and make a run on us, strafing topside. It went on and on.

It was a coordinated thing. One plane would make a dive-bombing attack, and the other two would strafe from two different directions. We had a string of sandbags up on the flying bridge, and we would get on one side of the sandbags when they came from that direction, and hop on the other side, and that sort of thing. One kid up there named Queneaux was killed.* A piece of shrapnel from the bomb that hit the fantail came up and took half his head off.

One bomb struck the fantail. I saw that bomb coming through the air towards the fantail, and I knew it was going to hit the depth charge rack. I thought we were going to have the biggest damn explosion the world has ever seen when

---

*Seaman First Class K. E. Queneaux, USN.

the bomb hit the depth charge. It hit back there and one of the depth charges caught fire. They rolled it into the water. I guess it wasn't fuzed or whatever; anyway, it did not explode. They rolled them all off. Then we were spinning around in the middle of this channel, barely enough room to spin around in. It was getting dark, and we were putting out a lot of smoke. The planes figured we'd had it, and they broke off. Our rudder was gone, so hand steering was set by chain of command voices from the bridge to the rudder hatch. Then we just went on up the channel.

Q: How did you find out it was Moorer in the PBY?

Mr. King: I saw a piece somewhere in some Navy publication--I may have that at home somewhere--but I have seen him since. I mean, I saw him when I was in the Pentagon, a couple of times. We sort of, in passing, reminisced about the good old days in the Asiatic Fleet.

Q: Did he feel any sense of chagrin over his . . .?

Mr. King: No, he had no reason to. He is a very great American and naval officer, in my opinion, and I've got a great amount of respect for him. I really think he's great. In fact, I wrote him a couple of fan letters years later on other activities of his.

But, anyway, that was about the size of it for the moment, for the Menado thing.

Q: After you survived the attack by the Hudsons, what next?

Mr. King: Well, it was, I guess, getting dark then. We had a fair amount of damage--none of it real critical, but we were in not too good a shape, and so the decision was made to beach the Peary. The captain picked out this island in the Halmahera group; the specific island, I think, is Ternate, or Madori Island. Anyway, we beached the Peary on this island, and the crew went ashore.

About the one kid that was killed up on the flying bridge, one thing that makes that stand out in my memory. He was killed instantly, but on the flying bridge on a destroyer there's not much room. There's room for maybe four people, if everybody makes room for one another. But when he was killed, we just left his body right there. So the three of us just had to kind of work around him during the course of the night. I'm not that much smitten with that kind of thing. I mean, it didn't really bug me, but it kind of sticks in my mind. It made for a long night.

We went ashore on this island and sort of took stock. A PBY came back to our anchorage and brought us some real critical things we needed to patch up the ship. I believe it was Admiral Moorer again, but I'm not sure about this. Contact was made with some Dutch military on another island in this group. They came to see us the next afternoon, and brought each one of us in the crew a quart bottle of ice-cold Heineken beer. I guess that was about the best beer I ever had in my whole life. We were there for the rest of that day, and a funeral ceremony was held for this kid Quineaux. Captain Bermingham made a very moving, moving, beautiful tribute to him. He was taken out in a launch and buried at sea there.

The ship was patched up and made, in some sense, seaworthy. They just pushed off from this sloping, sandy beach, just eased it back out. The stern was in fairly deep water, where it could get some propulsion with the screw, and we just slipped off fairly easily and went on to Ambon. These three pilots of the three Hudsons came aboard the *Peary* in Ambon, and expressed their regrets for the incident. I don't know of anyone that held any personal animosity towards them, the general situation being what it was.

We took on some fuel at Ambon--we were just about dry--and set out again right away for Port Darwin. These three planes escorted us part of the way to Port Darwin. I don't know what they'd have done if there had been any problems, but, anyway, they escorted us. The *Peary* arrived in Port Darwin, and I got off with Boaz and our gang, except for

Ensign Hirst, who elected to stay on the Peary as ship's company. His name is in that list of the flag there. He stayed on the Peary and did not survive the final sinking.*

The rest of us got off in Darwin. We set up temporary headquarters in the chief of police's house there in Darwin. An unusual incident that happened there. The police chief's house was our office, but we stayed in tents down further away from the office. We dug foxholes, because Darwin was supposed to be a prime target for Japanese carrier planes. We slept in these little tents that night, and the next morning when I woke up, I felt what I thought were leaves all over me. Then it got to me what was going on: a number one followed by 10,000 zeros of flying termites had invaded these tents that night before and shed their wings. We were just literally covered up by these brown, rustling, wings like little leaves. I don't know why I remember that, but I do.

Very shortly, that day or the next, the USS Langley arrived in the harbor, and we went aboard.** I should say that all of my personal gear was left behind in Manila. I had a lot of Asiatic souvenirs and all my uniforms, all that

---

*On 19 February, while operating out of Darwin, Australia, the Peary was attacked by Japanese dive-bombers and sunk. Of her crew, 80 were killed and 13 wounded in the attack.
**The USS Langley (AV-3) was originally a collier, later commissioned in 1922 as the U.S. Navy's first aircraft carrier. By the time of the outbreak of World War II, she had been reclassified as a seaplane tender. She was sunk in late February 1942.

kind of stuff. All that material was put on the Pecos earlier in Manila. Then when I was in Darwin I remember making inquiries about my gear that was on the Pecos. We were told that the Pecos was probably coming to Java and we'd get all our personal gear then. We didn't have any clothes to speak of. They gave us some clothes, and made up some dummy records and whatnot on the Langley. Then we went aboard the Boise, and we went to Surabaya on the Boise.* That was about a three-day trip.

The Boise, at that time, had the nickname of "The Reluctant Dragon." I don't know what really the background was, but it was not a complimentary term.

Q: I would gather not.

Mr. King: I remember that we didn't have any actual incidents, but there was some bordering on incidents, including the use of the term "reluctant dragon." Those of us in my little group there felt like we had sort of paid our dues. But, anyway, that's just sailor background.

Q: What did your group constitute? Were you just transient stragglers at this point?

---

*The USS Boise (CL-47) was a light cruiser, commissioned in 1938. She was 608 feet long, 62 feet in the beam, and had a standard displacement of 10,000 tons. Her main battery consisted of 15 6-inch guns.

Mr. King: I guess that's a good name for it. We were still together, that is, most of the flag allowance that rode the <u>Peary</u>. There were Harold Boaz, chief yeoman, and myself, yeoman first class, and, I guess, about four others.

Q: The Asiatic Fleet here just sort of dispersed.

Mr. King: Oh, it was ragtail, bobtail. They were all over the place; no one knew where anyone was. I don't mean chaos, but things were somewhat disorganized.

Anyway, we got to Surabaya, and there some kind of an organization began to shape up again. Admiral Hart and Commander Slocum were there with essentially the nucleus of the staff. A new overall command was formed, ABDA Com-- Australian, British, Dutch, and American. Sir Archibald Wavell was named ABDA Com.* Admiral Hart was ABDA Afloat, which was part of ABDA Com. I don't really recall now exactly how these commands shaped up by the time it wound up. I think Hart finally got relieved and went back to the States. I think I remember seeing that in his biography. And Wavell was the overall ABDA Com. ABDA Float was part of ABDA Com. ABDA Float was a couple of the Dutch cruisers. And the <u>Houston</u>, I guess, at that time it was still afloat.** We stayed in Surabaya and we had a fairly well,

---
*Field Marshal Sir Archibald Wavell, Supreme Commander, ABDA Command.

effective, and functioning headquarters there.

We were billeted in Dutch homes. I remember the home that I was billeted in. On Sunday there was a big formal Sunday dinner called a reistafel, brought by these servants called jongas. The jongas would come out to the table with large platters of many varieties of the same entree. There were beef jongas, the shrimp jongas, and the fish jongas. Each one would come by, four or five in each category, with a great big platter full of their specialty. You start out with a big plate of rice and one fried egg on top of the rice, and then you'd take some off each plate as they went by, until pretty soon you had a plate that was enormous--all of it very highly spiced. It was so good, it was just very good. But after you ate it, you had to just lie down and die for a while. You could hardly walk.

We slept in sort of a boardinghouse situation. And I remember that it was still fairly formal. We would get a pot of tea in the afternoon with a little padded cover on the teapot. And at night in our bunks we had what they call a "Dutch widow." It was a bamboo sort of frame like a big pillow, and you put that between your legs because it was hot at night, and you wouldn't sweat. So that was my introduction to a Dutch widow.

Well, things began to go downhill pretty fast there.

**The Houston was sunk early on the morning of 1 March 1942 in the Battle of Sunda Strait.

C. S. King #2 - 196

The Japs were moving our way awfully fast.

Q: As if things weren't bad already.

Mr. King: Yes.

Q: Now this is about late January '42, I would guess.

Mr. King: Late January, early February, along in there. The <u>Houston</u> was sunk in that battle of Sunda Strait. The <u>Marblehead</u> was damaged extensively and headed on back to the States. It became obvious pretty soon that things were going downhill fast, and we'd have to leave. On one day in particular, in the morning we were told we would be ground troops, part of this ABDA Com, a ground force that would stay there, which didn't suit me too well. But then it was a very quick shifting situation.

The next word we got was that the USS <u>Sturgeon</u> was over at Tjilatjap, on the other side of the island. Some injured burn patients off the <u>Houston</u> were going to be put on the <u>Sturgeon</u>. I was given a sack of classified items and instructed to go to Tjilatjap. At Tjilatjap, at least one night a bunch of us Navy guys were billeted aboard a Dutch ship named the <u>Zandam</u> out in the harbor. We were not on the <u>Zandam</u> too long. I remember, though, that we hadn't been paid in so long and all of a sudden we got paid. We got paid in guilders--we called them "gliders." We had no idea what they were worth. We had a poker game on the <u>Zandam</u> that ran all night long--playing for guilders--and at one time I had the most enormous stack of money in front of me. I broke even before the game was over, but I was rich beyond my wildest dreams at one point there.

I'm not sure now exactly how I got from the <u>Zandam</u> ashore to the <u>Sturgeon</u>. There was some difficult logistics in getting from point A to point B, whether you walked or bummed a ride. I damn near missed the <u>Sturgeon</u>, because I was late getting to the dock where she was. In fact, she was about to pull out. But, anyway, I remember getting on the <u>Sturgeon</u> and checking in. The doctor in charge of the <u>Houston</u> burn patients was a Dr. Wassell.* His name to us was "Shaky Jake," because he had a very pronounced tremor of his hands. Great guy. I mean, we liked him, but, we'd joke, "If you don't watch your P's and Q's, Shaky Jake will operate on you," and so on. Later on, they made a movie of him; Gary Cooper played Dr. Wassell.**

So we were on the <u>Sturgeon</u> several days, going to Fremantle. We were not under any kind of a direct attack that I was aware of. We apparently had some problems. It's not always great being a passenger. There were reports of

---

*Lieutenant Commander Corydon M. Wassell, MC, USNR.
**The movie was <u>The Story of Dr. Wassell</u>, released in June 1944. For more on the origins of the movie, see the Naval Institute oral history of Vice Admiral John L. McCrea, USN (Ret.).

Japanese submarines in that area, and I found out that what really worried a submariner more than anything else is another submarine. At least that's the impression I got--boy, when you mention enemy submarines, people take notice. They didn't worry so much about the destroyers as other submarines. I don't know why. I have no explanation for that.

We were on the Sturgeon then several days, but we couldn't surface for about two days because of where we were and the Jap forces around us. We were submerged for quite some period of time. Anyway, when we did surface, the fresh air was like champagne. I remember that was so beautiful. But then we made an uneventful trip to Perth. That really was the effective end of any Philippine or Asiatic Fleet adventures that I had. Because in Perth it was just 100% the opposite. We were just there, and all the Australian men had gone overseas. It was just 100 beautiful Australian girls to each American sailor. Just all of a sudden it went from night to day. Instead of being shot at and picked on by the Japs and everything, we were getting our autograph asked for, if you can imagine that--just overnight.

Q: Who was telling you where to go in all these things? Where was that direction coming from?

Mr. King: Up until the time I left Java, the direction came

from whatever remnant or whatever organization there remained of Admiral Hart's staff. When we got to Perth, that changed. I was put in an RPIO, registered publication issuing office. Then I had a designated commanding officer. So up until arrival in Perth, it was catch-as-catch-can. From Perth on, then I was part of an organized situation.

Q: When was your family informed that you were missing?

Mr. King: At one time in Java, an opportunity presented itself to make a phone call back to the States. We all lined up outside this telephone office to make a call home. None of us had communicated in a long time. But at that point was when I called home and talked to a telephone operator in Aransas Pass, Texas. The local phone operator, of course, knew my family and was more than a little surprised that I was not dead after all. My mother had sort of feared the worst from the very beginning. When she and my dad were officially notified that I had been lost on the Houston, she took it pretty hard.* It turned out that she and my dad had gone to Mexico for a sort of change in scenery. The operator got the wheels started, and the Mexican constabulary located them somewhere on the road in

---

*Even though the Asiatic Fleet staff, including Cecil King, had transferred ashore from the Houston in June 1941, official records in Washington, D.C., apparently still showed him on board. Thus, when the Houston was sunk, the Navy Department notified his parents that he was missing and presumed lost.

Mexico. Then they found out that I was okay. A little later, when I got to Australia, I called them up again at home and we got it all straightened out.

Q: So you didn't know you'd been declared missing?

Mr. King: No, I had no idea at all. It was a great shock to me. Of course, things were happening so fast during that long period of time there. Things were so disorganized that nothing surprised me. Every one of us made decisions of one sort or another, during an average 24-hour period, that determined whether you lived or died. I don't mean utter chaos but events were happening too fast.

Q: You couldn't plan. You just had to react.

Mr. King: React. We reacted from December 25 until whatever time I got into Perth. It was strictly a reaction. That's a good term for it.

Q: So you were having this duty at the RPIO and I imagine having some good liberty there.

Mr. King: Oh, great liberty, and that didn't last too long, because the decision was made to transfer this RPIO and reestablish it in Melbourne. I guess I hadn't been in Perth longer than a couple of weeks--if that long. Something like that. We flew from Perth to Melbourne. On that flight, at one point, we flew what seemed like hours, in an Australian commercial plane over one straight stretch of railroad. It must be the longest straight stretch of railroad in the world. We stopped somewhere in mid-Australia for fuel. It was an old gooney bird, Douglas DC-3 plane--Australian Quantas, whatever. A U.S. Navy captain was on board in passenger status. It turned out he was seriously interested in Australian aborigines. We stopped at this little, dusty strip of sand somewhere. He went out and made contact, and pretty soon--just sort of out of the ground--these aborigines appeared. This Navy captain was so excited; he was measuring their skulls and making voluminous notes. I never saw a man so happy over a development as he was to see these aborigines.

Q: Could he speak their language at all?

Mr. King: There was an interpreter of sorts there. But, anyway, we flew on to Melbourne. We were put in the Australian Navy Department headquarters called Victoria Barracks. An enormous safe was built and installed and all the security put in. We became a full-fledged RPIO.

C. S. King #2 - 202

Q: You might explain what an RPIO does.

Mr. King: Registered publications issuing office. We maintained, handled, and issued cryptographic material. Codes were issued to all the commands out there. Our office was a central repository and central issuing office for all the registered publications for the Southwest Pacific. Much of this material changed monthly, weekly, even daily.

Q: It's very exacting work. Everything's accountable.

Mr. King: Oh, my God. Oh, the nightmares we went through looking for something, until we found it. We had this great big room, with a safe door--something like Chase Manhattan bank in New York. We worked in behind the safe door, of course. We had shelf after shelf of all these publications and gear and various materials. We had to inventory quite often, but it was very exacting, very precise work.

We worked awfully closely with my brother Howard--not Bobby who was on the Peary--but my brother Howard who had been in that communications unit on Corregidor. He was also in Melbourne with me. Not in the RPIO office that I was in, but he was in the communications unit, which used our materials. So we didn't work in the same place, but we lived in the same apartment house in Melbourne.

My brother Bobby stayed on the Peary when I got off of it in Port Darwin and lasted maybe about a month. This is all in Dan Mullin's book.* The Peary was part of an escort operation that ran back and forth between Java and Australia. The Peary was in Port Darwin on the day of the 100-plane, Japanese carrier-plane attack and was sunk, very quickly and very specifically. My brother survived that. He was wounded and spent some time swimming in the water, which was covered in oil which was on fire.

He survived that and then wound up in a submarine. He was a radioman. He wound up in a submarine repair unit of some kind in Fremantle and stayed there for a year or so, I suppose, making cruises on submarines and working with communication gear, and so on.

I guess I lasted in Melbourne about nine months. That was really a time of intense action in the Pacific-- Guadalcanal and the whole works. I just got kind of antsy about this plush life I was leading when everybody else was out doing what they were supposed to do for the Navy, and so I put in for sea duty.

Q: I might ask you one question about that really hectic period you were in. Was there any briefing or instruction on what to do if you were captured?

---

*J. Daniel Mullin, Another Six Hundred (Mount Pleasant, South Carolina: J. Daniel Mullin, 1984).

Mr. King: I don't recall a single word to that effect by anybody. We had our own private plans. A couple of times it appeared imminent that I would be going to the hills, as they say. At one point I thought in the Philippines that I might wind up somewhere like that. I had my own sort of general idea what to do. On Borneo there was another possibility, and also in Java. It looked for a while there when we were going to be in ABDA Com that we were going to have to stay in Java and have the honor, and pleasure, and privilege of defending Java against the hordes of countless millions of Japanese. I just planned to go to the hills at that time. These were all my own contingency plans. But there was no organized setup. I'm not being critical or derogatory; I don't know who would have done that for us or who would have given us that kind of information.

Q: Since then, of course, there's the standard that you will provide only name, rank, and serial number, and all that.

Mr. King: Oh, yes. I think maybe that that was a fact of life--name, rank, and service number.

Q: But no specific training on resisting interrogation and what have you?

Mr. King: No. I think the whole idea of that was foreign. I guess I rejected in my own mind any possibility of being captured. I just always figured I'd go to the hills and from there somewhere else. I just didn't count on being captured.

Q: Well, you said that you found this life in Australia too enjoyable, so you had to leave.

Mr. King: That life was great. A little of it is okay, but my conscience began to hurt me. That doesn't sound very reasonable, but, anyway, it did. I just didn't feel that I was doing right. So I put in for sea duty and went back to the States on a ship of some kind--a transport ship.

Q: That must have been a long journey.

Mr. King: Yes, it wasn't a plane. It was a long journey. I think we left from Sydney. God knows what ship. But we landed in San Francisco, and in San Francisco I saw my first WAVE.* There were a whole truckload of us chiefs. We were going from Goat Island to somewhere. One guy said, "Hey, look, there's a lady sailor." We all looked over there, and sure enough there was a WAVE ensign. We hooted

---
*Navy women in World War II were known by the acronym WAVES, Women Accepted for Voluntary Emergency Service.

and hollered and yelled, and I guess it was the most embarrassing moment of her life. But that was kind of a shock to me. I wasn't ready to accept that fact.

Q: At what point had you become a chief petty officer?

Mr. King: I had taken the regular peacetime exam in late 1941 sometime. When we got to Perth, all of the first class--all of the ones that were still around, three or four of us--were all made chief. I don't know by what authority or what. Whether it had something to do with the exams we took, or whether because of wartime, we all made chief at the same time.

There were no American uniforms to be bought in Australia. So we bought Australian CPO uniforms and put American insignia on. It was the craziest looking thing you ever saw. I made chief sometime in February or March of '42.

When we got to Frisco, we were made available, and I sent a telegram to my old boss, Commander Slocum, who by that time was a captain in the Bureau of Personnel. I was a friend in need, so I sent him a telegram and said, "I'm back in the States." I think I asked for an aircraft carrier. Sure enough, a set of orders came in and I got transferred to USS Carnegie, which was a CVE going in commission up in

Tacoma, Washington.* I was in the so-called pre-commissioning and fitting-out detail for a couple of months. But she never went into fleet service, because she was turned over to the British right after she went into commission.

Q: What experiences do you remember from Tacoma?

Mr. King: Well, not a great deal. It was a period of pretty high, rather intense activity. They were trying to get the Carnegie to sea the day before yesterday, and I don't remember much except just working pretty hard and trying to get this ship ready. I didn't much care for being on one of these jeep carriers. That didn't sound too good to me. So I was very pleasantly surprised when the British took her over.

Q: I'd be interested in other examples of culture shock you encountered. You saw the WAVE. I mean, this was a vastly different United States than you had left.

Mr. King: Ten thousand percent different. In fact, all these chiefs that I wound up in this detail with, that all hit San Francisco at the same time, we had more money than

---

*The escort carrier Carnegie (CVE-38) was commissioned on 9 August 1943 and three days later was turned over to the Royal Navy, for which she served as HMS Empress. In January 1946 she was returned to the U.S. Navy.

we'd ever had in our whole life. All of us were getting back pay and this sort of thing.

Q: How could they possibly know what pay was due you?

Mr. King: I'd hate to have that job. But we had a lot of money. On Turk Street in San Francisco was the Turk Hotel. We took over that hotel--lock, stock, and barrel. There were enough to completely take over the hotel. I think we had a 72-hour liberty--three days off. We immersed ourselves into the civilian wartime environment. On the telegram I sent to Captain Slocum I said my return address was Turk Hotel, Turk Street, San Francisco. And that's where I got the answer back to. I think in three days we got pretty well acclimated. We immersed ourselves in United States, circa 1943.

When I was in Tacoma, I got a very sudden set of orders to go to the Hornet, in Newport News, Virginia. A group of CPOs all got on the train to go to Norfolk, Virginia.* We hadn't had any laundry in several days because of the rapid turnover of time and events. I had a zipper bag with six or eight white shirts in it, none of which were clean. That train trip across country took about four or five days, I guess. So each morning I would reach in this bag and pick out the cleanest of all the dirty shirts, and put it on for

---

*CPOs--chief petty officers.

that day. That night I put it back in the bag, and the next day I'd go through the same selection process again.

Another memory I have from the train is that there were Army MPs--which I thought was a hell of a note--Army MPs telling Navy guys what to do.* They made a little trouble for us. Not bad trouble, but there were several of us chiefs that had one compartment, I guess it was. We were playing poker, and somebody had a bottle. The Army MPs came in and found the bottle, and poured it right down the face bowl in the little compartment. That really came close to combat, but we all held our peace. I was really upset about that.

I remember another thing about that trip. I don't think we'd eaten anything from the time we'd left Seattle to the time we'd gotten to Cincinnati. We just played poker and enjoyed ourselves. One of the guys was nominated, in Cincinnati, to get off the train and go get some hamburgers for all of us. He didn't have much time. He jumped off the rear end of the train and went out--into this enormous depot in Cincinnati. He lost himself somewhere, and the minutes ticked by, and it got closer and closer to train time, and we didn't see him. Finally, at the last minute he came running up, and he had a big wicker basket full of hamburgers--each one wrapped in one piece of paper with no pickles, no nothing in it. We all were so ravenous from not

---
*MPs--military policemen.

having eaten in all that period of time, that--I'm not sure this is true, Paul, but later on we said no one took the paper napkins off--that we ate the hamburgers, paper napkins and all. I don't know.

We went on to Norfolk and then to Newport News, and I was in the fitting-out detail of the Hornet. I guess my overriding memory there is of the Hornet, besides meeting my wife . . .

Q: She had come out from Texas?

Mr. King: No, this was my second wife. I got divorced from the one I met in Bermuda.

I met my present wife then in Newport News for the first time, which really made that a memorable experience. Not only was I deliriously happy to be on the Hornet--I thought that was the greatest ship in the world--but I met the greatest woman in the world. And, you know, it was really a climax for me.

Q: Describe the circumstance there. I mean, you certainly had a dramatic meeting with your first wife.

Mr. King: Well, my second wife--there were two or three of them, and the whole schmear of the service records. A lot of our people had been sunk on the old Hornet. There were two or three of us chiefs in the fitting-out detail of the Hornet that were living at the receiving station outside of Newport News. We were going into town one night and were waiting for a bus. This big Buick car stopped with these two beautiful girls, ladies, women in it. I guess there were three of us chiefs. During the wartime atmosphere, you know, we were boys in blue, so they said, "Can we give you a ride?"

We gladly accepted, and during the course of the trip from the receiving station, we got better acquainted. So one thing led to another. Beer was almost unattainable in those days, in ordinary circumstances, but you could get it in the receiving station. So we got some beer from the receiving station, and we all repaired to their house and just really had a grand time. These two ladies were sisters, both beautiful, both delightful, and both just everything.

My wife-to-be, Emily, found out that I had been in China. She had this thing on for China. I found out that she was Tom Wolfe's cousin.* I had read every word he wrote, so it was love at first sight in more ways than one. So during the time I was in Newport News, putting the Hornet in commission, our romance blossomed, shall we say. I guess there was no doubt in my mind that I had met the one person

---

*Thomas C. Wolfe was a noted American novelist. Among his works were Look Homeward, Angel (1929), Of Time and the River (1935), and You Can't Go Home Again (1940).

that I really and truly wanted to marry and live with.

So we put the Hornet in commission.* There wasn't much time for extracurricular activities on the Hornet. It really was a high-velocity period. They were trying to get that thing to sea, because the first Hornet had been sunk.** This Hornet had originally been named the Kearsarge, and they renamed it the Hornet. Miles Browning was going to win the war with one airplane with the new Hornet there.*** He was a hard driver. I guess I worked almost as hard as I ever did in my naval career in that brief period of time, getting the Hornet ready to go to sea.

Q: Doing what?

Mr. King: I was the chief yeoman in the ship's office, as opposed to a chief yeoman in the captain's office. I was chief in charge of personnel for the Hornet.

Q: So you had to check in every new man.

---

*The USS Hornet (CV-12) was one of the first ships of the new Essex class of carriers that formed the nucleus of the fleet during the upcoming Central Pacific campaign. The Hornet was commissioned 29 November 1943. She was 872 feet long, 148 feet wide on the flight deck, and had a standard displacement of 27,000 tons and top speed of 33 knots.
**An earlier Hornet (CV-8) was sunk on 26 October 1942 in the Battle of Santa Cruz Islands, part of the U.S. effort to defend Guadalcanal.
***Captain Miles R. Browning, USN, was first commanding officer of the Hornet.

Mr. King: All that sort of stuff. Check them in, account them, and the whole schmear of the service records. A lot of our people had been sunk on the old Hornet. There was a lot of work for a personnel person--a lot of work. This was in the fall of 1943. Our commissioning date kept being upped, and we were just really going at it. Secretary of the Navy Frank Knox was at the commissioning. A lot of dignitaries were there. We were commissioned, and four months to the day from our raising the flag in Newport News, we were in a full-fledged action in the Pacific. I think Palau was our first one.* So we went from four months in Newport News in the Navy yard to full operating capacity in the Pacific.

Q: How did you spend those four months?

Mr. King: I guess about half of it at GQ and the other half of it sorting out the personnel, getting things organized.** One of the hardest jobs in those days, for me, was in going to sea when we had to get a list of everybody on board ship off the ship before we left. And I cannot describe to you the tension when you've got the harbor pilot on board, when you've got the air groups on board, and you're trying to get to sea, and the captain

---
*Planes from the Hornet laid mines in a harbor at Palau at the end of March 1944.
**GQ--general quarters, that is, battle stations.

wants to go, and the passenger list is not ready.

Q: How do you physically go about doing that job?

Mr. King: I put every yeoman on that ship on notice that when we did this, it was all-hands GQ for the yeomen. I didn't care which yeomen--navigator's yeoman, captain's yeoman--there were no teacher's pets. Every one had to take part in this. My crew and the ship's office would have a 3x5 card on every person on board, to the best of our knowledge. We would put those in rough alphabetical order, and I would put them in stacks of 100. I would run around the ship myself and give 100 to the navigator's office, 100 to the captain's office, 100 to the log room, and 100 to somebody else. They had to get right at it then--type those 100 names, type them on the embarkation list. By that time, we were ready to dump the pilot, and the pilot would take the passenger list back in with him. If you're out there making circles and waiting for the passenger list, well, the poor guy in charge of the passenger list is not a very popular individual.

Q: How often did you have to do that?

Mr. King: Well, every time we left port. But, of course, the first time was the toughest. After that it was keeping up with changes. I don't know how many times we did that during the time I was on there. It wasn't that many times, because we didn't make that many departures. I guess maybe from the time we left Newport News until we went through the canal and on to the West Coast, maybe five or six times. I'm at a loss to give you the exact number, but it was a heck of an operation.

Q: But it was more often than once a month?

Mr. King: It was probably more often than once a month. The more we operated after commissioning and everything, the easier the job became and the less new people we had involved. It was still before the days of computers. It was still a hands-on job from top to bottom.

Q: Did you have a battle station in that ship?

Mr. King: Yes, I did. On the Hornet my battle station was what we called Batt II or secondary conn. I guess that was one of the best battle stations on the whole ship because, boy, you saw everything up there. When the planes came in and landed, we were looking right at them from Batt II.

Q: This is in the after part of the superstructure, the island?

Mr. King: Right, yes. The bridge, Batt I, forward; Batt II, secondary conn, aft. The purpose of Batt II or secondary conn was to take over from the bridge in case the bridge was shot out. We had all the communications and that sort of thing duplicated in Batt II. As a matter of fact, when we would get under way, part of my job was to go on the circuit and pick up all of the stations and see if they were ready.

Q: You were a phone talker?

Mr. King: Yes, JV phone talker.

Q: Yeomen have traditionally filled that role.

Mr. King: Always been the talkers, always been the talkers--and I don't mean that in a pun sense.

Q: Presumably that job is because yeomen are more articulate than others in the crew.

Mr. King: I suppose so. But I always enjoyed that, because I always felt on top of communications, knew what was going on.

I recall a lot of incidents on the Hornet that were

spectacular. There's a scene that I've seen 100 times, I guess, on "Victory at Sea"--and every wartime aviation movie I ever saw--where this one plane comes in and breaks in two.* One like that was taken on the Hornet. I remember that actual incident very vividly.

Another time, one of our planes came in and had been pretty badly damaged; the pilot was shot up. I believe it was a TBM.** He hit the deck, one of his landing gear gave way, and he was going from side to side. He lost consciousness and hit the firing button. He sprayed the Batt II, secondary conn. We tried to put our profiles in the steel deck.

Another time we were at flight operations, and I was walking up the ladder to the bridge, up the catwalk with my back to the after part of the ship. I heard these things flying past my ears--buzz, buzz, buzz--and an explosion at the same time. One of our planes had come in, and a 500-pounder bomb, I guess it was, broke loose from the rack. When it hit the deck, the bomb cartwheeled, and it kept hitting nose down, tail down, nose down. It armed itself about the first time it hit. And then it went off 20 or 30 yards farther up, and we had some severe casualties.

---
*"Victory at Sea" was a popular television series produced by the National Broadcasting Company in the early 1950s. The series was built around U.S. Navy combat films of World War II.
**TBM was the General Motors version of the Grumman TBF Avenger, the standard U.S. carrier-based torpedo bomber during much of World War II.

Q: Did it blow a hole in the deck?

Mr. King: Yes. It blew a hole in the deck and also blew the legs completely off one of the flight deck crew. I don't think we had any deaths from that particular incident. From the time the ship was commissioned until I left, I spent every hour of every action back up there; it was a perfect picture. I mean, if I had said, "I want to have somewhere where I can see everything," I couldn't have picked a better spot.

Q: Did you feel vulnerable in that spot?

Mr. King: Well, not so much because we had a 1/2-inch steel waist-high shield up there. I just enjoyed being up there where you reported the action. I really enjoyed that.

Then at one time when I was on the Hornet, an opportunity came up for me to help debrief the pilots in VF-2--Fighting Two--by taking shorthand when the air intelligence officer got their statements after missions. I found that I had trouble writing down what they said. I was so wrapped up in what they were saying, I'd almost forget to put it down. I did that quite a number of times. I found it utterly fascinating.

Q: What do you remember about the shakedown period?

Mr. King: Miles Browning was such a driver. One thing I remember was that our navigator, a lieutenant commander, got cross-wired with Miles Browning. The day we left Norfolk to come around to the West Coast, Miles Browning put him off the ship with a set of orders. I thought to myself, "You can't do things like that. He is an officer. That's BuPers."* But he went off with a set of orders, and the orders said for him to report to any ship or station, something like that. I mean, I didn't see them myself, but that impressed me mightily. I didn't know that you could do that.

Q: Did Browning have a reputation throughout the ship?

Mr. King: Well, it was kind of a mixed thing, because he had such a reputation from Bull Halsey that I think his reputation, generally, was of a martinet and hard driver.** But it was not necessarily sort of image. He was very strict, and he acted as if he was going to win the war himself with one airplane. He was really a dedicated guy.

---
*BuPers--Bureau of Naval Personnel.
**Captain Browning had been chief of staff to Vice Admiral William F. Halsey, Jr., USN, when Halsey was Commander Aircraft Battle Force and later when he was Commander South Pacific Force.

C. S. King #2 - 220

Q: He's been portrayed as almost a fanatic.

Mr. King: I would say fanatic comes pretty close to it.

Q: Was he perceived as such by the crew at that time?

Mr. King: Well, no, not really. Maybe I'm just speaking for myself now, but he was perceived more as a guy who was just so damn gung-ho. I could understand why he felt that way because it was serious business, and I guess my sympathies were for him a little bit. I didn't have any negative feelings towards him, but he was hard on the officers. He wasn't so hard on the crew. That is to say, he was not nearly as hard as our skipper of the Davis was, for example. He demanded an awful lot. He demanded perfection in drills and so on.

Q: Well, he and Jocko Clark are viewed in that same aggressive vein, but somehow Clark's methods were considered legitimate, and Browning went beyond what was accepted.*

Mr. King: Yes, Jocko Clark was as different from Browning as day is from night. I think he got the same results but in a different way. That brings on a lot of other things that I remember. Jocko Clark was part Indian, and his lower

---
*Rear Admiral Joseph J. Clark, USN, Commander Task Group 58.1, who was then using the Hornet as his flagship.

lip just stuck way out, and it was always sunburned. Finally the doctor on the Hornet gave him no choice but to wear a gauze 4x4 with a string over his ears so the 4x4 would hang down over his lip. Jocko did it, but it made him madder than hell. I've seen him snatch three or four of those things off in the course of a couple hours. "Goddamnit." He'd tear it off and throw it down. And here would come the doctor and make him a new one.

Jocko was such a colorful guy. Whenever he came out on the bridge--GQ or any other time--he was wearing the sick bay pajamas that he slept in. Sometimes his hairy stomach would be sticking out, but he was oblivious to his appearance. He was totally oblivious to his appearance. He was just universally loved, respected, and admired on the Hornet. He had a great feeling for the pilots. More than once, when a pilot landed aboard the Hornet, shot up or whatever, the doctor, the emergency crew, and Jocko would get to him all about the same time. Jocko would bend over the stokes litter and pin a medal on the guy right there on the stretcher. You know pilots appreciated that. He was really and truly a great man.

Another time on the Hornet, some Japanese ships were sunk off of Saipan. Survivors were collected out of the water by various ships and put on a tanker and then put on

the <u>Hornet</u>. So we wound up with a couple hundred POWs.*
I don't think they were military. I think they were a
mixture of military and . . .

Q: Fishermen, perhaps?

Mr. King: Anything. We had them for a couple of days, and
Jocko didn't like that a damn bit because it interfered with
the readiness of the ship. We got rid of them in a couple
of days. They had never, of course, seen American food
before. They were struck by it, and what they really loved
was bread. They saw our mess cooks making sandwiches, so
the POWs would make sandwiches. They even made sandwiches
out of hotcakes. They had the same breakfast we had, and if
the breakfast was hotcakes, they'd ask for bread and make a
hotcake sandwich. That's the God's truth.

They had one little guy on there, a funny little Jap--
I'm sure he's been written up--who professed to be just
deadly against the Japanese. I think he said he was Korean,
but he would write obscene phrases, Japanese, in chalk on
bombs on the planes. They would let him. He would write,
"To hell with Tojo," and stuff like that.** At least I
hope that's what he was writing. He was kind of a mascot.
They thought a lot of him.

---
*POWs--prisoners of war.
**General Hideki Tojo was the Japanese Prime Minister.

When the time came to get rid of the prisoners, Jocko was so relieved. We were taking fuel from a tanker, and they put them off on this tanker by a highline. Taking on fuel under way is a split-second operation. So they rigged a canvas bag. They would put two or three Japs in the bag and send them over to the tanker. And about the third bag, one of the early transfers--I didn't see this myself, but I know it happened--one of the Japs hollered "Banzai" or something and just dove over the bag and into the water.

There was not that much distance between the tanker and a carrier refueling at sea. You just go backwards in these great big churning whitecaps, and you get back there and you got these screws--one or two screws on the tanker and four screws on the carrier, and it's just a meat grinder. So this first guy that fell down there, that's all she wrote. Just some pink foam. So the decision was what to do. Jocko said, "Let's keep them going. If they want to dive over, we got to get going."

So I don't know how many jumped over. These tales grow in telling. I'm satisfied at least one of them did. Maybe more but, anyway, the transfer went on till they all got off of the Hornet.

Gosh, the more I talk about these things, the more I remember.

Q: Well, keep telling it. Was that a comfortable ship in

which to live?

Mr. King: It was. The Hornet and the Midway were the two best ships I think I was ever on.

Another thing that happened on the Hornet was that we had a small group of real no-goodniks on there. I mean, these kids who were not necessarily honest-to-God gangsters. I don't know what they were, but, anyway, they were involved in anything that was seriously wrong on the ship--heavy gambling and extortion. One of them one night was thrown over the side. It was common knowledge around the ship that that's what had happened. He was officially listed as being lost at sea, but there's no doubt in my mind what happened. Those people he ran around with just threw him over the side. The exec was convinced of that too.

Another memory I have on the Hornet was that on one occasion, maybe more, our damaged planes were just pushed right over the side. At the time I thought, "Well, hell, that's the only way we can win this war. That's how we can win it, by being able to do that, because you can't take up valuable fighting space on the ship with duds." So they just pushed them right over the side.

Another time one of our pilots, one of our Hornet pilots, came back badly wounded and died. He was buried in his plane. They pushed the whole plane over the side. That was a very moving, very moving ceremony. Pushed him over the fantail with full honors.

Then we had one other burial at sea, when one of our firemen--a big beefy guy--had heat prostration down in the firerooms. When he went berserk, he had this heat seizure. He was wearing phones, was a talker, and it is said that he took those two lines from his phones and wrapped them around his hands, and pulled the heavy phone wire right in two. He had that much strength, and it took six or eight men to buckle him down, to get him to sick bay. He was completely out of his mind and had the strength of ten men.

In the sick bay, his temperature got so high that they could not take his temperature with a medical thermometer. They had to use some kind of thermometer from the engineering department to take his temperature. He had some tremendous temperature. He died, and we had a formal burial at sea, where they wrapped him in canvas. That was my first experience seeing that kind of funeral at sea. Because when that kid died, who was killed on the <u>Peary</u>, they took him off on a launch and buried him. I wasn't on the launch.

Q: How was the bulk of your time spent once you got out into action? Now you didn't have this business with having to send off a personnel report every time.

Mr. King: No, no. We spent so much time at condition I-A. That was the condition immediately before GQ. At I-A you're semi-GQ but not entirely buttoned up. When we first got out there, we spent more time at I-A, I guess, than an ordinary ship did because we were new. We spent two or three days almost, either at I-A or GQ. Our chiefs' quarters were back on the fantail about three decks down. We had a cook, a reserve ship's cook, who was really great. I think he owned a restaurant or something in civilian life. About the second day, the word got around to all the chiefs through the grapevine that there were steak sandwiches in the chiefs' quarters. So, a few at a time, we would trickle down and break watertight integrity on I-A and get our steak sandwiches.

So my time came, and I got relieved and went down. This guy had made some hoagie rolls, made them himself, and these steaks were just gorgeous. So I got in line and got my steak sandwich. Just as I put one end of it in my mouth, the alarm sounded for GQ. I don't like to be below decks at GQ. I do not like it at all. I feel claustrophobia and everything else. But we were under a pretty well sustained attack for about, I guess, five minutes. You could hear the bombs going off in the water. You could hear the noise against the hull. The ship was making sharp turns, and it was that sort of thing, antiaircraft firing, and just a lot of stuff going on. After about five or ten minutes it was all over. I looked down, and my sandwich was gone. I had eaten that entire sandwich during that period, and I didn't remember taking one single bite of it.

Q: It was wasted.

Mr. King: It was wasted. I remember I was mad. I thought, "Damn! I wasted a whole steak sandwich." These things are not in sequence. My memory after 50 years--I guess things just come to the surface from time to time.

Q: What do you recall from experiencing an air attack when you were topside?

Mr. King: That was before the full-fledged kamikaze days, and I don't think that, in itself, was an overriding fear. But I remember several occasions when we were under fairly heavy attack. It just seemed like the sky was full of planes, projectiles. Just as far as you could see, planes going in the water here, planes going in the water there, the tracers going through the air, just an intense moment of bright colors. During those moments, I seemed to get sort of a second sight. I could see farther and kind of sharper; it would go into slow motion kind of. These really were moments that I can close my eyes right now and see.

One time, it might have been the New Jersey that was with us. We didn't operate with a battleship that much, but on this occasion we did. Along towards sunset, the New

Jersey got in between us and the setting sun. We also had some tin cans and I think a couple of cruisers, and maybe a jeep carrier--a regular task force situation. But I remember the comforting feeling I had looking at that battleship against the setting sun. I thought, "You know, I'm just like I'm home in church." I thought that was such a great thing.

I think that very same night we were under attack. The carriers were not supposed, in ordinary circumstances, to open up our deck guns at night because the guns would silhouette the flight deck, and the Japs would know it was a carrier. I mean, that was the idea. We didn't ordinarily open up at night, but on this one night, the _New Jersey_ did, and it looked like a gigantic Christmas tree. I never saw so much fire and tracers coming from one place in my entire life. I don't know how much armament the _New Jersey_ carried, but everything on that ship just opened up. It was just a big cone up here, and the cone would move around. And then you'd see a plane light up and go down, and that cone would just keep on going. It was a spectacular sight.

Q: Do you have any idea chronologically when that might have been?

Mr. King: That must have been in early '44, something like that.

Q: What do you remember about the demise of Captain Browning?

Mr. King: I guess it was kind of common scuttlebutt that he was in a heap of trouble. And it was no great surprise, I guess, that he went. But there was regret on my part. I still have a vision today that that guy was a dedicated fighting man. He had one idea in life, and that was to get that ship out there and win the damn war. But I don't remember any specific circumstances about it. Captain Sample came to us in his place.* Sample was later killed in the Pacific. He was going from Point A to Point B, and the plane crashed. Sample's widow married George Anderson.**

Q: Was there a sense of relief after Browning left?

Mr. King: There definitely was amongst the officers. In my particular circle, in the crew, I guess I just felt a sense of a little bit of regret, but understanding. I mean, I knew that he had gotten himself in trouble. But I still had

---

*Captain William D. Sample, USN, relieved Captain Browning as commanding officer of the Hornet.
**The second wife of Admiral George W. Anderson, Jr., USN, was the widow of Rear Admiral Sample, who was lost in October 1945 when the plane in which he was flying failed to return from a flight over Japan. Anderson was Chief of Naval Operations from 1961 to 1963.

a residual feeling of loyalty to the guy because of his dedication, I guess that kind of thing.

Q: Did you work for him directly?

Mr. King: No, I'd been on the bridge with him. I was not in the captain's office; I was in the exec's office. That was Commander Dutch Duerfeldt--great guy.*

I've got a document here somewhere, which I'll show you later on that Miles Browning wrote, that took us to sea. This is one of these, "Let's do it. The Hornet's going to be the most effective ship in the Navy, and we're going to do it and we're . . ."

Q: Do you remember the incident with the stampede in the hangar deck during the movie?**

Mr. King: I remember that very well. I was not at the movie. I was back in the chiefs' quarters. But the accounts were that a noise of some kind occurred, something fell and hit the deck.

Q: I think it was a fire extinguisher.

---
*Commander Clifford H. Duerfeldt, USN.
**This incident was the straw that broke the camel's back in the case of getting Browning relieved as commanding officer of the Hornet. For details, see Commander Harold L. Buell, USN (Ret.), "Death of a Captain," U.S. Naval Institute Proceedings, February 1986, pages 92-96.

Mr. King: Maybe that was it. Then somebody hollered bomb; somebody hollered fire; somebody hollered something else. A perfect stampede developed on the hangar deck. My recollection is that the chiefs' quarters were back by the sick bay. We found there was a commotion going on, and I went up the ladder. I couldn't go up because they were carrying guys that were bunged up, bloody noses, eyes, nothing serious. They were just carrying all kinds of people down to the sick bay from this stampede up on the quarterdeck. I wasn't in it, but I had that exposure to it.

And, also, I remember one time when an aircraft engine got loose, out at sea. We had a hell of a time with it. It was an aircraft engine in a crate. It broke loose, and we were in pretty heavy weather. There was a famous book, or story, by Victor Hugo about a loose cannon. It was some ship way back in his time, and what a time they had getting this cannon pinned down. I thought of that at that time, because that damn aircraft engine was running across the deck and the sparks would fly. And on the hangar deck, you don't want sparks. Hell, there's napalm and everything else there.

I wasn't up there, but I was close enough to it where you could hear some of the sound effects from guys yelling. And we'd go this way, and that damn engine would cross the

C. S. King #2 - 232

deck, and just whammo! But, finally, some honest-to-God hero somehow got a line on that engine and made it secure to the bulkhead and gradually pinned it down. That aircraft engine tore up a lot of planes. It caused an enormous amount of damage.

Q: Did you get ashore on any of the atolls for liberty?

Mr. King: No, never did. As a matter of fact, the Hornet was one of the first carriers to fuel at sea, take on ammunition at sea, replenish at sea, everything at sea. I've forgotten the exact amount of time now, but at one time we set some kind of a record by being the longest operating carrier--eight months or some damn thing--just continually going all that time.

Q: Did you get into Ulithi at all?

Mr. King: No. I left the West Coast on the Hornet. Except for Pearl Harbor, the next time I got off of it was when I was transferred. I don't think I got ashore anywhere off the Hornet anywhere else in the Pacific.

Q: How long were you on board?

Mr. King: I was on the Hornet from September 1943 until

October 1944. I spent a lot of time on there in the Pacific without ever leaving the ship. I didn't really notice it. I mean, it wasn't that kind of a hardship, but nobody else did to speak of.

Oh, one time Jocko Clark, because of this very fact, got some beer ordered officially for the Hornet. And we worked out a system where one division at a time could have a beer party up on the forecastle--this is at sea in wartime. They could drink two beers a man, three beers a man--something like that--and that was it. I think the first time the first division had it; second time, second division--like that. They had a couple hundred cases of this beer stowed down in a storeroom up forward.

The first night it was on board, all they had was a padlock on the hatch of this storeroom. I guess by 9:00 somebody had broken the padlock and stole a few cases of beer. The supply officer was very upset, so the next day he had the shipfitter come around and put four hasps on that hatch, square hatch, and put four padlocks on those. Probably took the guy about five minutes the second night-- all four padlocks off, and they got the beer. So the next day the shipfitters came up there and put a bead of weld.

Q: Tack welded it.

Mr. King: Tack welded that whole damn hatch. And when they

took the beer out, they just hammered it up and took the tack off. That's how they kept that beer for our beer parties. That's the kind of thing that made Jocko so beloved. That's just the kind of thing that he would do.

Another thing I remember about Jocko--we had movies at night on the hangar deck in port. And you don't smoke on the hangar deck. You don't smoke anywhere topside on a carrier at any time for any reason. That's worse than a magazine. Jocko would, I guess, have a couple of horns in his room, go up and go to the movies, sit in the front row there. Jocko would put a cigarette in his mouth, reach over and with a kitchen match, scritch and strike that kitchen match on deck, light up his cigarette, and sit there, and smoke cigarettes at the movies. And not one person ever said anything about that. And I've seen him do that more than once.

We picked up this guy Ray Tweed off of Guam, who had hidden out in a cave from the time the war started to the time when he came aboard the Hornet in '44.* I had an acquaintance with the guy before the war. He was a first class radioman who had been on the published list of chiefs before the war.

When he came aboard the Hornet, he was very edgy at first. You couldn't get behind him or anything, and he was

---

*Radioman First Class George R. Tweed, USN. For Admiral Clark's version of Tweed's recovery and promotion, see Joseph J. Clark, Carrier Admiral (New York: David McKay Company, Inc., 1967).

very spooky because he'd been by himself that long. But because I knew him, I tried real hard to really give him the first-class treatment, anything he wanted. I had the barber come up to the ship's office while I was making out his record, and give him a haircut. We were giving him the first-class treatment. And when he told me that he had been on the list, I said, "Well, hell, I'll fire off a dispatch and we'll get you your chief's rating right now."

So I made up a dispatch, because you couldn't promote a chief without BuPers authority, even in those days. I made up a dispatch--all the usual stuff--request authorization, and so forth--and got it released, and cleared, and sent. I even got a priority precedence, I think, on it, because it was big stuff. I told him about it and he was pleased as punch. Then, several hours later on, he was asked to go up and see a guy named Rosenblatt, who was Jocko's flag secretary.* Rosenblatt was kind of a colorful guy, and Rosenblatt wanted to take him in to see Jocko. Pretty soon someone said, "Hey, Rosenblatt wants to see you" to me.

I thought, "What in the hell have I done now?"

So I went up there, and Rosenblatt said, "How come Tweed's not a chief radioman?"

I thought, "I'm ahead of him." I told him, "We sent off this dispatch, and I expect an answer back tomorrow."

He said, "How come he's not a chief right now? Admiral

---
*Lieutenant Herman S. Rosenblatt, USNR.

Clark wants him to be a chief."

So, hell, I don't need a brick wall to fall on me. I went back down to the office. I typed out the whole thing for him. I put down there, "Authority: verbal orders of CTG 58.1." The paymaster was an ensign. I gave him all the paperwork, and I said, "Now, this guy's got three years' back pay coming, retroactive, as a chief."

The ensign said, "I ain't going to pay him."

I said, "You can have the same experience I did, if you want to." I told him what happened to me with Rosenblatt. So he went grumble, grumble, grumble, but he went ahead and paid the guy all his money.

Q: That would be a pretty good sum.

Mr. King: It was a good sum. It was thousands of dollars, not 50 or 100. It was, I guess it was several thousand dollars.

Q: I take it BuPers approved of this.

Mr. King: Never heard a word about it. [Laughter]

The reason that kind of sticks in my mind now is that when I was down in Panama there was a yeoman first class named Elton Flowers down there. He was a good friend of mine. Back in the Thirties, Elton Flowers had been on the

Sequoia, FDR's yacht.* FDR loved the Navy, and they had a handpicked crew on the Sequoia. They had a coxswain, a third class boatswain's mate, who was probably the best seaman in the Navy. He probably could sign his name, but he had no academic background at all. He was a damn good seaman; that's why he was on the Sequoia.

So one time FDR came aboard the Sequoia and was piped aboard. The coxswain had the watch that day, and his cap was shiny white, squared over his eyebrows, and his boatswain's mate whistle, shiny--the very picture of a seaman. Roosevelt went to his cabin and said, "I want to see Flowers." So Flowers came up, and FDR said, "Flowers, that guy at the gangway--why does he only have one stripe up here on his arm and four stripes down there on his sleeve?" He had four hash marks on and was still only a coxswain, which wasn't too unusual those days.

Elton said, "Sir, he doesn't have one over there. He's got three over there." So he spun around and went out of the office. He got busy on the typewriter made out an immediate promotion from third class to first class. It was unheard of in those days to advance someone--much less jump over a rate--with no authority. Elton put down, "Verbal orders of the President of the United States." Elton said he never heard a single word about it. The next time FDR saw that guy, he had three up here and four over here.

---
*FDR--Franklin D. Roosevelt.

C. S. King #2 - 238

Q: He was a first class from then on.

Mr. King: I thought about that. So when Rosenblatt said to me, "How come he's not chief?," I remembered what happened to Elton. I don't know why in the world I didn't have the gumption to go ahead and make him chief, and quit arguing about it.

Q: Well, you satisfied your conscience.

Mr. King: But that was dumb. That's what happened to Elton too.

Q: Are there any of the big battles that stand out in your mind? For example, the Philippine Sea Battle--the "Turkey Shoot?"*

Mr. King: The one that stands out is the "Turkey Shoot." That's one that really stands out in my mind, because it was a spectacular thing from the spectator's standpoint. I remember very vividly when they were out there on, mixing up with the Japs, and we'd get these fragmentary reports in: splashed two, splashed three, and so on. It just seemed

---

*On 19 June 1944, the carrier pilots of Task Force 58 shot down more than 300 Japanese planes. The event came to be known as the "Marianas Turkey Shoot."

like this was what we went out there to do. We were shooting up the whole damn Japanese Navy. It just seemed like that was the greatest thing in the world.

The next day, it was high feeling and emotion about the distance our planes had to go in trying to intercept the Jap fleet as it steamed away. I was just close enough that I could sense that this was a big damn decision, about whether to send them off or not--and the distance involved, and all that kind of thing. I remember all the suspense involved in that.

That night, when they came back in, I was up topside, at my battle station. It was a memorable evening, because there were planes landing all over the place. It didn't matter what carrier they were from. The minute anybody flashed ready deck, somebody landed on it. Almost every landing was some kind of a deck crash. They were running on fumes. There were planes going in the water everywhere. That's when Mitscher lit up the fleet: searchlights--the whole damn thing.* It was just a spectacular, memorable occasion.

I remember on the Hornet they passed the word to throw over anything that would float--wooden orange crates, anything. These guys out in the water--there were just people everywhere. It was just an extremely dramatic

---
*Vice Admiral Marc A. Mitscher, USN, Commander Task Force 58, ordered the carriers' lights to be turned on to aid the pilots in the return from their long flight toward the Japanese fleet.

occasion. I just couldn't believe what was happening. When it was all over, that's when we went down to chiefs' quarters and said, "Boy, this is it. We're going to break three or four regulations." Somebody had some booze of some kind.

Q: Where had that been stored?

Mr. King: God knows. [Laughter] But it got resurrected for that moment. We all gathered in the compartment I shared with several other chiefs. I had a guinea pullman. So we all had a drink of some kind. A good friend of mine named Duke Helms was the chief photographer's mate. He'd often wanted to take a picture of my tattooed feet. He said, "We're going to make this a real occasion. I'm going to take a picture of your damn tattoos." So he had me take off my shoes and socks, and took a picture. I remember that battle more than anything else that happened all the time I was on the Hornet. It was a great occasion.

I used to be very proud when they would put up our new decals on the bridge structure for ships sunk, planes shot down. That kept growing, and growing, and growing.

Q: Did you get to know any of the pilots?

Mr. King: I got to know several of them fairly well, especially when I was working with the combat intelligence officer on debriefing the pilots. Then there were a lot of hero stories always passing around, like on every carrier, I guess. Some guy would do something spectacular, and by the time he got back to the ship, we'd have increased it by ten planes and everything. There was a kind of gung-ho spirit, and I just couldn't believe my good fortune at being on a carrier and with all that kind of stuff, and shooting, and all the things going on. This was a big change from when I'd spent the first three months of the war skulking around from island to island all over the place. Now I was on the winning team. That's the way it's supposed to be in the first place. That's the way it really should have been.

Q: Well, now, finally, it was a fulfillment of that vision you'd had of the U.S. fleet coming back.

Mr. King: It was. It was and I remember it so many times. I've always been kind of a kidder, kidding people around. When we would be going into a particular operation--and we had a couple of kids in the exec's office on there that were kind of spooked by the war and so on--I would tell them terrible tales. I'd break out a map and I would say, "We've got to go from here to here. And there's ten Jap battlewagons here, and ten Jap cruisers right down there," and all this kind of thing. And I know you shouldn't do things like that, but I did it because in my own mind I never had the slightest feeling there was any kind of a problem. This was what we were supposed to do in the first place, and I was so glad to be a part of it.

Q: Were you still around for the Battle of Leyte Gulf in the fall?

Mr. King: I left her in October 1944, shortly before the battle. I left her at sea. I went to Manus, New Guinea, to get transportation back to the States. And that's when I told you I ran into McCain that time.

Another thing on the Hornet, when I was talking about kidding those youngsters--there was a guy, a young boy named Edwards from Hershey, Pennsylvania, who was a yeoman striker in my office. We were all pretty fond of him. He sort of enjoyed being kidded. We did our duty.

Q: Interesting way to put it.

Mr. King: He had a picture on his desk of his girlfriend in Hershey. And every time I came in the office, I would say, "Gosh, that's a nice looking picture of your mother, Eddie."

And he would, "No, that's my girl. That's not my mother; that's my girl." I guess she was a year older than he was. But I would always act like I really thought it was a picture of his mother. But, anyway, later on he bugged me about getting a battle station. He said he wanted to be on a 40-millimeter gun. He wanted to shoot. I tried to talk him out of it. He was adamant. He wanted to see and smell the smoke, and shoot down the Japs.

Well, I finally gave in. I went to the gun boss and asked him about it. So we got him a battle station on the 40-millimeters. He hadn't been on it more than a couple of weeks or so until we had some kind of a fracas and he came back after the session, and told me all about it and how great it was.

About a week and a half or two weeks later--he wasn't on the 40-millimeter more than a month--a Jap plane strafed the flight deck and a tiny piece of shrapnel hit this kid in one side of his stomach and went out the other. It just tore his insides up. He was the first combat casualty of any kind to the crew that we had on the Hornet directly at that time. It caused quite a stir, and, God, I felt bad about that. So I went down to see him in sick bay as soon as he could see people. He was lucid, felt good about it, and was proud of himself. I really felt bad. The kid died that very same night. I guess that's about the most negative thing in my mind about the Hornet. I felt a very deep sense of personal responsibility about that, even though that's the kind of thing I guess everybody runs into in a combat situation.

I went to Hershey with my wife several times with an idea of going to see his folks. One time we went there and I saw they had a list in downtown Hershey of all the people killed in action in World War II. There was about five Edwards on there. I should have done it, but I didn't. It always stayed in my mind, and it still kind of bugs me.

Q: Well, if it hadn't been him, it would have been somebody else.

Mr. King: I suppose so, yes. But after that I had a new feeling about skippers who have a direct involvement in the matter of plane and personnel combat assignments where. I guess it's brought home to them pretty clearly.

Q: It just goes with the job.

Mr. King: It goes with the territory, as they say.

Q: Were there moments for relaxation amidst all this action?

Mr. King: Oh, heck, yes. Although our combat time was fairly compressed, it was not all grim fighting and everything. I guess most of our time at sea was, to some extent, combat oriented. I mean we were very seldom at condition IV.* Very seldom.

Q: A lot of training.

Mr. King: It was almost always III, II, I-A, or I. We had a lot of training, and also a hell of a lot of dead time, so to speak, back up in Batt II on the battle station. We spent a lot of time just cruising. Because we had reveille every day one hour before sunrise. All the time I was out there, it was an hour before sunrise. So, you know, every day, an hour before sunrise, back up to battle stations until an hour after sunrise. I'd be up there every day. So a lot of time was just sea time, up there at Batt II: watching the planes, watching what was going on. That kind of thing.

I also recall that in the case of a normal predawn GQ, which was usually around 0430 or thereabouts, when the boatswain's mate of the watch up on the bridge would press the button to activate the mike, there would be a split second or so of background noise before you could hear his voice. Then he would say the usual, "General quarters, general quarters. All hands man your battle stations."

While we did not actually dilly-dally, there was not an instantaneous reaction. We would get our uniforms on and

---

*Condition IV is peacetime steaming.

head toward battle stations. Not sluggish, but not breakneck speed either. However, if the GQ was sounded at any other time, by the time the background noise was over and the BM of the watch could say, "General quarters," we were out of our bunks, in our shoes, and heading topside. When the GQ was the real McCoy, regardless of the time, there was just about instantaneous reaction.

Q: I think we're going to run out of tape here, and we'll get the next duty station next time.

C. S. King #3 - 247

Interview Number 3 with Chief Warrant Officer
    Cecil S. King, Jr., U.S. Navy (Retired)

Place: Mr. King's home in Arlington, Virginia

Date: Monday, 11 August 1986

Interviewer: Paul Stillwell

Q: Last time we just got you detached from the USS <u>Hornet</u> after your adventures in the Pacific. Then I believe you headed out to the Midwest.

Mr. King: A whole bunch of us--there were several hundred in this particular group--finally wound up at NAS Alameda.* On the day our assignments came in, there were some theatrics involved. They would say, "So and so, where would you like to go?"

    A chief would stand up and say, "So and so."

    Then they'd say, "Well, you got this instead." Everybody would clap and cheer. It was kind of a fun thing.

    So when my turn came, I said I wanted to be somewhere on the East Coast. They said, "Well, you've got the Naval Air Station Minneapolis." A hurrah went up, because a lot of guys think of being in Minneapolis as being in heaven. That's the Midwest, not too close to the ocean. So I duly went to Minneapolis. I had been in the Pacific for a number of years then and was fairly well accustomed to the tropics.

---
*NAS Alameda--Naval Air Station Alameda, near Oakland, California.

I was assigned to Minneapolis, and I got there in January. I can't tell you how cold it was.

Q: Below zero probably.

Mr. King: Way below zero. But it was a nice station, a home away from home. There was not much wartime atmosphere about it. It was just a homey place to be.

Q: Well, you'd been on a wartime footing for about five years, so you could afford to take a little break there.

Mr. King: Well, for a while I did. But I just didn't vibrate to the reserve air station climate. I got edgy, and so I finally put in for a transfer to sea duty.

Q: What did you do while you were there? I think we should cover that.

Mr. King: I was in the captain's office, captain's writer. I worked for a guy named Mendenhall, who had been commissioned ensign from chief yeoman.* After a couple of months, I'd just had all I wanted of it, and I put in to go to sea. The request for a transfer didn't go over too well. There was a little problem with that.

---
*Ensign Gerald W. Mendenhall, USN.

Q: What was the role of a reserve air station during wartime? Was it just a place for planes to pass through?

Mr. King: Yes, sort of a transient stopover place. As I recall, there wasn't a big maintenance section. There was not much of an operation about it. There was a fair number of planes, but I think we were kind of a stopover, more or less.

Q: Obviously, there was no aircraft carrier stationed nearby.

Mr. King: No. We had some makeshift carriers on the Great Lakes during the war for training ships. But I just don't recall much about NAS Minneapolis. It was a nice place to be, in a beautiful town, and so on, and so on. But I just got edgy after a while--there's a Navy term for that--and so put in for sea duty. Mendenhall was very helpful. As a matter of fact, I found a couple of telegrams the other day. One of them is where Mendenhall wired me at home and said, "Your request for the Midway. They can't do it, but you can have the Princeton. Let me know right away. ComAirLant wants to know."*

---

*ComAirLant--Commander Air Force Atlantic Fleet, the type commander for aircraft carriers in the U.S. Atlantic Fleet.

Q: Those were both new carriers at that point.

Mr. King: Yes. So the exact wording of my telegram back to Mendenhall was, "If it floats, I want it. Request extension. Grandmother broke her leg. The fishing is swell." I knew him pretty well, so I got another ten-day extension out of it. I went back to Minneapolis and then headed for Philadelphia, where the Princeton was going into commission. CFO, the commissioning and fitting-out detail, was at the Philadelphia Navy Yard.

Q: How far along was she when you reported?

Mr. King: I guess she was two or three months away from commissioning, something like that.

Q: At that point, you still didn't know when the war was going to end, so it was probably still pretty hectic.

Mr. King: Still going full bore. I was very happy to be assigned to the Princeton, because she was a CV and I had been on the Hornet. So I was glad to get the Princeton.*
But the Princeton was not a happy experience for me. I don't wish to speak ill of the dead--Captain Hoskins was the

---
*The Princeton (CV-37) was essentially an Essex-class sister of the Hornet in which Mr. King served earlier.

skipper.* The chemistry between Captain Hoskins and me was not great, and this was exacerbated by his aide, a mustang lieutenant, Richard P. Lewis, also deceased.** Again, I don't wish to speak ill of those who have gone before, but I didn't get along with Lewis worth a damn. Because of him, I didn't get along with Hoskins either. It's kind of ludicrous for a chief yeoman to say he didn't get along with the captain. You don't do that. But, I mean, it was not a happy relationship from my standpoint.

I tried very hard to get off the ship. My wife Emily was in St. Augustine with her mother. And our firstborn was fixing to come along, and I wanted to get back. Except for Minneapolis, I had never had any assigned shore duty in the United States. It was all sea or foreign service, and I didn't think it was out of the way to put in a request to get off of the Princeton and go ashore.

I tried every way in the world, and the more I tried, the deeper I got on the list. So I got pretty far down on the list, which is not normal for me. Normally I got along pretty well with my peers and with the skipper. As a matter of fact, on the Davis with Captain Carr, I got along okay with him. He was a martinet, and he was eccentric--sort of

---
*Captain John M. Hoskins, USN, had been slated to take command of the previous Princeton (CVL-23). He was on board during the Battle of Leyte Gulf in October 1944 when that Princeton was sunk.
**Lieutenant Richard P. Lewis, USN, had previously been a yeoman. "Mustang" is a Navy term for an enlisted man who becomes an officer.

a Captain Queeg--but, I mean, there was never any problem. But there was a big, fat problem with me and Lieutenant Lewis and Captain Hoskins.

Q: How was this manifested? I mean, what sorts of difficulties did you have?

Mr. King: Well, when it became obvious to Lieutenant Lewis that I wanted off the Princeton, that just didn't sit well with him. Captain Hoskins had served on the old Ranger for a long time--flight deck officer, air officer, and whatever else. Then he went to the first Princeton, and then to the second Princeton after number one was sunk. The crew was divided up on the Princeton. There was three groups: there were the "privileged few," who had served with Hoskins on the old Ranger and the first Princeton. Then there were the "thieving many"--those who had served with him on the first Princeton. Then there were the "hungry horde," who had never been with him before. And there's more truth than poetry to that. I mean, there were three separate castes on the Princeton. They were as distinct as they are in India.

Q: His foot had been blown off when the Princeton was hit at Leyte Gulf.

Mr. King: Right. Yes, and, you know, he was renowned in the Navy. But those of us in the "hungry horde" did not share the universal admiration. I mean, he was our captain, and in the Navy, as you know, the captain is the captain is the captain. I guess I dug my own hole in trying to get off of there. That was probably the root of the whole thing.

Q: Did any of the other people show any animosity as in, "We were all through this together, and you're a newcomer"?

Mr. King: Well, there was a little of that sort of thing. I mean, it became kind of the typical Navy joke, laughing thing on the ship, where you would say, "Hey, you're in the hungry horde."

"No, no, the thieving many." It was a fun thing, and people kind of enjoyed it in a way. However, if you were not in the favored castes, you didn't enjoy it. I don't mean it was terribly overt in that you were punished if you were not in it. It was just kind of a vague thing.

Q: Was it good-natured?

Mr. King: I cannot paint it as anything but being good-natured, and it never bothered me. That kind of thing never did bother me. What bothered me was this business between Lieutenant Lewis and Captain Hoskins and me about my efforts

C. S. King #3 - 254

to get off.

Q: What was your specific job? Were you running the captain's office?

Mr. King: I was the captain's writer. Lewis was my boss, and the captain was my skipper--that was my job.

Q: So you couldn't avoid him?

Mr. King: Could not. And that didn't help the situation at all.

Q: How would you describe his personality, other than your relationship with him?

Mr. King: As his writer, I did a substantial amount, much more than ordinary, personal correspondence for him. He would dictate to me literally by the hour. He had a voluminous correspondence with many, many people. And I guess that shouldn't influence you. But at the same time, he was not unaware of his ego, and I guess it kind of fed on itself. I mean, whatever negative feelings there were in the beginning just grew on both sides. I never let it affect my professional calling. I mean, we had a good captain's office on there, because I knew what I was doing.

C. S. King #3 - 255

We had a good, very smooth-running captain's office, procedural-wise. I put in various things that I knew worked and that sort of thing.

Q: Such as? What sorts of things?

Mr. King: Oh, correspondence control. I designed some buck slips for handling the correspondence and things that I knew that worked better than some of the standard ways of doing things--standard forms, standard procedures, and everything.

Q: Are these like ticklers and things to make sure things get answered and reports sent off in time?

Mr. King: Yes, that sort of thing.

Q: Did you resent that the captain was using you for personal correspondence rather than professional?

Mr. King: No, I didn't resent it. I was quite accustomed to that, because in a given job with an admiral or a captain there's always a sprinkling of personal correspondence. You don't resent that. I mean, that's part of the job. I never gave it a second thought. I just went ahead and did it and thought about the World Series or something. I mean, that didn't bother me at all.

C. S. King #3 - 256

Q: Is this considered sort of one of the perks that he rates, just like a steward or whatever?

Mr. King: Sure. That's a very good relationship sometimes, that the captain and his writer get along. It works out very fine both ways. I've enjoyed some great relationships like that--for example, Admiral John Dale Price, one of the greatest guys that ever lived.*

But, anyway, this situation was unfortunate from the beginning. And I made it worse, and he made it worse. I'm not minimizing. I mean, I played a pretty good role in continuing my efforts to get off there. Because I was going to get off. I was going to get off there. My wife needed me, and she let me know that. I wanted to respond.

The Princeton went west. The next pickup I have of the sequence of events that sticks in my mind was in the Pacific. The Princeton got the job of taking President Quezon's body back to the Philippines.** He had died in the early 1940s. We made a special flagship deal, taking his body to the Philippines, and Justice Murphy of the Supreme Court was on board.*** That was a big event in the

---

*Mr. King later served with Vice Admiral John Dale Price, USN, in two separate tours of duty.
**Manuel Quezon served as President of the Philippines from 1935 until the nation fell to the Japanese in 1942. After that he headed the Philippine government in exile. He died in the United States in 1944, and the Princeton returned his body to the Philippines in July 1946.
***Frank Murphy was an associate justice of the U.S. Supreme Court from 1940 to 1949.

Philippines, to get his body back.

This was quite a homecoming to me. I mean, I hadn't seen the Philippines since I had left there in rather ignominious circumstances years earlier. This was a great occasion to me, and I enjoyed very much going ashore and trying to resurrect some of my old friends. I ran into a couple of them, I guess.

Q: If we could go back just a little. What do you remember about the commissioning and then the workup period for the ship in the Atlantic?

Mr. King: Well, I don't recall which dignitaries were involved in our commissioning ceremonies. It was a major event, the commissioning of a first-line carrier.*

Before she actually went into commission, V-E Day took place.** This put a different light on the Princeton. My thinking at the time was that although the war with the Japanese was still very much in evidence, the European peace sort of broke the dam. I didn't feel the same full-bore effort; I didn't think it was going to last a hell of a lot longer. I just really didn't. Also, President Roosevelt died while I was on the Princeton.***

But then your question about the commissioning, I don't

---

*The Princeton was commissioned 18 November 1945.
**V-E Day, victory in Europe, was 8 May 1945.
***President Franklin D. Roosevelt died 12 April 1945.

recall any particular circumstance of the commissioning out of the ordinary. We went through a standard shakedown cruise to Gitmo, that sort of thing.* And I just don't recall anything out of the ordinary. I think we headed to the West Coast fairly soon, because it was still a wartime situation as far as the Japanese were concerned.

Q: With all the new ships that had gone into commission, had the talent and experience been diluted by that point? What kind of people did you have, for example?

Mr. King: I think there were more experienced people on the Princeton than there were on the Hornet. Because the Hornet, I guess, in that day was really a full wartime footing. We had an awful lot of new people and reserves and that sort of thing. But on the Princeton, I think there was a fairly substantial difference in the makeup of the whole ship's company, officers and crew. There were a good deal more experienced people on there.

Q: I guess by that time there had been enough of the war that people had gotten that experience.

Mr. King: Yes, from that standpoint. We had a crackerjack chiefs' bunch on the Princeton, just some great guys. I

---

*Gitmo is a nickname for Guantanamo Bay, Cuba, site of a U.S. Navy base devoted largely to underway training of the crew of ships.

have real good feelings about the chiefs' quarters and my peers on there, and about the ship's company. We had a good bunch of airdales, and we all got along. The only negative was the problem I had with Lewis and Hoskins. But the ship itself--I have very good memories of that. I don't recall anything specific that stands out in my mind from the commissioning to the West Coast. We went through the Panama Canal, of course. We were headed to the Pacific as fast as we could go. I'm fuzzy now about V-J Day, where we were when that happened.* It was kind of anticlimactic, really, so the next thing that sticks out in my mind is the Philippine trip.

Q: How were Americans received in the Philippines at that point?

Mr. King: Well, it was, of course, not like the old Asiatic Fleet days. But it was a good relationship and some of the old band of Americans--there weren't many of them around. I went to Whitey Smith's place, which was still open. There were very few people around who were there in the pre-World War II days.

The city of Manila was almost unrecognizable. It had just been beat to death; there were very few things that I

---

*V-J Day, victory over Japan, was 14 August 1945.

recognized in Manila. I'd just get disoriented when I went ashore, not knowing exactly where I was. The situation was that different. But the atmosphere and the ambience were such that I just really felt like I was home again. I really enjoyed getting back there--not to see any one person, or persons, but just to be back in the Philippines. I always have such a warm feeling in my heart for the Philippines.

Q: Did the people there seem bedraggled after this ordeal they'd been through?

Mr. King: Yes, they did. They sure did. There was a feeling, just sort of recovering, and getting over the shock, and getting back to a normal way of life. Yet, on the other hand, it was a bustling place. It was really a feverish activity.

Q: Were there warnings against black marketing and that sort of thing?

Mr. King: I'm sure that that sort of thing went on, but I don't recall anything specific like that.

Q: Was there a ceremony connected with the President's body being returned?

Mr. King: There was a big ceremony, of course, with Justice Murphy of the Supreme Court. As a matter of fact, I kept a whole stack of newspapers of those days. Then about three or four years ago, in my work with American Cancer Society, we set up a hospice here in Arlington, and the moving force behind it was a Filipino doctor, a great lady named Dr. Jo Magno. I gave her all these papers. I don't know where she is now, but that's what happened to them.

When we were in the Philippines, my oldest boy was born. He was born with a severe physical defect. He had a problem with his spine. He had some vertebrae out of place in his spine, and he was curved back with sandbags. That just really capped the climax, so to speak. Hoskins was adamant. He wouldn't let me off there, not for leave or transfer.

The naval hospital in Jacksonville, Florida, recommended civilian treatment. My wife did go to a civilian doctor. When Hoskins finally sent a message through channels to the Red Cross to verify that my son did have this problem, the Red Cross formally replied that Emily had been discharged from the naval hospital, and that was the end of the trail. So Hoskins took that as another example of my diabolical scheming to get off the Princeton. That just put it in concrete. So this was not too happy a time for me.

C. S. King #3 - 262

I remember very distinctly an episode that stands out. I showed you that CSC the other day, the continuous service certificate. I had gotten in such a predicament with Hoskins that I felt very uneasy. I felt very bad about it affecting my professional standing. I didn't want whatever was going on family-wise to color the fact that I was doing an effective job--or I thought so--as his writer. I requested a special audience with him, and he received me. Although I was his writer and saw him often, this was different. He received me in his cabin in a formal setting, and I brought my CSC.

By that time, CSCs were no longer used. A few of the people had them but just as souvenirs. The point I was trying to make with my CSC was that my service was nothing to be ashamed of over the years. The CSC reflected that. I always had good marks--4.0s and a number of commendations. This was all laid out in my CSC. The point I was trying to make to him was that, aside from my efforts to get off the Princeton, I still, in my opinion, was an above-average chief yeoman. I didn't want the two to get mixed up.

Captain Hoskins took my CSC, and he didn't open it. He just dropped it in his trash can beside his desk. He said, "You're going to stay on this ship as long as I'm on this ship. When I leave this ship, whoever relieves me, I'm going to tell him to keep you on this ship. You're going to stay on this ship just as long as you're in the Navy or I'm alive"--something like that. And I think he referred to the man without a country--Philip Nolan. He said, "You'll make that look like a shakedown cruise"--something like that.*

This was not said between clenched teeth. I mean, there was no extreme emotion, but the point he was making was unmistakable, loud and clear, and there was no humor in it. That was just before we got to Pearl. I fired the last arrow out of my quiver, and wrote to a guy who, I guess at the time, was either in BuPers, or somewhere in D.C. Only a couple of weeks later, I got a set of orders to be transferred from the Princeton, transferred to ComAirPac based in Pearl.** Of course, Hoskins couldn't argue with that. I never saw him again until I left the ship. I mean, the deed was done, and I guess Lewis relayed to him that these orders were something that couldn't be tinkered with. So when we got to Pearl, I left the ship. My leaving was swift and silent, and that's the way I wanted it.

That was an unusual situation. Again, I know that this was something that was between Captain Hoskins, and Lieutenant Lewis, and me. And they're both dead now. And I don't want this record that I'm making now to be a

---
*During the Civil War Edward Everett Hale wrote a novel on patriotism. It was titled The Man Without a Country and told of the fictitious Philip Nolan who was sentenced to spend the rest of his life moving from ship to ship because he had condemned the United States and said he didn't want to hear it mentioned again. In the novel he was continuously at sea from 1807 to 1863.
**ComAirPac--Commander Air Force Pacific Fleet, the type commander for aircraft carriers in the U.S. Pacific Fleet.

reflection on them. I guess what I'm saying reflects on them, but at the same time, I want it made known that I respected both of them as naval officers. It was just this situation that arose that kind of got out of hand. They were both competent people, but I just didn't get along with them.

Q: What was your job then at ComAirPac?

Mr. King: Well, gee, the sun came up over the horizon and everything was rosy. I was chief in charge of the flag office. That was a great job, and I just enjoyed it immensely. I brought my wife out to Pearl. She came out, and we lived on Ford Island for about a year and a half.

Q: Was that where you worked for John Dale Price?

Mr. King: Yes.

Q: What do you recall of him as an officer?

Mr. King: He was a guy that really stands out. He was a great guy. He was something like Jocko--not really like Jocko, but he enjoyed that kind of respect and admiration from everybody that was around him. He was kind of easygoing, and sort of a cowboy old kind of guy. I just worshipped the ground that he walked on. I just thought he was great. I didn't know him personally before that time.

Q: How much of a personal relationship did you have with him?

Mr. King: I guess about the same I had with Admiral Hart, for example. I was not his personal writer. There was a Lieutenant Wainscot who was called Scoop, Scoop Wainscot (short for Windscoop).* Scoop Wainscot was the flag lieutenant, and he was my direct boss. My main job was running the flag office and that sort of thing.

Q: Did this include distribution of personnel throughout the carriers?

Mr. King: No, I had very little to do with that aspect of it. My duties were primarily as chief in charge of the personnel in the flag allowance, however many they were, and running the mail operation for the flag office, and this kind of business. It was an enjoyable job, a good job, and I really enjoyed it. It was interrupted about a year and a half later when Lieutenant Wainscot came to me. He knew the whole circumstances about the Princeton and everything. He said, "I just got wind that Admiral Hoskins is coming to

---
*Lieutenant Charles H. Wainscott, USN.

ComAirPac as chief of staff." Scoop said, "The scuttlebutt is that you're going to be his first or second order of business after he gets here."

Q: What was life like in Hawaii then for someone with a young family?

Mr. King: Oh, it was just beautiful. We had quarters on the base, on Ford Island, that cost $18.75 a month--great, big house. The Navy furnished it lock, stock, and barrel. They had a small commissary that worked kind of on the honor system there. You just went up and down the shelves, getting things yourself. They had an enormous garden there tended by some local gardener. You just went anytime you wanted to, picked what you wanted to, and left what you wanted to in a tin can. Creature comforts were wonderful. They had a beautiful chiefs' club there, and I gravitated through the chairs and got to be head bartender at the chiefs' club. It was just a great existence.

We didn't have a car then. You could check out Jeeps and take your family for a ride around the island. I finally bought a car that, I guess, had been owned by a series of people who had been at the air station Ford Island since the Thirties. I think I paid $40.00 for it; it was a Buick. God knows how old it was. It didn't have any headlights, but, anyway, we used that to just knock around town. I don't know what happened about license plates, anything like that. That was in 1946, '47, '48--in that time frame.

Q: That was during the great demobilization period. Did that have an effect on your office work, the drawing down of the aviation commands?

Mr. King: Not a great deal. Our particular section was not primarily involved in that. I don't recall any crisis circumstances or things like that. Those were busy times, but I don't recall anything terribly out of the ordinary.

I think the demobilization was mainly people going from the Pacific direct to the States. I don't remember much effect in Pearl of that sort of thing. Tremendous amount of air transportation. When we left there, we left by plane. I got another set of orders transferring me to ComAirLant, and I went to Jacksonville.

Q: Had you managed to escape before Hoskins came?

Mr. King: Yes. I forget who I wrote to then, but, anyway, I got a set of orders out of ComAirPac, and I think I left Pearl the day before he got there, or some damn thing.

Q: Had you begun at this point to think about getting a

commission?

Mr. King: Yes. I submitted an application for a commission, and that sort of perked along.

At first my wife and I and our youngster went to Jacksonville, but we were not there long. I was assigned to one of the ComAirLant commands there, CNaVanTra, as it was known. Admiral Litch, E. W. Litch, was Chief Naval Air Advanced Training.* He and his staff were transferred to Corpus Christi, Texas, a few months later, and I went with him, lock, stock, and barrel.**

And a kind of an aside there--the skipper at Corpus was pretty rough on uniforms. We got word to be careful. We flew from Jacksonville to Corpus in kind of an overnight weekend operation to get there and set up. We got there on a Saturday. Admiral Litch and his wife--and I think they had a grown daughter--were leaving the base on Sunday morning to go to church in town. The Marine at the gate was involved in carrying out the skipper's orders about civilian clothes. When Admiral Litch attempted to drive out with his wife and daughter, the Marine sentry stopped them. I guess they didn't have base stickers yet, and he was in civilian clothes. Admiral Litch identified himself, and the Marine said, "Just a minute." He went in the shack and called the

---
*Rear Admiral Ernest W. Litch, USN.
**The Naval Air Advanced Training Subordinate Command was established at Naval Air Station Corpus Christi, Texas, on 1 January 1948.

sergeant of the guard. He said, "Sarge, I've got a guy here with his wife and their daughter, and he claims he's Admiral Witch or Litch, or something like that, and he wants to get out the gate. What'll I do?"

The sergeant said, "Well, the first thing I want you to do is go out and salute him, and let him out the gate. And the second thing is get relieved, and come down and see me. I want to talk to you."

Now, I don't know whether that's true or not. But that's a good story that was told about Litch.

Corpus was a home base for the Blue Angels. The Blue Angels were a small outfit, but they had a pretty good-sized publicity section. I was chief yeoman, and that's what I did. I worked with a lieutenant who was sort of their advance man. That didn't last very long, then I got a set of orders to the head shed in Pensacola.

Q: Chief of Naval Air Training?

Mr. King: Chief of Naval Air Training, who was Admiral Black Jack Reeves, very colorful guy.* I guess you've heard a lot of stories about him.

Q: Yes, but I want to hear yours.

---

*Vice Admiral John W. Reeves, Jr., USN.

Mr. King: Well, a personal story that I was involved in, so this one I can vouch for. Reeves was a big fisherman. Loved to fish. Went fishing often. The boat shed was his baby. He would crank up these weekend trips to go fishing; anybody that loved fishing was welcome. Rate or rank, it didn't make any difference. I guess I qualified, because I really loved fishing.

On this one trip that I recall, it was pretty rough that day. Had a strong wind. We went out by the wreck of the old Massachusetts, which is real good fishing, a lot of bottom fish around: grouper, snapper, and things like that. We were making passes back and forth in the area of the Massachusetts. We were just sitting around on deck and whatnot, just casting all around, and doing pretty well. Admiral Reeves was just sitting there with three or four of us. Something happened--the boat rolled or pitched--and he lost his line, everything. The whole rod and reel went over the side. A tremendous hush went over the whole boat. Nobody said a thing; nobody knew what to say.

I was sitting next to him, and I had my tackle box open. He looked in my tackle box, and I had what they call a mullet hook. It's like a small grappling hook that has four or five spokes on it with sharp points, made of lead. You use it to cast out and yank through a school of mullet to snag them--a snagging hook. He just picked it up, and picked up another rod and reel there and put this snagging apparatus on his line. He stood up and just kind of looked around and got his bearings, and he cast way out. We were in fairly deep water, I guess 30 or 40 feet of water. He made one cast, and let it sink through the water, and then he began to pull it in. Pretty soon he gave it a little jerk, and then he pulled on up. When it came on up, it brought up that rod and reel that went over the side in the snagging hook. He went over and got the line and pulled it, and here came his rod and reel.

Q: That's quite a feat.

Mr. King: I mean, we just all felt that even the wind and the waves obey Admiral Reeves. He was a very colorful guy.

Q: Did you ever see his temper in action?

Mr. King: Yes.

Q: I've heard he was a very demanding officer.

Mr. King: Oh, he was demanding. Well, of course, I was still a chief yeoman then, so I didn't get the full effects of it. But I was told many times that when a new officer came on board that Admiral Reeves was like Admiral Rickover.* He had a personal session with them, and it was meant to tell them that there were two kinds of officers in the Navy: can-do and no-can-do. "If you're a no-can-do, I'll help you get to wherever you want to go and wish you well. And if you're a can-do, welcome aboard and glad to have you." He laid it on the line on that sort of thing, first out.

There's a thousand stories about him. I was under the impression that he had a volcanic temper. And while I never saw it in action myself, I heard many accounts of the fact that nothing stood in his way. He was so mission oriented that nothing was impossible to him.

Q: He also took on another mission, that of fighting the Air Force, at that point.* Did you see any evidence of that?

Mr. King: I saw some evidence of it. Our print shop was where all this material was turned out. That was kept pretty much under wraps, and it wasn't terribly well known. I do recall some night operations, when the print shop worked all night long cranking out various pieces of paper connected with that operation. They would then be flown the

---
*Admiral Hyman G. Rickover, USN (Ret.), headed the Navy's nuclear propulsion program for many years. He had the reputation of being both demanding and unpleasant.
*In the late 1940s, 1949 in particular, the U.S. armed services were squabbling over roles and missions. Among the proposals was one that the newly formed U.S. Air Force would absorb naval aviation. The Navy strongly resisted.

next day to Memphis, Tennessee, for further distribution. There was a Tennessee newspaper involved. I think Captain Thach was quite involved.*

Q: Thach was his point man, making speeches all over the place in favor of the Navy.

Mr. King: Yes, I remember Thach was involved in getting out these bales of these very fancy publications. The Bomber Myth was the name of one of them. These were slick paper-- nice publications. I knew it was sensitive, and I didn't go around talking about it. It was something that sort of fit in with Reeves's personality. I mean, that's the kind of thing I would expect him to do.

Q: Well, he expected of himself this can-do attitude, obviously.

Mr. King: Yes, indeed.

Q: What was the nature of your specific duties?

Mr. King: Again there was a flag allowance, and Lieutenant Paul A. Terry was flag lieutenant. I had a very good

---
*Captain John S. Thach, USN. Thach's oral history is in the Naval Institute collection.

relationship with Paul Terry. He was a great guy. I guess Paul was the guy that got me the set of orders out of ComAirLant to Chief of Naval Air Training when I escaped from Pearl. Paul Terry was a guy who also was completely oblivious of hours. When he worked, he worked--when the work had to be done, he did it. I worked along with him. So I just did it out of a sense of duty, not out of a personal thing with Terry. I just kept those same hours.

A lot of the extra work we had to do was simply a reflection, again, I guess, of Reeves's personality and the fact that hours didn't mean anything. He just stayed until everybody went home at night. At some point there, John Dale Price relieved Reeves.* I think Terry was probably more associated with Price than he was with Reeves.

Q: Did the atmosphere change any when Price came in?

Mr. King: Yes. It got to be less of a kind of almost combat atmosphere under Reeves, to more of a duty operation with John Dale Price.

Q: Well, Reeves was really doing two jobs. He was running the training establishment on one hand and fighting this battle with the Air Force in addition to that.

---
*Reeves retired on 1 May 1950 and was relieved by Vice Admiral Price.

Mr. King: I guess my feeling is that the Air Force thing got to be more of a job going on than his other job.

Q: That would account for the long hours.

Mr. King: Yes. I don't recall any of that Air Force stuff connected with John Dale Price. He was the kind of a guy that sure did inspire a lot of loyalty. Finally, I became his writer and traveled with him a lot. As a matter of fact, the only time I ever got flight skins, I got a half a set of skins when I was flying around with Admiral Price to all the different commands, doing inspections and things like that.

Q: Why just half?

Mr. King: Well, they were kind of scarce, you know, and you'd have to divide them. Because I was a chief yeoman, that was kind of a gray area. I wasn't really entitled to skins. I mean, you could do it, but they were getting awfully tight then. For a while, during the war, anybody got flight skins. Flight skins, of course, was this money you get for flying.

Q: Hazardous duty pay.

Mr. King: By that time, they were getting pretty scarce. And I was very privileged to get a half a set when I flew with John Dale Price.

Q: What experiences do you remember from serving that closely with him?

Mr. King: Well, I remember one time we went off to Corpus, or Jax, or somewhere to do an inspection.* John Dale really had an outlook on life that was refreshing. We were going through a series of shops: the metal shop, this shop, that shop. Navy shops in those days, and I guess maybe today, are great on pinups. They're just all over the place. Everybody's desk had a big sheet of Plexiglas, and under the Plexiglas were all these pinups. At one point we went from one shop to the second shop, and Admiral Price looked down at the desk top, and there was this great big Plexiglas and all these girls under it. He turned to me, and he said, "Only the faces change."

He would deliver little philosophic asides from time to time. I cannot personally vouch for this, but I was told that Admiral Price, in Pensacola, had a growth behind his ear that was diagnosed as malignant. He was going to have it removed, and the story goes that the morning of the

―――――――――
*Jax--Jacksonville.

operation, they got all the way into the operating room. In the operating room, before the anesthetic was administered, he said, "We're not going to do it." The story that we were told was that the operation itself was very iffy, that the location in the mastoid area behind the ear was very tricky, and it may go, and it may not. I think Admiral Price decided not to go with it. Either the diagnosis was not accurate, or whatever, but, anyway, he lived years after that.*

I guess it was later on--it was after I lost track of him--that he was the naval adviser for the movie Mister Roberts.** I've seen it on the late, late show a couple times and with credits to Admiral John Dale Price, naval adviser.

The reason I left Pensacola was that finally I made warrant. I took the exams for warrant, and my number came up. Terry and Price made much of it. They were very kind about my making it. We had, you know, all sorts of wetting downs and everything. Of course, I got my orders, because in those days you got instant orders when you shifted from enlisted to officer status. And so that's when we left. I did very well on my examination for ship's clerk. When the Naval Register was published and for the first time I

---
*Admiral Price died 18 December 1957 at the age of 65.
**Henry Fonda and James Cagney starred in the 1955 Warner Brothers film Mister Roberts, based on the Thomas Heggen novel about a wacky supply ship that operated in the backwaters of the Pacific in World War II.

appeared in it, I was number one ship's clerk in the Navy. I'd done fairly well on my examination.

Q: Was there some reason that you sought that out rather than LDO, or was that an option?*

Mr. King: At that time, I believe that I put in for LDO, and my number came up for warrant. I don't really recall actually going up and bucking for warrant. I know I went up for LDO. It's a blank in my mind. I remember I was very surprised when the warrant came back, because I was getting kind of long in the tooth, so to speak then, as far as a change in status. I'd always been very happy as a chief, very happy, and it was with mixed emotions that I made warrant. But, you know, I could see the many advantages. But there was some terrible financial changes connected with it, because there I was, with a half set of flight skins, public quarters on the base, head bartender in the chiefs' club again, and just rolling in money, so to speak. When I went to sea, I got orders to Midway--lost my flight skins, lost my bartending, and public quarters. That was a pretty good drop in income. We damn near starved to death there for a while when I was first warrant.

Q: Can you explain the difference in duties, status,

---

*LDO--limited duty officer.

obligations, and so forth, between a chief and a warrant officer?

Mr. King: Well, my first duty station as warrant was the Midway, and that's part of the game, I think, the change in scenery, because it would be a little difficult on your home ground to shift over.* Not difficult, but there are some adjustments there. But I was pinstripe, of course; I was W-1.** That doesn't fill anyone with great dreams of grandeur by being a pinstripe. I don't mean to derogate it, but it's not a full-fledged officer. But at the same time, I viewed it as a change of distinction, so to speak. I was very much aware of the difference. I was being made aware of the sea change between enlisted and officer status.

Q: What were the distinctions? I mean, did you have greater responsibility in your new job?

Mr. King: Yes, there was really a substantial change. In fact, I went aboard the Midway as personnel officer.

Q: This is for ship's company rather than flag?

---

*The USS Midway (CVB-41) was commissioned in September 1945. Originally she was 986 feet long, had a beam of 113 feet and 136-foot-wide flight deck. Her standard displacement was 45,000 tons, with a top speed of 33 knots.
**At the time, warrant officer grades ran from W-1 through W-4. The sleeve stripe insignia for W-1 was only half as wide as for the other three grades, so those in W-1 were customarily known as pinstripe warrants.

Mr. King: Ship's company personnel officer. There was a chief personnelman on the Midway who was in charge of the ship's office. On the CVB class carriers then--I'm not sure about the CVs, but the CVBs had two warrants: one ship's secretary and one personnel officer.* I had no choice about the Midway. I went aboard as personnel officer. While the basic work that I was involved in was not that different from a chief's duties, nonetheless, there was a substantial difference in responsibility. Living in the warrant officers' quarters instead of the chiefs' quarters was a substantial difference. Having a stateroom instead of a bunk was a difference.

Q: I'd like to pin down, how did your responsibilities differ from those of the chief personnelman?

Mr. King: Well, going back to my previous jobs as chief of a flag allowance or on the Hornet, when I was chief, when I was personnel chief--on the Hornet I had a lieutenant I reported to. On the Midway the chief personnelman that ran the office of some 15-20 people reported directly to me. I, in turn, reported directly to the exec. And there was a little bit of a gray area there, because there was the exec
. . .

---

*Up to the time of the Midway, fleet carriers were classified CV. She was the first to carry the designation of CVB--large aircraft carrier.

Q: Was this Commander Ashworth?*

Mr. King: Yes. And I was determined in my own mind to really be a good warrant officer. I mean, I was determined to do that. And I kind of went the extra mile in doing that. We had a good outfit on the Midway. There was a lieutenant (j.g.) on the Midway--and I forget his title now--who reported to the exec, but he was not really in the chain of command. I guess it depended on the personality of the guy, as to whether or not he, in turn, was in charge of the office, and then to the exec, and me to him. But there wasn't any kind of a problem.

This was also a part of this transition period, in just going aboard, like jumping in the cold water, from a chief petty officer to a warrant officer. When I came aboard the Midway, I was a warrant officer; that's all there was to it. I wasn't a new warrant officer; I was a warrant officer. The other warrant officer, a guy named Curly Dixon, that I was going to relieve was an old W-2, a hell of a good guy.**

We had a couple of months' transition period with Curly and myself. That helped a heck of a lot, because he was a very decent guy and smoothed over a lot of rough edges.

---
*Commander Frederick L. Ashworth, USN. Ashworth eventually retired as a vice admiral. He has been interviewed as part of the Naval Institute's oral history program.
**Chief Ship's Clerk Joseph R. Dixon, USN.

Otherwise, I think I might have stubbed my toe a couple of times. When I came aboard he gravitated pretty fast from the office to the warrant officers' quarters. After our little shakedown between Curly and me, then he became sort of a pastor. And that's right and proper to do so. That's the way it should be, and I didn't resent it.

Q: He was there to be consulted, but he wasn't there to boss you.

Mr. King: Exactly. And that worked out very fine. I appreciated that. He was a very decent guy.

Q: What did your duties entail? I mean, you speak of reporting to the exec. What sorts of things did you report on?

Mr. King: Well, all of a sudden, I tried to run the personnel part of the ship in such a manner that the exec would not ever have to have any details. I tried to just not ever bother him with anything except matters of substance. If in a certain rating, say, it looked like from the orders in and orders out we were going to be short in black gang or something like that, I might go to him.*

---

*Black gang—the engineering force that operated the ship's propulsion plant.

C. S. King #3 - 283

But I tried really to have it a self-contained thing, so that he was never even aware of the fact that we had a personnel office. I mean, he had big things to do.

Q: You tried to keep the problems from reaching his level.

Mr. King: Yes, I guess it worked out pretty well. I don't ever recall having any kind of a problem where I had to go to him and say, "We've got a problem." I just tried to have it so he never had a problem. And he didn't have a problem either. That worked out very well as far as our relationship went.

Q: There's a great deal of routine work to be done, but you had a lot of subordinates to do that, I take it, to fill out service record pages and transfers.

Mr. King: Oh, yes. I spent a lot of time in the office. I guess I must have acted like I was duty-struck when I first got aboard, because I spent an awful lot of time in the office. I was running a little scared. It was quite clear to me that the personnel officer was not a chief in charge of an office. I didn't go ashore too much; hell, I couldn't afford to go ashore. But as a matter of routine I would just do my day's work in the office. I would stay there until it was time to eat. I didn't walk out at 4:00

o'clock. I'd just stay there in a leisurely kind of way.

It wasn't any feverish pace, but just kind of acclimatizing myself to what was going on, and just kind of getting in the routine of what a personnel officer does. After dinner, we'd sit around warrant officers' country and solve major problems, tell sea stories, and all that kind of stuff. Then I'd wander back to the office every evening. Again, I would just sort of sit around in more of a relaxed way, but there was always something to do. I could sign quarterly mark pages or other things. I mean, there was always stuff to be signed, and I never did go for the rubber stamp thing. I always wanted to sign everything I had to sign, so I spent a lot of time just mechanically signing my name.

But on the other hand, that was very much a learning operation for me. I learned an awful lot on there, just sort of self-taught. I quickly began to sense where the pitfalls were.

Q: What were the pitfalls in that job?

Mr. King: Well, the pitfalls were, I guess, just to spend too much time in the warrant officers' country, and all of a sudden wake up and find you've got a problem. I tried to anticipate anything that happened.

Q: You can't supervise everything personally. Did you follow the practice of spot checking records from time to time?

Mr. King: Yes. I didn't just hover over the chief personnelman, watching every move he made. I tried very much to have relaxed situations where he ran the office; that's fine. But, nonetheless, there was enough business for the two of us, and it was a good relationship. It worked out very well. After a fairly short while, I felt comfortable in knowing that I knew what was going on, and that I could not foresee any problems where I'd have to go to the exec in a panic, saying, "We've got this, we've got that."

Q: Now, you had two groups of visitors on board, as it were. You had the air group and the flag allowance. What was your relationship with those two?

Mr. King: The air group might as well been in Timbuktoo as far as I was concerned, because the air group ran its own personnel shop. I had to turn in to the commissary department every day an accurate, right-down-to-the-man, listing of bodies on board who were eating. That was vital to the supply officer's work in knowing how much money they'd need, and that sort of thing. It was terribly important to account for the number of bodies on board. The air group would give me a listing. They were pretty good about it. That worked out fine.

Then we always had, on every carrier I was ever on, cats and dogs, civilians, you name it. These are always under the ship's secretary who keeps track of civilian passengers. So the air group had enlisted people, but I just got numbers from them. They came and went as a totally independent body. In the captain's office, the ship's secretary--we had a great guy, CWO Andy Forsling.* We got along just beautifully. I would just get numbers from him--bodies on board.

The only time there was any kind of a joint operation was when we would have man-overboard drill. That got awful hairy at times, because I had to turn in the final report to the captain that there was nobody missing.

Q: Was there some demand to do that pretty quickly?

Mr. King: Yes, there was a hell of a demand to do it quickly, because in a real, legitimate drill like that, the skipper didn't want to sit around all day making circles, waiting to get under way. If it was a real or an imagined man overboard, whichever--we had both kinds--you had to be accurate in your numbers. That's when I would take the

---
*Chief Ship's Clerk Andrew Forsling, USN.

number from the air group as gospel. If they said everybody's here, then everybody's here. And I would take the numbers from the ship's secretary as gospel--everybody accounted for. Then the rest of the ship's company--which was 2,500 to 3,000 people--was my own baby. Then I relied on heads of departments for their numbers.

Q: That's a situation where you can't be off just one or two and let it slide by.

Mr. King: You can't be off one. I recall some author once --I think it was Faulkner or Michener--was asked, "Isn't it easy? How in the world do you just make these enormous amounts of money by just writing?"

He said, "It's easy. Just sit down in front of your typewriter, and put a piece of paper in it, and just stare at it until drops of blood come out on your forehead." Well, in trying to get a number for the skipper to say, "We can move now," was when drops of blood came out of my forehead, because I had this awful specter of actually leaving somebody out there. That's when it really got hairy. But that was kind of the cutting edge in getting back under way after a man overboard.

Q: You described this experience before where there was a lot of pressure to get a list off the ship before you

C. S. King #3 - 288

sailed. Was that still a requirement?

Mr. King: No, not by that time. We had to get it off, but it was not under the same pressure at all. Because we had a much better accounting of our people, and I don't recall ever feeling much trepidation at giving a getting-underway list. I was fairly competent at that.

Q: Was there any automation yet in the personnel-handling business?

Mr. King: Not on board ship there wasn't. We didn't have any PAM installation or anything like that.* As late as the FDR, which is the ship I retired off of, it was still pretty much a mechanized, hand operation--on board ship, that is. Now, of course, we knew that on the beach there was a shifting. Back when I was in Pensacola, they were setting up one of the first primitive PAM installations.

Q: You served in a number of carriers. Did you seem to enjoy the carrier life-style?

Mr. King: Yes, I did. I used to feel like being on the destroyers was a young man's game. Carriers were for the time when you got a bit older. It's a much more comfortable

---
*PAM--personnel accounting machine.

living condition aboard a carrier. Some of my happiest memories are of tin cans. I felt more in the Navy on a tin can. But that's not a fair statement. I spent more time on carriers. I just always seemed to enjoy every ship I was ever on. You know, I had some problems on the <u>Davis</u> that turned into kind of sea stories after a while--and the problems with Hoskins and Lewis on the <u>Princeton</u>. But, by and large, the association with the people and that sort of thing--I kind of like carriers.

Q: Well, you don't get a sense of knowing everybody in the ship. You can't possibly.

Mr. King: No, you don't.

Q: You just have these little enclaves.

Mr. King: That's right. You know the colorful people. And you know there are colorful people on every ship. You're right. It's kind of like enclaves. But those that stand out in one enclave, or other people are aware of them, and that kind of business. But the life on a carrier is fairly comfortable, and it's a good life.

Now, the flight deck is do or die--peacetime, wartime, anytime. I mean, that's where it's life and death, and it's every second--and this atmosphere kind of permeates. You don't ever take it for granted. Even if you're not on the flight deck, you still know what's going on up there.

Q: In the chiefs' quarters, everybody has his particular specialty, whether it's engineering, or weapons, or yeoman. But you all have something in common, and that's the chiefs' hat and there's a lot of cronyism there. Was there that same sort of feeling in the warrant mess?

Mr. King: No, I don't guess there was. Yes, you're right. There is a difference between the two. There were so few warrants. Very few cases of duplication. There were two ship's clerks, for example, but there'd be one gunner, one aircraft gunner, and that kind of thing. So most of us had our single areas of concern. And there was a kind of camaraderie in the warrant officers' country that I had not seen before. You were more aware of the fact as a warrant that you were kind of a craftsman in your own trade. And one was aware of the fact of the responsibility that each of us carried in our own mind of what we did. But it's easy to extrapolate that to someone else, so you know that the guys you're associating with are guys that know what they're doing. And that was kind of nice too. That was kind of nice.

Q: I'd be interested in how much a degree of respect you

received, both from above and from below.

Mr. King: Well, the skipper would come down and have chow in the warrant officer mess. And he would make the usual remarks about the warrant officer, the backbone of the Navy. When I was in the chiefs' quarters, the skipper would have chow in the chiefs' quarters, and he would say the chiefs are the backbone of the Navy. I mean, some of that was sort of pro forma.

On the other hand, I think that it's a fair statement to say that most of the crew, enlisted, and most of the officers have that degree of feeling about the warrants, based on the fact that they're people who are good at what they do. We didn't sail under any false colors as far as knowing everything about everything, like a new ensign out of the Naval Academy. That's not a proper comparison, but it's not like being a qualified OOD under way. We had our own single job, and that's what we did, and I think by and large that people appreciated that both above and below.

Q: Well, you don't plow many furrows, but you plow yours pretty deep while you're at it.

Mr. King: Yes, that sort of thing. When a crisis occurred and they hollered for the chief boatswain, the chief machinist, or someone like that, you knew that it was going to be fixed. The guy was there that was going to fix it. That kind of thing rubbed off of me, and on the Midway--my first ship as a warrant--I used to go up to the forecastle on getting under way and anchoring, to watch our chief boatswain in action. He was a great chief boatswain--a tremendous seaman. I just liked to go up there and see that guy, with that damn anchor that must have weighed as much as a destroyer, and handling the getting under way. I just liked to watch that, and I would go down into the main engine room sometimes with the machinist. I mean, it always kind of pleased me to be around these guys and see what they do on their home turf. I didn't do that all the time after a while. But when I was first aboard the Midway, I did that quite a bit, just to kind of get a feel for what goes on in the warrant officers' world.

Q: Those were the biggest carriers in the Navy. Were they treated special by others off the ship?

Mr. King: Well, let's see. When we went to the Med, they used to have a kind of a ceremony.* Like if we relieved the Coral Sea or the FDR, somebody would come over dressed up as King Neptune. It was not like crossing the line, but it was something like that. But that was really confined to the CVBs; that was between the Coral Sea, the FDR, and the

---
*Med--Mediterranean Sea.

<u>Midway</u>.

Q: Was there a special status associated with those ships?

Mr. King: I guess we kind of felt so on the ship, because of the size, I guess, more than anything else. On a typical Med cruise, there's a pretty good amount of time spent in underway exercises, and things like that. You don't just go from Nice to Golfe Juan to Istanbul. You spend a lot of time at sea, and it's military time. There's some good liberty over there, but at the same time, it's kind of a gung-ho operation. You don't lose sight of that.

Q: What specific incidents do you remember about the <u>Midway</u>, both from the Med and back in Norfolk?

Mr. King: Well, let's see. I joined the <u>Midway</u> in the Med, flew over, and had a flight from wherever it was to Port Lyautey. At Port Lyautey, I remember sitting in the terminal there waiting for a lift to Malta in the late afternoon. Somebody looked out the window and said, "Look over there." I looked over there, and there was a long string of camels with people riding them, just out in the desert, just kind of like a movie scene. But, anyway, then we flew from Port Lyautey to Malta. The <u>Midway</u> was anchored in Malta.

I got on a passenger plane--four-engine R5D--and we just landed here and dropped two and took on one and landed there and dropped four and took on six.* It was a travelling Greyhound bus kind of thing. We were pretty close to the end of the line, and we were down to about three passengers. One of them was a photographic enthusiast, and he got the pilot to fly down inside of Mount Etna--go right down inside the damn crater. At that time Etna was not acting up, but I remember that was kind of hairy. I like to fly and all that, but I didn't enjoy that too much.

I remember then landing at Malta was like landing on an aircraft carrier--the landing strip there--just a sheer cliff landing in Malta. I joined the Midway in Malta, and that was sort of in midstream for her Med cruise. So I didn't get a full-fledged Med cruise--got maybe a couple months, something like that. I guess the Midway and the Hornet are the two carriers that I have the most affection for and enjoyed the most. Midway was a great ship. The time in the Med was not combat time, of course, not in the full sense of the word. Anyway, it was more of an operating situation, while the time in Norfolk was not. The time in Norfolk was mostly Navy yard time in Portsmouth.

Q: Who do the warrant officers go on liberty with, each

---

*R5D was the Navy designation of the Douglas C-54 Skymaster transport.

other?

Mr. King: Each other. As a matter of fact, the first liberty I ever made off the Midway, I was kind of on my best behavior, you know, my first trip ashore with warrants. There was a custom then that sometimes fellows would take cigarettes ashore. I don't mean everybody on the Midway smuggled cigarettes, but it was not unheard of for someone to take cigarettes ashore. And there were about six or eight of us warrants that landed in the boat at Cannes. I guess the French customs work like American customs. They know what's going on. They don't have to do a lot of work on the beach.

But this one warrant pay clerk--we called him Ag, short for agitator, because he was the biggest agitator in the world. Anything he could stir up, hate and discontent, he would do it. Ag had a little loot bag full of cigarettes, unbeknownst to me. So this French customs went right to Ag as he got off the gangway. The rest of us knew that something was going on that wasn't too good, so we kind of hung around but at a discreet distance. And this guy had a beret on like a typical French movie type. The bottom line was that Ag had to give him 1,000 francs duty on each carton of cigarettes. I guess he had about 20 cartons of cigarettes. That's what they sold for on the beach--1,000 francs. Ag didn't have 20,000 francs. So we all got together and chipped in all the money we had and we made up the 20,000-franc kitty. Then Ag paid the customs guy 20,000 francs, and the guy gave him a receipt for the cigarettes and said, "Vaya con dios," or French equivalent.

So then Ag went up the dock and sold the cigarettes as soon as he got up the first bistro he walked into, got the 20,000 francs, paid us all back the money, and then we went ahead and went on our liberty.

Q: He didn't make anything; he didn't lose anything.

Mr. King: No. But that was a lesson to me if I ever had an idea about doing something like that. There was something about that French customs guy that was strictly business.

On the *Midway* now I did some work with the customs in coming and going and that sort of thing. Another time in Norfolk, coming back from that Med cruise, I guess, the customs came aboard. They knew exactly who had what: "We want to see this guy, that guy." There was a lieutenant commander in the engineering department that had an accordion that was on the verboten list. They put out a list every time you go to the Med--don't bring this, don't bring that--and this accordion was on the verboten list. And it was the name of it--a Spinelli, or Parenduli, or something like that. So the customs just said "We want to see Lieutenant Commander [whatever his name is]," and they said, "We want to see that accordion you've got."

So he showed it to them. The customs guy took out a little leather kit with a couple of chisels and a little hammer, and he just chiseled the mother-of-pearl script on there for the name of this accordion. He just chipped it off and said, "Okay, it's all yours." It's not worth a thing, I guess, then.

That also happened sometimes in perfume, where people would bring back excessive amounts. Well, the customs would just scrape the label off and give it back to you. But they knew long before we got to Norfolk who had what on there.

Q: How did they know?

Mr. King: I guess that's skill; they just seemed to know. Now, I make that as a statement of fact. I know there were people there with things that they didn't declare that they got away with. I don't mean dope, but I mean things that they declared. But, by and large, a significant contraband would seem to be known to the customs before we ever hit port. I got accustomed to that.

Q: You mentioned working with the executive officer. What do you remember about him.

Mr. King: I established a good relationship with Ashworth right off the bat. I mean, we seemed to just get along fine. I went the extra mile, and a few miles beyond that, in trying not to ever let him have any problem with the personnel office.

My wife and--by that time--our two children were living in Asheville, North Carolina, where her folks lived. When we got back to Norfolk, Ashworth would, as often as not, check out a plane and drop me off at Asheville.* I mean, it was really a great situation. All the time I was on the <u>Midway</u>, I had a real good setup where I could go to Asheville just like I go to Clarendon here. I mean, I had a pretty good batch of friends in pilots--ship's company pilots and that sort of thing--who needed the flight time.

I especially remember one time Ashworth and I went to Asheville. We landed there at night, and Asheville's got a kind of a rough airport. It's in the mountains. Apparently it's not widely loved by strange pilots going there. I guess civilians are okay. But we landed, and when I got out of the twin-engine Beechcraft, SNB, Ashworth said, "The next time you come here, you take a helicopter, goddammit."** He said, "I'm not going to land at this airport anymore."

---

*Even though he was part of ship's company of the <u>Midway</u>, Commander Ashworth was still considered to be in flight status. To maintain his flying proficiency, he periodically checked out a plane, such as the SNB trainer, to get in a number of flight hours each month.

**The SNB was a trainer-type plane, rather than a fleet aircraft, but it was suitable for allowing aviators to maintain their flying skills.

Q: Any other recollections of Ashworth?

Mr. King: Yes, Ashworth was a real gentleman. That guy was a real soft-spoken gentleman. He was also a guy that I admired very much. He was of the Chick Hayward school but in a low-key way.* He was not flamboyant. He was very low key, very soft-spoken, very understated, but another guy of unmistakable substance. I really had a great feeling for him. Ashworth was, I guess, as instrumental as anybody in getting me a favorable hearing at the Atomic Energy Commission when I put in to go to work for them--because of his background.** He had a long background in special weapons, and he was good enough to give me a nice little letter when I applied for an interview at the Atomic Energy Commission.

Q: You get into a position with these senior officers, and they know you've got this experience in a specialized field. Do they wind up calling on you for advice and suggestions? For instance, did Ashworth or the skipper ask you for inputs

---

*Captain John T. Hayward, USN, was commanding officer of the Franklin D. Roosevelt (CVB-42) when Mr. King later served in that ship.
**In August 1945, Ashworth was the weaponeer for the atomic bomb mission against Nagasaki, Japan. Later he served with the Atomic Energy Commission and in the atomic energy section of the OpNav staff. He and John Hayward were involved in the first carrier-based Navy squadron capable of delivering atomic weapons.

on a captain's mast case or what have you?

Mr. King: Well, I think the role of the personnel officer on a carrier in the mast situation--it's kind of like they have pre-mast. It's not exactly legal and proper, but they still go on. I mean, the personnel officer can do a certain amount of screening within limits on something that really does not merit the attention of the exec or the skipper. At the same time, he can buck things up to the exec who has the same right again. But the skipper really is the one that should hold it, but nine times out of ten, the guy that goes to captain's mast is the tip of the iceberg. A lot of the stuff has been sorted out and solved at the exec and personnel officer level. There is communication, of course, between the skipper and the exec and personnel officer on given cases--a repeater or something like that.

I tried to take the initiative on things like that. On the *Midway* I got in the habit of making an unsolicited presentation to the heads of the departments every few months. I gave them a status report on what the personnel picture looked like--what we had on board, what we had ordered out, what we had ordered in, possible gaps, and that kind of thing. That went over pretty good. That's the kind of thing where I tried to do things in advance. I think that might have taken the place of someone asking a specific question. I don't mean I knew all the answers, but I knew those problem areas that I tried to get on top of before they became . . .

Q: So they didn't get caught by surprise.

Mr. King: Yes, so they didn't get caught by surprise.

Q: Was there a problem that far back in shortages of people in the technical ratings?

Mr. King: Yes, indeed. Yes, indeed. That was a real problem. That was a problem on the Midway, and it was very much a problem later on the FDR. Every time I'd do one of those dog and pony shows with the vacancies, this caused great alarm. "What are they going to do? We've got to do something." But at least by flushing them out ahead of time like that, we didn't get the after-the-fact kind of problem.

Q: As time passed in that ship, were you getting more and more confident as a warrant officer?

Mr. King: Yes. That seemed to come pretty fast. I think it was part of the Med cruise and being able to just immerse myself in the job. By the time we got back from the Med cruise, I felt pretty comfortable in my job.

Q: You've talked about the emergencies in which the warrant officers are summoned. I can imagine fires or a combat situation. What kind of emergencies come up for a personnel officer?

Mr. King: Oh, a sudden draft of people comes aboard. I can't paint that as an emergency, but when they would pass the word for me, which didn't happen too often, it would be something like that. Maybe somebody just came aboard, that there was a big problem checking them in, or a draft of people, that kind of thing. But there was never any kind of substantial breakdown, crisis, and problem for the personnel officer.

Q: Do you get in the business of emergency leave, and verifying deaths, and illnesses, and that sort of thing?

Mr. King: Yes. I tried to keep that also. I tried to not have the exec be involved in ordinary things. And this falls into a distinct pattern. I mean, if there are 3,000 people on a ship, after a while when the captain holds mast, they're almost all repeaters. You very seldom see a new face at mast. As a matter of fact, after I went to mast a couple of thousand times, I just knew what they were going to say before they opened their mouths. It falls into a distinct pattern. And I used to wonder why in the hell they wouldn't take 100 people, that I could very easily identify, off the ship. We'd never have mast anymore. Because on an average ship--and this holds true on every ship I was ever on--99% of the crew keep their noses clean, do their jobs, and never get in trouble. Most of the trouble cases at mast are repeaters.

Q: You have the occasional guy who has an emergency or can't get back on time for something, and it's an isolated instance.

Mr. King: Well, something we did on the _Midway_--and I don't mind taking credit for this--we instituted a system on the _Midway_ where we had a problem because kids would take a weekend in Norfolk and they'd go to Cincinnati. They'd go all over the United States in some ramshacklety car. They'd drive 12 hours to get somewhere, and spend 12 hours there, and drive back. It was terrible. We had a couple of bad wrecks. So finally we instituted a system on the _Midway_-- which later was copied--of basket leave. When anyone went out of the area where there was any doubt about getting back on Monday--providing that they had a good reputation--they could sign a leave chit for a 72, and it would be okayed. Then it would be kept in the basket. If the guy got back on Monday morning okay, they'd tear it up. If something came up, and he couldn't get back, then he'd be charged a day of leave.

Q: He was covered.

Mr. King: He was covered. So we started that. I had a commendation of some kind for that basket leave thing, which seemed to take a lot of the pressure off these kids driving ungodly hours in ramshacklety cars.

Q: You probably had to work with the chaplains in these emergency leave situations, didn't you?

Mr. King: Yes. We had a kind of guarded relationship there, because I think that the personnel officer would have a more pragmatic view--and this comes with the territory--than the chaplain. You know, the chaplain . . .

Q: A little more gullible?

Mr. King: Yes. And not only a little more gullible, they have to do it, you know. If a guy goes to a chaplain and gives him some terrible story, well, unless the chaplain knows better, he believes him. So then the chaplain and personnel officer go nose to nose. And the personnel officer would say, "That guy is a phony from the word go." But these things can be worked out, and they were worked out. But you're right; it's like a kid in a family that will go to the parent most likely to say yes. You go to the chaplain. But that worked out pretty well. I never had any big problem with it.

Q: Where did you go from there?

Mr. King: The *Midway* was in the Navy yard. And we went to Gitmo for our regular ORI, operational readiness inspection. Again, I dwell on something that's self-serving, but I remember it very well and took some pride in it. You get an inspection down there. Every department gets inspected. I was determined to get an outstanding mark for the personnel office. So I went ashore and cultivated this chief ship's clerk in the ship's company down there at Gitmo--not in a cozying way, but I mean in a practical way. "I want to have a good report. What're you guys looking for?"

So he told me: "Be sure your manuals are up to date. We spot check this, spot check that." Well, I went back, and we had a kind of GQ in the personnel office the day before inspection. We sat up that night, corrected all our manuals, spot checked our records, and all the different things that they checked us on. We got an outstanding mark for the personnel office. The exec was very pleased about that.

Q: One advantage that those inspections have is that they give you a stimulus to do the things that you should have done anyway.

Mr. King: That's right. In the real world you understand that, too, and you don't mind it. There were a couple of plus things about Gitmo--for officers--where I really enjoyed that prestige. You could buy bulk rum from the officers' club in Gitmo for $1.00 a gallon if you brought your own gallon jug. So we would go down to the gedunk stand in the ship and get these empty jugs that had the Coca-Cola syrup or whatever, take them ashore, get them full of rum for $1.00, bring them back to the ship, hide them in some convenient spot. Then when you hit the beach, you had a little storehouse built up to take home, which I thought worked out very well indeed.

I guess I'm about running out of ready memories of the *Midway*. I forget exactly where we were, but I got rotated in normal fashion. I'd finished my tour on the *Midway*, and I was due for shore duty. I got a set of orders to the D.C. area, and I was assigned over here to the Naval Station Anacostia.*

Q: It must have been unusual to leave a duty station in a routine fashion at that point.

---
*Anacostia is part of the District of Columbia, across the Anacostia River from the city of Washington.

Mr. King: Yes. I guess I hadn't had too much of that. But the <u>Midway</u>, from beginning to end, was pleasant memories. I enjoyed every bit of it. I don't have one bad memory about the <u>Midway</u>. I left her in good fashion, and all the warrants gave me a wetting-down party, farewell. You know, it was a good deal.

Q: So you finally got some shore duty. Except for that brief stint in Minneapolis, it'd been a long time.

Mr. King: Yes. I was glad to get the Washington area. Not that I had any connection or roots here, but it's fairly close, I suppose, to Asheville. Also, that's where the action is--Washington. That was kind of interesting to me.

Q: Well, Anacostia was a lot more thriving then than it is now, wasn't it?

Mr. King: Yes. Actually, when I say Washington was the center of action, Anacostia was a dead end. It really was a backwater place over there. It was a receiving station, pure and simple, and not even much of a receiving station. Not much activity there, and not too many people.

It was a beautiful place to graze for a couple of

months. I wasn't actively seeking a transfer, but I was not all that pleased with it. I went ahead and tried to buy a house. Emily was going to join me with the kids pretty soon. Curly Dixon, that guy I relieved on the <u>Midway</u>, occupied a spot over in the Pentagon on the staff of CNO, known as OP-002. There was OP-00, CNO; and OP-09 is VCNO.* OP-002 is the administrative assistant to CNO, runs the little CNO mail shop for the front office--handles mail for the VCNO and the CNO, and that's all. Curly was OP-002, and we ran into each other, and so he said, "Why don't you come over here and relieve me?"

I said, "Hell, be fine with me." So the very next day I got a set of orders to report immediately, no delay and so on and so on. Here's another case where I got a set of orders, and I didn't really connive to get it, Curly did it. The exec over there at Anacostia wasn't too pleased about it. He didn't jump up and down, but he was unhappy. But I think I convinced him that I wanted a faster pace and this was a normal sort of thing for me.

Anyway, I went over to the Pentagon and reported in. And, gosh, the difference in the Pentagon and the naval air station, or the Naval Station Anacostia, beggars description. That really is the big leagues, speaking of CNO's office and all. I enjoyed it right away. I knew I had found a hell of a good job. Fechteler was CNO when I

---

*VCNO--Vice Chief of Naval Operations.

got there.*

A little bit later, Carney came along as CNO.** And with Carney came his amanuensis, or his right-hand man, Lieutenant Herbert Carroll, Herb Carroll, who had been with Carney since year one.*** Herb and I got along real well. So I had a good, very good job there. I enjoyed being in the Pentagon, and all these things--seeing the famous people--famous in the Navy terminology.

Q: What was your job specifically?

Mr. King: Well, specifically, we had this little office--there was a lieutenant; Lieutenant Mike Murphy was in charge of the office. Then there was a warrant billet, two chiefs, two first class, and one WAVE--five people. What we handled really was that paperwork that the Chief of Naval Operations saw, for the most part, and some that the Vice Chief had. But we were the CNO's own mailroom. Not personal, but everything that went to him came through us. The bulk of it was classified; we had ample security and that sort of business. It was a busy place, very busy, but rewarding. It was the kind of job where, when I would take in a stack of stuff for Admiral Carney, then I felt like I was involved

---
*Admiral William M. Fechteler, USN, was Chief of Naval Operations from August 1951 to August 1953.
**Admiral Robert B. Carney, USN, was Chief of Naval Operations from August 1953 to August 1955.
***Lieutenant Herbert C. Carroll, USN.

in something fairly important.

They later abolished Lieutenant Murphy's billet so that the top dog was the warrant. So then they had a warrant, two chiefs, two first class, and a third class. This guy Murphy was a senior mustang lieutenant, who spent his time, I guess, in an imaginary chiefs' quarters, warrant quarters, whatever. He just sort of grazed along there; everything was fine with him, whatever happened. Everybody liked him, but he just didn't do much work.

Murphy was a great baseball nut, and he was a great creature of habit. Every noon hour, he would go down to the Pentagon concourse and get the day's little tabloid paper-- <u>Washington News</u>. He'd bring it back up to the office, and that was good for the afternoon. One time the headlines on that paper said, "Reds Trade Otis for Steel Mill." The story behind it was that an American named Otis had been captured in Czechoslovakia, and was imprisoned, and through some kind of diplomatic shenanigans, he was released a couple years later in return for a steel mill being turned back over to the Czechoslovakians, or something like that. But the big headline was "Reds Trade Otis for Steel Mill." So Murphy came up and sat down, and he opened his paper out and saw the headline. He said, "Well, hell, the Reds don't have anybody named Otis in their lineup." The steel mill didn't bother him. He didn't know Otis, but, I mean, that was Murphy--a likable guy.

Q: One-track mind.

Mr. King: One-track mind. Then, when Carney left and Arleigh Burke came in, things changed. Things really changed. I guess Arleigh Burke was the hardest-driving naval officer I've ever been around in any capacity, any time, anyplace. Not offensively so. I mean, everybody that worked for him felt privileged to do so and was intensely loyal, but, boy, he was a driver. He had two shifts. He had one shift that came on regular working hours. Then another stayed late. In effect he worked right on through from in the morning until late in the evening. So we had a kind of port-and-starboard arrangement.

We would all of us work his hours one day, and the next day half would get off at the end of regular hours. Like I'd get off one afternoon at 4:30, whenever it was, and the next night at 9:00, 10:00, whenever. But we didn't mind, because Burke was that kind of a guy. We felt like we were really doing something that was important, worthwhile, and he was very visible to everyone. While it was a period of intense activity, it was not negative. I remember it with very positive feelings. And I remember going out in that south parking lot at 10:00 o'clock at night, and I would just be wiping out my tracks, but I felt good about what I was doing.

But at that same time, I was still a pinstripe warrant. I think it was two years from pinstripe to W-2, and I was really suffering financially. I don't mean I was ready for the poorhouse, but we were having a hell of a time of it. Finally, it became obvious to my wife and I that we just couldn't cut it on warrant officer's pay, and I had to have some more income. I really tried to find something I could do that I could do every other night, because you couldn't work at something else on the nights for Arleigh.

After a number of experiments, I started selling Guardian Service Cookware, which is a kind of heavy-duty aluminum cookware. We had some of it at home, and I knew it was good. I figured I could sell something if I knew it was good. So I started selling Guardian Service Cookware, and Emily would go with me. The deal is that you get a prospect, and then you put on a dinner in their house, and they invite people. See, I paid for the food and I paid for my expenses--it was strictly 100% commission basis. So I would cook the food, serve the dinner for this crowd of people, and then get their names by giving out a door prize. And I would call on all of them to sell them cookware. Whatever I sold--it had a hell of a markup--was mine.

So I would make $200.00, $300.00, $400.00 some months out of it, and it made the difference. It really kept us humping--I mean, you're doing a dinner one night, when you were not working late for Arleigh, and then skipping a night, and making your prospect calls the second night. I don't want to paint that as a terrible hardship, but it was interesting. It made the difference. We got along just fine, and moved into this house here because of that.

But, anyway, to get back to Navy business, that was just a very joyous time for me. I made W-2 in due course and got a bump up in pay, to where we were getting along okay financially. I think the tour in those days was three years, something like that, on the beach. And I got an extra year. So I did four years altogether for Fechteler, Carney, and Burke.

Then Captain Hayward came by one day--Chick Hayward. We were just talking about whatever we'd talk about, and he said, "By the way, I got the FDR, and we're going to go to sea in Bremerton next [whenever it was]. Why don't you tag along?"

I thought, "Boy, wouldn't that be great." So I said, "I'll see." I began to think about it. I guess when you think about something, all of a sudden you've got to do it. And I kind of felt like the time was right. Four years was enough. So I went in and saw Admiral Burke and told him that I had been talking to Captain Hayward who was going to get the FDR, and I wanted to go to sea with him.

He said, "Cecil, my boy. Never ask for anything, because if you do, you're liable to get it. Go ahead." I've remembered those words many times. I guess they'd been said before, but that was a lot of wisdom.

Q: Before we get to that, I wonder if you could go back and discuss each of these three CNOs individually--the personalities of each and the types of work that you were doing.

Mr. King: Well, let's see, Fechteler was a kind of breaking-in period. Fechteler was a big man--big man physically with a big, booming voice, and bluff, hearty, outgoing manner. I had very little personal contact with Fechteler as such, but we saw a lot of him.

Q: Did he delegate more than Burke did? It sounds like Burke tended to take more things on himself personally.

Mr. King: Yes, Fechteler did. Fechteler delegated more than Burke did and spent more time in his office. Burke was all over the place, but Fechteler spent about all the time in his bailiwick, which is a huge office--a great big office.

Q: You probably had to decide what should go to the boss and what shouldn't, didn't you?

Mr. King: That's a problem that I guess I have lived with,

and it's a terrible problem. I was getting in more trouble by pointing it in the wrong direction. But that's what you get paid for. You really do. And also what's wheat and what's chaff, sending in trivial stuff.

Q: You say you've had problems. Is that because you made the wrong guess on specific things?

Mr. King: Well, I guess the most shining example was later on the Atomic Energy Commission when I was caught between two guys who were jockeying for power. But it's really a question, number one, if you have the final option of not sending something to someone who shouldn't receive it, who in turn will bugger it up, and then the boss man says, "What in the hell did you give it to him for?" That sort of thing. It comes with the territory. But I've always been very sensitive, first, to not sending in trivia, and secondly, to not sending it to the wrong person. At the beginning, there were several people between me and Fechteler himself. It went through two or three hands, so that was never a problem that really intimately involved me. Although in a reverse way it could if I started it off wrong. It would be my little red wagon, so to speak.

Q: I would think that they would expect a great deal of discretion in a job like that, because you obviously know a lot of things that could be of interest throughout the Navy. People might have a tendency to pump you.

Mr. King: Well, that kind of comes with the territory too. That goes back to any job you ever have, wherever you're an admiral's writer, or something like that. You know, to a greater or lesser degree, there are those people who would like to get in on the inside, but if you handle it properly, you never have any trouble. But woe be unto whoever violates the unwritten law and does use their job to drop a little goody where they shouldn't drop it. That's like blasphemy; that's the unforgivable sin as far as I'm concerned. But no, on Fechteler, I just recall that he was a big man with a big, booming voice, and he kept pretty well to his own office.

Carney, who came after him, was a little bit more outgoing in terms of the parameters of the job. That is to say, I think he delegated more than Fechteler did. And Carney was sort of inclined to be a bit of a colorful guy. I think he was kind of aware of it. He was sort of PR conscious--not in a negative sense--but he was very much aware that he was Mick Carney. I remember from time to time people would write him that didn't know him, and would address him as "Dear Bob." His name is Robert B. Carney. That was a good criterion. If somebody said, "Dear Bob," the boss never saw it. If it said, "Dear Mick," then he got the letter. There was exceptions, of course. But he was a colorful guy.

Q: I've heard he was very gifted in the use of words.

Mr. King: He was. For example, one time Herb Carroll, his long-time trusted lieutenant, was up for a fitness report, and Admiral Carney wrote it himself, as he properly should. He just penned it out, and that became the official document; we didn't type it. He had one sentence in the fitness report, and that sentence was: "I have used up all my encomiums on Herb Carroll." That was all; that was the fitness report. And everything was 4.0, 4.0, 4.0, 4.0. He was very gifted, and I think that his public appearances--I think he pretty well wrote and orchestrated everything himself. He didn't delegate that.

Q: I've heard he had the ability to dictate the draft of a speech, and it was so good that it didn't need any polishing.

Mr. King: Yes, that was his reputation. Herb Carroll was very much aware of that, and that became a fact of Herb's job. I mean, he knew when to let something get tinkered with and when to let it be the admiral's words. He knew that very well and good from years, and years, and years.

That was part of Herb's stock in trade. That kind of relationship, which is built on years of acquaintanceship, that's good.

One other anecdote I can remember about Carney was one time in his outer office, his aide, Captain W. J. Marshall, who later made admiral, was on the phone.* He always talked in a loud voice on the phone--and I guess Carney could hear his voice inside his room. So Carney opened the door and said, "Who are you talking to, Bill?"

Marshall said, "I'm talking to somebody on the Hill."

Carney said, "Why don't you use the telephone?" We all thought that was very funny.

Q: Do you remember any of the substance that was going on during this period? For example, the atomic submarine was coming along during that time, the first guided missile cruisers were being developed, the Rickover issue surfaced.

Mr. King: I remember to some degree some Rickover problems. I'm not sure whether they went from Carney to Burke or were entirely in Carney's time. After Burke arrived, it kind of crystallized in my mind; everything was an issue. But between Fechteler and Carney, I cannot recall, going back at this point and thinking about some clear-cut issue that would be a good example of one or the other. The guided

---
*Captain William J. Marshall, USN.

missile cruiser was one. Rickover's too well known for me to go into it, but there were Rickover problems. And other than that, I think that Carney was much more Congress-oriented than Fechteler was. Carney kept a very close eye on the congressional relationships aspects of his job.

Q: Would you say Fechteler was much more of a rough-hewn type?

Mr. King: More of a rough-hewn type and more of a no-nonsense type. I guess he was, to some extent, just a kind of a black-shoe admiral that was very much mission oriented.* He was not much for detail, or not much for relationships with the Hill, per se, or social life--that kind of business. He was kind of rough-hewn.

Q: More of a sailor man than a bureaucrat.

Mr. King: Much more. He was not as colorful nor articulate as Carney, but I think probably he had more substance. Probably he had more substance than Carney did. Burke had both. He had the whole tamale.

Q: Any specific issues you remember from the Burke years?

---
*A black-shoe officer is one with battleship-cruiser-destroyer experience, as opposed to being a naval aviator. Naval aviators are known as brown shoes.

Mr. King: Well, there were still some residual problems on the Air Force side when Burke first came in. And other than that, for a specific issue--let's see, we're getting into the 1955-56 era. I think probably there were some, there were some issues on the shipbuilding side, not necessarily guided missiles. I think that concerning small ships, for lack of a better word--destroyers, frigates, smaller--Burke was very much, again, black-shoe oriented. He didn't seem to me to have the feel for the aviation Navy that a brown shoe would have. Burke, I think, to me comes off probably as being more of a surface-ship admiral.

Q: Well, he was, of course. But I'm surprised to hear you say that, because I have heard from others that he did have a view that embraced the whole Navy, because he'd served with the fast carrier task force and Mitscher in World War II.

Mr. King: Well, at the same time, I think he was sensitive to the big maritime or naval strategy. I'm drawing an awful fine distinction here. I mean, he didn't treat the aviation navy with neglect or anything. But I think his first love-- you could always get his attention with an issue having to do with small surface ships.

Q: Now, when he was demanding that people work these long hours, did he show appreciation or consideration, or did he just expect that as a matter of course?

Mr. King: More of the former than the latter. He was not generous with praise, but he wasn't sparing. I mean, there were times when I'd leave the office at some ungodly hour at night and would just happen by accident to be in the hall with him. He'd say something nice, or give you a pat on the shoulder that made you feel like he really knew what the hell was going on. But I never felt like he was just being arbitrary or capricious. I always felt like--well, he did it himself. I mean, none of us kept his hours. I just felt that was part of our job with him to work those hours. I didn't resent it. I don't know anybody that did, anybody.

Q: Did you work with his aides, people like Commander Weschler or Commander Peet?*

Mr. King: Commander Peet, I guess, is more of a name than Weschler. There was always in the front office, on the personal staff, so to speak, of the CNO, there was a four-striper.

---

*Commander Thomas R. Weschler, USN; Commander Raymond E. Peet, USN. Both retired as vice admirals, and both have been interviewed as part of the Naval Institute's oral history program.

C. S. King #3 - 322

Q: The senior aide.

Mr. King: Yes. I forget now who the four-striper was for Burke. But my bifocals were pretty well centered from our operation in there with the ebb and flow of papers that were designed for Burke's eyes, so that I didn't aim them or direct them at anybody else except Burke. What people did with them after that was one thing. But I pretty well kept my eyes in the boat, as far as that sort of thing. I mean, I didn't have a whole lot of business with people other than--in the case of Carroll, in the case of Carney, Carroll; in the case of Burke--I guess it was Peet probably. I guess I've got Alzheimer's disease; I've forgotten the name but it was really that kind of relationship.

Now, Donald Duncan was VCNO for Burke a little bit.* Burke had an awful high regard for him. Had a very high regard for him. And once in a while Burke would send me off to deliver something--some eyes-only stuff, or whatever, to one of DCNOs.** Once in a while, I would get dispatched to one of them to some inner sanctum thing. I remember that when Burke would say, "Give this to John," or "Charlie," that kind of thing, that's who got it--nobody else. I would sometimes have troubles at the delivery point. But I took Burke very seriously, and that's what he meant. He meant the name he gave me and not anybody else.

---
*Admiral Donald B. Duncan, USN, Vice Chief of Naval Operations.

Q: I hear he had almost a fetish about prompt responses to written correspondence.

Mr. King: Yes, indeed. Yes, indeed. He had a low boiling point when anybody that worked for him was dilatory in a reply going out for his signature. He liked it prompt, and he didn't like interims or acknowledgments. He liked the substance back as soon as they could get it out, or sooner. And if that wasn't good, he'd do it himself.

Q: Was he a bug on style and the presentation of the typed and written matter?

Mr. King: My memory is that he was not to the extent that Carney was. Carney was more style-oriented, I think, than Burke was.

Q: Carney was more of a wordsmith.

Mr. King: Yes. I think to Burke, as long as a message got to whoever it was supposed to get to--by word of mouth, whatever--he was satisfied. If he felt, in his own mind, that so-and-so had gotten the word, then it was all right

---

**DCNOs--Deputy Chiefs of Naval Operations.

with him. That's how I felt about Burke.

Q: Were there any special privileges that went with working that close to the CNO?

Mr. King: I think, probably, the only special privileges were in the eyes of our peers; I mean, it was that kind of thing. You know, if you were in one of the inner sanctums--well, if I came down the hall to go to some vice admiral with something--after a while it became, "That's fine, you know, right on in." It was that kind of thing.

Burke's style is not something that was hidden. I mean, everybody in the Navy and the Pentagon knew his style. Those of us that worked very close to him were given the accoutrements when you work for a guy like that. Because you didn't work for him unless you cut the mustard, and that was also known and appreciated too.

Q: So you got a little reflected glory.

Mr. King: You got a little reflected glory, and that made up for the late nights as far as I was concerned. And we had a good working atmosphere in his office. I mean, we all had a damn good morale, because we all felt like we were members of the club. And it wasn't just 100% grind all the time. We had our light moments, and it was, I guess, something like a pro football team. It was that kind of business, where we didn't all just consider ourselves just burdened down creatures. We had a lot of fun, and Burke was quick to pick up on that sort of thing. If something funny went on, he wanted to know about it.

Q: Well, anything else on that before we get you to the FDR?

Mr. King: I don't know. I guess not at the moment. I found out, in these tapes that we do, that after I finish one with you and I have a moment to reflect, I probably think of a thousand things that I should have said. But for the moment I guess I've about beat that horse to death.

Q: Well, what difference, if any, was there between your time in the Midway and that in the FDR?

Mr. King: Well, it was an unusual thing. When I reported to the FDR, she was temporarily out of commission, was going back in commission.* It was a recommissioning thing in Bremerton.

When I reported in, the job was kind of open as to

---

*The Franklin D. Roosevelt was decommissioned 23 April 1954 to undergo a two-year modernization. During that time she received a hurricane bow, angled flight deck, steam catapults, streamlined island, and updated electronic gear. She was recommissioned 6 April 1956.

which one of the two ship's clerks would be ship's secretary and which would be personnel. Having been personnel on the _Midway_, I was kind of thinking about being ship's secretary on the _FDR_. But when I got to the _FDR_, the ship's clerk, who was already there--and I was way the hell senior to him, and had my pick if I wanted it--but he was a hell of a good guy.

I could see that he didn't want to be personnel officer. I think he was yeoman oriented and wanted to be ship's secretary. He was such a hell of a good guy, and I liked him, so I thought, "Oh, hell, I did it before, and I can do it again." So I decided I would go ahead. I'll never forget the look of gratitude in his eyes when I told him. He was really grateful. And it worked out fine. He was a nice guy, and we got along real well.

The _FDR_ and _Midway_ were sister ships right down to the last bolt and nut, except that the _FDR_ was built in New York by the naval civilian employees, and the _Midway_ was built in Newport News by civilians. I'm not an engineer, but the difference was like light and dark. Although similar, the _Midway_ was such a much better constructed ship. Even I could sense that it was a hell of a better ship.

Q: In what ways? How would you illustrate that difference?

Mr. King: Well, by the number of problems that we had

engineering-wise. On the Midway, the maintenance was always just taken for granted; she just ran like a clock. But the FDR, we had one problem after another. You kind of got tired of people saying, "That damn New York Naval Shipyard. They ought to build buggies or something instead of a battleship. They just can't build them." That kind of thing. The FDR did her job and everything, but it was a pack of troubles for maintenance.

Q: What about cleanliness?

Mr. King: The Midway was a cleaner ship, a tighter ship to my recollection, with all the vagaries of memory. It just seemed to be a better operating ship. Now I liked the FDR. I mean, I don't have any bad memories of that. It was a good tour of duty and all. But the Midway stands out in my mind as much the better ship by any criteria that I can recall.

The warrant officers were in the same location on both ships. I had the same stateroom, the same bunk, the same everything on the FDR as I had on the Midway. I used to walk down the hangar deck at night, out at sea, going from my office back to the warrant officers' mess, and I felt like I was in a twilight zone or something. It was really kind of weird. I had that feeling so many times--a feeling of deja vu, or whatever.

Q: Different ships have different personalities.

Mr. King: Every ship I was ever on had a distinct personality of its own, just like a person. Every ship I was ever on had a distinct personality.

Q: What difference might you see in those two ships?

Mr. King: Well, the Midway was more of an operating ship. One had a feeling on the Midway that no matter what the hell came up, she'd do a damn good job of it. And the FDR, there was always a bugaboo of question mark in the background--would it hold up? Would something happen? That kind of business.

This is a generality, but to me a ship almost always reflects very accurately the personality of its captain. Not its exec, but its captain. I've always felt that I could go aboard any ship for five or ten minutes, just wander around doing most anything, and have a fairly good picture in my mind of the skipper of the ship. It's a very nebulous kind of thing, but the captain's personality is kind of reflected in people. You know, if the captain is a disciplinarian and all that sort of thing, then you know there's a kind of an air of don't get in trouble. I mean, if it's a happy-go-lucky, that's good, gung-ho, then you get that—it's a kind of reflection. It takes a while to develop, but once it's there, it's fixed, and it's very easily identifiable.

Q: What kind of personality did Captain Hayward impart?

Mr. King: Captain Hayward was, I guess, to some extent, out of the sort of the Burke school, you might say. He was a guy who attracted the confidence of his people. He was supremely confident in his job and what he was doing. He was polished and smooth and witty, and had a kind of style about him. He just kind of exuded confidence. People around him felt the same way.

Q: He seems to know everything about everything.

Mr. King: Knows everything—I couldn't put it any better myself. But not offensively so. In a very positive way. Just a great guy. I liked him when I met him in Coco Solo, Panama. Didn't know him that well. But I always had the same feeling about the guy—that he had class. What impressed the hell out of me was in Bremerton, shortly after we'd gone into commission, for some reason Admiral Burke was in town and had gone out to the FDR to visit Hayward as kind of a protege of his. I knew he was aboard, but I was back in the warrant officers' mess. It was after hours.

All of a sudden, somebody came and got me. They wanted to see me in the wardroom. I went to the wardroom, and Burke was having a chat with all the officers, kind of philosophizing, as he liked to do. Captain Hayward took me in, and said, "Here he is." Burke gave me a big hug, and I just thought, "What class." That really impressed the hell out of me. Because Burke gave me a great big, warm greeting from the good old days. It was Hayward's idea. And I guess that really impressed me, both those guys to do that.

Q: That's the kind of person you want to put out the extra effort for.

Mr. King: Anything they ask me to do, I'll do. I don't care what. And, very well, that's exactly what I felt about it.

Other than that, the tour on the FDR was very much like the Midway. I had the same job. I really did the job on the FDR as I did on the Midway. In fact, in the Navy yard I even had all the desks torn out of the ship's office on the FDR and rearranged like they were on the Midway. Just felt better that way and I knew it worked.

Q: On the other hand, that's not as much as a challenge, because you know you can do that easily enough.

C. S. King #3 - 331

Mr. King: Yes, and that's what kind of bugged me a little bit. I enjoyed the FDR, but there was no challenge to it. I began to think, "What the hell am I doing here, doing the same job twice in six years?" That's when it really began to be clear to me that I'd better haul off and leave the Navy.

Q: Had you looked into getting a commission at all?

Mr. King: No, no, I was very happy as a warrant officer. In my 24 years in the Navy, I spent eight years as a white hat, eight years as a chief, and eight years as a warrant. It just seemed to be a tidy way of doing things. Each one of those three categories had their own charms, their own good features, and their own bad features. The decision, to me, began to come along when I finished 20 years, which was in 1954--three years before I retired. At that time, you have to think about it. I mean it began to become an option: do I do it, do I not? For the next three years I did my job as best I could. I still had this business in mind about what to do if I should do it, about leaving the Navy.

Q: Now, the Franklin D. Roosevelt came back around to the Atlantic. What do you remember about that trip?

C. S. King #3 - 332

Mr. King: I remember a lot of things about that trip. One was Norris Bradbury, who was a civilian scientist in charge of the weapons laboratory at Los Alamos.* He was a big buddy of Chick Hayward. Chick had a background in special weapons.

We had a very adventurous trip. We went around the Horn.

Q: Couldn't go through the canal, so you had to.

Mr. King: I'd always heard about going around the Horn, and that became a great thing. We had a ceremony in which you became shellback and went around the Horn at the same time. Anyway, you qualified twice. You qualified as a shellback and a golden dragon. I was Davy Jones, head of the ceremony. Years later, when I was on the Atomic Energy Commission, Norris Bradbury came to Germantown one day, and we were just talking about ships and shoes and sealing wax. He said, "I want to show you something." And he took his wallet out and showed me his shellback card, which I had signed as Davy Jones on the FDR.

But that was a very exciting trip, because I had always dreamed about going around Cape Horn. It was very strange weather. At one time we had just nothing but ice--not big,

---

*Physicist Norris E. Bradbury was director of the Los Alamos, New Mexico, scientific laboratory from 1945 to 1970. From 1941 to 1945 he served on active duty as a Naval Reserve Officer.

thick ice, but small ice--as far as you could see. We had very stormy weather around the Horn. We had an exciting, adventurous trip. I remember it very well.

Q: What do you remember about the liberty ports on that trip?

Mr. King: I guess the last port I recall is when we hit San Diego. We just went to sea from San Diego. And I don't recall if we stopped anywhere on the way around or not.

Q: Nothing in South America?

Mr. King: We might have stopped at Rio, on the other side, but I don't recall a single port on the Pacific side.

Q: Anything else about that ship?

Mr. King: The FDR was the ship on which I did put in my request for retirement. The men in the warrant officers' mess were awfully good to me. We had a wetting down party and I really had a feeling then that this was it. I mean, this was not a transfer; this was the unmistakable leap off the deep end. That was very much on my mind. I was never easy in my mind, when I did it, about leaving the Navy. I never was easy about it, because I hated to leave the Navy. I didn't want to leave the Navy. My wife and I had many spirited discussions. She's not really a nomad at heart, and you know the old saying, "Three moves are equal to a fire." She didn't like to move around. So when I got my 20 years in, she thought it was time. Logic told me it was time, but sentiment said, "Don't ever leave the Navy. Stay with it. That's your mama, your papa, your chow-chow, your whiskey, soda." I mean, it was everything.

Q: This had been your life since you were a teenager.

Mr. King: Yes, it was everything to me. So I wasn't at all comfortable. It was something where I knew I had to do it. I put in my chit and signed it, but I had great misgivings about it. I think this was kind of epitomized by an experience when I was being processed at the New York officers' separation center, or whatever they called it. There was a lieutenant commander off of the FDR that happened to be with me. We went along every stage of the game. A long checkout slip--see the chaplain, the library, so we went through the numbers.

The last number on this long laborious checkout sheet was the ID card room. We were with each other, and we got down in line there, looked at the head of the line, and there was a little kid about 18 years old--some yeoman striker--and that was his job. He had this guillotine machine. As each man stepped up, he would take the green ID card, put it in the machine, and go whack, whack, whack, and cut the picture out.* Then he would take a gray one out, put the picture in it, laminate it, and hand it to you. That was it. When you got that, you were no longer a person.

This lieutenant commander in front of me--I think he and I were thinking the same thoughts--so finally, it came his time. He was in front of me. He reluctantly handed his green ID card to this kid. The kid went whack, whack, whack, and those four pieces fell on the floor. This lieutenant commander said, "Damn." Because that was him on the floor. You know, that green card takes you on the ship, off the ship. That's your identity. That's you. When somebody just cuts it up, all of a sudden you realize, "That's me." That little bit of trauma was the one thing that told me I was not in the Navy anymore.

Q: That symbolized the whole thing.

Mr. King: That symbolized the whole thing. After I got out of the Navy, in this very house, for the longest time--I guess a matter of months--I'd come home at night after a hard day's work at the Atomic Energy Commission because I

―――――――
*Identification cards for active-duty U.S. armed services personnel are green; those for retired personnel are grey.

just really was knocking myself out trying to make it. I would come home, just worn out, and sitting down with a newspaper and be looking at it. And all of a sudden I would physically just jump up. I felt I had to check in somewhere. I had to show somebody a piece of paper. I mean, it was a momentary thing. It passed right off, but I would get a physical start, and thinking "My God, I've got to go . . ."

Q: So you had some withdrawal symptoms.

Mr. King: I had some definite withdrawal symptoms, and they went on and on for the longest time. It was a diminishing thing--after six months or so.

Another thing that I remember very, very vividly about that transition period was that something told me when I went down to the Atomic Energy Commission headquarters in my uniform--before I left the Navy--to be interviewed. As Tom Wolfe would say, a voice came to me in the night and said, "If you go to work for this outfit, let the Navy be behind you." I don't know why, but I had a definite feeling about that. I did that and I never under any circumstances in the beginning days of my new life ever said anything like, "Oh, this is fine, but in the Navy this . . ."

It was a temptation sometimes, because there were some

things that I thought could be improved the Navy way. But I never said it. I never said I was going to the commissary. I never said I was going to the PX.* I found out that was one of the few smart things I did in my whole life, because, in general, the civilian world is not that crazy about the military. I was one of these terrible double dippers and all that stuff.** I didn't keep it a secret, but I sure didn't flaunt it.

Q: You gave them less reason than they might have had to resent you.

Mr. King: I gave them no reason at all. I just busted my butt for them and never said a word about the Navy. It turned out that that was a good thing, because I saw so many guys come in and do the opposite, and just really get in all kinds of trouble. I don't mean serious trouble, but just took twice as long to do something than if they'd just kept their mouth shut.

Q: I think they expect to be recognized in the civilian world for their Navy achievements rather than making it in the civilian world.

---

*PX--post exchange.
**"Double dippers" is a slang term for individuals who work for the U.S. Government while also drawing retirement pay from the government.

C. S. King #3 - 338

Mr. King: That's a very good way of putting it. But, boy, my earnest advice to anybody that ever leaves the Navy and continues their activity--in the government, anyway--is to very low-key it.

Q: Without going into as much detail as we have on the Navy aspects, could you summarize that AEC experience and your work with the American Cancer Society, please?

Mr. King: The Atomic Energy Commission--at the time I went into it in 1957, there was no break. I left the Navy on Friday and went to work for the AEC on Monday. The AEC at that time was really a hard-driving, mission-oriented outfit that I felt thoroughly at home in the atmosphere. It was really a no-nonsense place. It was not like the good, gray government--agriculture, labor, something like that. It was scientific and technical with a hell of a big mission to do and let's do it. And I liked that. I liked everything about it. I really felt good about the Atomic Energy Commission. I went to work in the secretariat as a kind of a paper-shuffler, which is what I was. I made it my primary goal in life to knock myself out, because I felt very much the keen difference between--there were so many educated people in the Atomic Energy Commission, Ph.Ds, I mean. That was the norm, almost.

Q: Nobel Prize winners even.

Mr. King: Everything. And here I was a high school graduate. I felt that very keenly. I didn't go around crying in my beer, but I was aware of that distinction. I thought the only way I can make up is just to run when everybody else walks. And so I did. I wouldn't go straight home at night if there was still work to do. I felt like that was the only substitute I had for a sheepskin, and it helped. It helped a hell of a lot, because as the years went by I began to pick up grades for hard work and I could see other people much more academically qualified than I were not getting them. I saw just plain old effort helped a hell of a lot.

After I'd been in the secretariat a little while, a new chairman came to the AEC named John A. McCone.* I guess he had as big an impact on my life as anybody I've ever met. McCone was a hard-driving, tremendously energetic man who had made not millions, but B for billions during World War II in construction with the Bechtel Corporation, which at one time was Bechtel-McCone. Although the Atomic Energy Commission was a five-member commission, under McCone there was a single administrator. He just did that by the force of his personality.

**John A. McCone was chairman of the Atomic Energy Commission from 1958 to 1961.

McCone's style was to travel a lot. I don't mean travel for travel's sake, but he wanted to see what was going on. He would be in Paris one weekend and Moscow soon after that. He just went all over the whole damn world. And wherever he went, he ran the AEC out of his hip pocket. He was just as much in command. He used to appoint a commissioner as acting chairman, but that didn't mean a damn thing. McCone was still the chairman.

In his traveling like that, he was comfortable with a non-female companion. He had a guy named Terry Lee who had done that for him in all his jobs throughout his whole working life until he came to the AEC. Then I became a type of Terry Lee. I traveled with McCone. I was with him every waking hour, no matter where he was. He was comfortable with that. He liked it. I don't mean he liked me, but that's the way he liked to do things.

Again, my shorthand came into play. It just saved my skin in more ways than one. I took shorthand in high school to be around the girls, and I think how much good it did me later on.

But, anyway, McCone worked every minute. We'd be in a helicopter over Germany, and he would give me dictation. I would go to every affair that he went to, and I was supposed to keep a complete record. I would make notes and the next day give him a little transcript.

We got along great. But as far as intense effort goes, I never worked so hard in my life as with McCone. He was just that kind of guy. He was never a warm man. I don't mean he was uncaring. But when you worked for him in the capacity that I worked for him, you were aware that he appreciated it. But if you wanted him to pat you on the back every day, that wasn't his style at all.

Q: All business.

Mr. King: All business, 100%. But I liked that in a guy. I admired it in him. I think I learned more from him in the two years I worked for him than anybody I ever knew, just watching what he could do. He could accomplish the impossible, and I've seen him do it time and time and time again, through just force of his personality and what he knew. That's just the way he was.

A small example--we were two weeks in Russia, and we went all over the damn place. Before we left from Washington, I spent a lot of time getting ready for the trip--preparing data books and backups and stuff like this. Our last stop was at Brussels for a meeting with an outfit called EurAtom, which is all the European members of the atomic community. So I went over to the State Department. I got him a book about that thick, all tabbed on EurAtom. I had everything about EurAtom there. So when that point came in the trip--we were about three days from Brussels--I said, "Mr. McCone, I've got this thing on EurAtom."

"Okay, fine." So I put it away.

The next day I said, "Mr. McCone, I've got this thing on EurAtom."

"Fine." Okay. I put it away. And the closer we got to Brussels, the more panic-stricken I got, because I could see myself and him going to a meeting with EurAtom commissioners and saying "What the hell's going on here?" So in the limo, going to the meeting of the EurAtom commissioners, I said, "Mr. McCone, this briefing book on EurAtom."

He said, "Cecil, I know about EurAtom. Put that goddamn thing away." So I put it away, and he sat down with those guys and he talked about kilotons this and kilotons that. He was on top of it. He knew as much as they did, if not more. How he knew it, I don't know. But that's just the way the guy operated.

Q: Did you have any contact with David Lilienthal?*

Mr. King: Not direct contact. Lilienthal was a commissioner. I'm not sure whether he was a commissioner when I came in. When I came in, there was Strauss as

---

*David E. Lilienthal was chairman of the Atomic Energy Commission from 1946 to 1950.

chairman before McCone, and Gordon Dean, I think.* Anyway, Lilienthal was one of those guys that was around for a while. You'd see a lot of the former commissioners. And people like Edward Teller were always around the headquarters.** I got accustomed to seeing just really so many things, my eyes stuck out as I'd walk down the hall.

Q: How about Seaborg.*** Did you know him?

Mr. King: Worked for him personally when he relieved McCone as chairman.

Q: What do you recall about him?

Mr. King: Seaborg was as opposite from McCone in working philosophy as a person can be. I don't mean to say Seaborg didn't work, but he was a 100% different guy than McCone. If McCone gave a speech, you could do drafts for him for days. The day he went to give that speech, he'd pay some attention to it. Not too much, if it didn't suit. If Seaborg was to give a speech in September, he wanted to

---

*Lewis L. Strauss, a Naval Reserve rear admiral, was chairman of the Atomic Energy Commission from 1953 to 1958. Gordon Dean was chairman of the Atomic Energy Commission from 1950 to 1953; he died in an airplane crash in 1958.
**Physicist Edward Teller played an instrumental role in the development of the hydrogen bomb and in the payload for the submarine launched Polaris missile.
***Glenn T. Seaborg, Nobel Prize winner in 1951, aided in the discovery of nine new chemical elements. He was chairman of the Atomic Energy Commission from 1961 to 1971.

draft it in June. I mean, he was a very methodical guy, very methodical. He had eight children, and one of his children came when there was no doctor around, and he delivered the child himself. He knew exactly how to do it because when he got married, he took time off to look at a book about what to do. Anyway, he kept in his pockets at all times a stack of 3x5 index cards that told him every eventuality of every trip he was going to be on. He was always prepared for everything in that sense. Whereas with McCone, it was always spontaneous.

Q: In his head.

Mr. King: In his head. But they were different people. Seaborg was really difficult to be on a trip with because he was very much conscious--I don't mean he was egotistical, but he was a guy that didn't like to have anything arise on a trip that took any of the emphasis off of his role. He didn't want trouble with the podium. He didn't want trouble with lights not being on. He didn't want trouble with small type that he couldn't read or had to use his glasses. Everything had to be precisely done, precisely done. Now, I'm talking about details. He's a Nobel laureate and a very great scientist. And I don't mean to minimize that for a second. I'm just talking about that man you see when you work for him, travel with him, and so forth.

McCone was a Republican. He was relieved by Seaborg when JFK came in to relieve Eisenhower.* A guy named Howard Brown and I were the two people that survived the transition. Seaborg kept most of us on, because the agency still was scientific and technical and not political, but at the same time there were shifts. I worked for McCone two years in a personal capacity as his administrative assistant, and four years for Seaborg in somewhat the same job.

Q: How did you come to make the transition from that to the Cancer Society?

Mr. King: The Cancer Society is volunteer work after I retired. But, anyway, about three or four years into Seaborg's term, I had been in "mahogany row," working for the commissioners for a number of years, and had acquired a number of grades. I'd gone from GS-11 or GS-12 all the way up to GS-15, I think it was. But the last several grades that I had picked up were all Schedule C, not permanent. I served at the pleasure of the commissioner. So I saw a chance working for a guy named Dwight Ink, who is still very much active over in Washington. Dwight Ink came back on the staff as assistant general manager, and he asked me to come

---

*Dwight D. Eisenhower was President from January 1953 to January 1961. John F. Kennedy was President from January 1961 to November 1963.

and be his assistant. If you work on the staff and you make that transition, your grade becomes permanent. So it was a question of giving up the perks of "mahogany row" and commissioner's life to work for the staff to preserve my grade. So with Seaborg's blessing, I went to work for Dwight Ink as assistant general manager's assistant. You used the word assistant about 19 times, but it was that kind of role, and so then I worked on the staff until I retired.

In 1971, President Nixon created something called the Price Commission.* Just made a speech and created the Price Commission and also the wage board. The Price Commission was formed out of detail people from all agencies in town. Dwight Ink was instrumental in seeing that I was taken from the AEC to work with the Price Commission, because it was the President's baby. So I went to the Price Commission as deputy director of administration. Had a great job, a challenging job, worked around the clock.

I worked so hard I found myself in the hospital with a bleeding ulcer, and that concluded my government service. When I tossed the coin, it came up on the side of no ulcer. I was not ulcer prone, I didn't think, so I was surprised to get one. But I was going a little bit too hard, I guess. So I left the Atomic Energy Commission and fully retired.

Q: At least you didn't have to sell cookware anymore.

---
*Richard M. Nixon was President from January 1969 to August 1974.

Mr. King: Hell, no. The AEC was very good to me. I enjoyed every second of it and miss it to this day. But it was a different life than the Navy. It was a different career, a different life. The whole thing was.

When I left the AEC, I again went through the kind of trauma I did leaving the Navy, to a little bit of an extent. This time I didn't know if I had enough money to live on. It turned out I had more than I needed. But I went to work as a management consultant, whatever the hell that is. And I still do that to this day. I'm working on a contract for AID right now.* But I only do it now when I want to do it. Again, I'm working for Dwight Ink; that's the same guy I'm working for at AID.

Back when I left the AEC, my wife was very community oriented. She used to march up and down our street for the Cancer Society. One year she couldn't do it, so I did it for her. I did it the next year, and the next year, and so on. The next thing I know, I'm neighborhood captain, and I'm this, and I'm that, and I keep getting different jobs. I wound up as president of the Arlington unit, and the next thing at the state level. I've been almost full-time Cancer Society since 1972. But I now think I've wound that up, because I'm concluding my two years as state chairman. So I'm about to put that to one side.

---

*AID—Agency for International Development.

Q: It's a remarkably long way from firing at a Model T Ford in Texas.

Mr. King: Yes, it is, it is. You know, in talking to you, so many things come up that my mind has just been churning a lot, and I remember these haphazard, disjointed incidents. And I remember people's names I hadn't thought of in I don't know how many years. It's just amazing to me. I think I could probably start over again.

Q: Well, you'll have the chance when you get the transcripts so you can fill in some of these things.

Mr. King: Well, I guess that brings us up to date then.

Q: You had a remarkable talent for landing on your feet, despite the occasional problems put in your path.

Mr. King: Well, I've had my problems. I sure have. But on the whole, when I look back, I've been a very lucky guy. I've been a fortunate man. I've been fortunate beyond belief. I've been fortunate in the jobs that I've had. And I've had so many good jobs. I've been fortunate in my family. I've been fortunate in my health. I just really consider myself a very lucky guy at this point. I really do.

Q: Well, from what you've said, you derive both satisfaction and enjoyment from you work. That is a very rewarding life.

Mr. King: It is. It is. Didn't put meat on the table, but it makes you feel good. I've enjoyed it, and I've made more money than I should have made. If my father had any idea today of how much income I get--and I don't get that much, but I mean by our standards back in Aransas Pass--he'd come out of his grave, I think. I remember now when I said to him, "Dad, I'll get $63.00 a month when I retire from the Navy at age 37." I thought he was going to faint. But, anyway, I've been very fortunate by every parameter that I can think of. The Cancer Society has been very rewarding to me because there's a great benefit to being a volunteer in the Cancer Society. You don't get paid, so you can tell the truth with the bark off. You do what you think is right for logic's sake, with no obstacles of any kind. That's a great way to do business.

Q: There's also a special pleasure in doing something for others.

Mr. King: That's true. It's kind of a selfish thing there. My dad and two brothers died of lung cancer, and I feel like I'm paying my dues to some extent. Of course, there are as many health agencies as there are diseases--kidney, heart, lung, all of them--but, you know, you work with the one you like.

Q: Well, on behalf of myself and the Institute, I very much appreciate the time that you've put into this. Others will have a chance to enjoy reading this, as I've enjoyed hearing it from you.

Mr. King: I feel kind of bad about things I've said about Captain Carr, Captain Hoskins, and Lieutenant Lewis. All three of them are dead now. But they have relatives, and I don't want them to read these transcripts and think what an ungrateful bastard I am. But, I mean, those are the things that happened.

Q: You're bound to run into a few of those in the course of a career.

Mr. King: Yes, and I'm sure if they were interviewed, they'd have as much to say about me as I said about them--if not more.

Q: Maybe wherever they are now, there is an oral history program.

Mr. King: If so, I hope they get into it.

C. S. King #4 - 352

Interview Number 4 with Chief Warrant Officer
Cecil S. King, Jr., U.S. Navy (Retired)

Place: Mr. King's home in Arlington, Virginia

Date: Monday, 23 October 1989

Interviewer: Paul Stillwell

Q: Good morning, Mr. King. It's a pleasure to see you. I think one thing I could say to characterize the previous interviews: they were not only productive but enjoyable. So I enjoy the relationship from that standpoint, as well as what we're adding to naval history.

What sorts of reviews have you made as a result of going back over the first three transcripts?

Mr. King: Kind of an overview thought struck me after having gone through all three of them. That was that this account that we've made of events covers a period going back some 50 years ago. All this is receding at an increasingly rapid rate--at least in my mind, or what's left of it. I have reviewed this history at some length and attention to detail, both in the initial stages and again recently. There's probably not a page that I couldn't double or triple with no difficulty, and I would have been proud to do so.

However, I think these efforts do provide sort of a broad-brush picture of a period that I was privileged, highly privileged, to be a part of. I have viewed with some surprise, even astonishment, the record of, and public reaction to, the Korean War, but quickly realize that the people of World War II, of my years of experience, enjoyed some substantial differences. The enemy was clear-cut and recognizable. He hit us first a Sunday punch, as we would have termed it--God knows, no pun intended. We enjoyed the full support of the general U.S. population, and in most cases were proud of the chance to be of service in the service.

But, anyway, the period going back to when I got out of boot camp and finally wound up on the <u>Portland</u>. Again, I was struck by the lack of any kind of knowledge that we recruits had of what the Navy was all about. I didn't know anything about the Navy before I shipped in. When we were going to be assigned, we really didn't have any constructive knowledge of the fleet. We knew a battleship was big and a destroyer was small--that kind of thing--but we didn't know much about the operations of the Navy. Not that that was necessarily a point of criticism, it was just that the thought that struck me again of what decisions we made, or what decisions we were a part of that really were rather substantial. Yet we were just like kids in a candy store, and, actually, I think it worked out pretty well.

Q: Well, even after you'd been at it for a while--this was my experience--you get to know your specific job very well,

C. S. King #4 - 354

but other types of ships, other parts of the Navy, you have virtually no knowledge of.

Mr. King: That's true. Not only no knowledge of, but one of the enjoyable things about the Navy was--as far as liberty was concerned, and just general socialization--was how much fun it was to talk with someone off some other ship, some other Navy activity that was just totally unknown to me. We would drink beer by the hour and go over sea stories and that sort of thing. That was one of the real fun things about the Navy, was being a part of it. At the same time, it was a total learning process all of the time.

Q: Sort of the disciplinary pattern was what you do ashore is your own business as long as it doesn't impair your ability to do your job on board ship.

Mr. King: That's true. And, also, that was observed not only as sort of a fact of life, but the Navy had that sort of philosophy about it. That is to say, if you made a big thing out of yourself on the beach, you'd probably be hauled up short by some other sailor. It was done really as something that I thought was invaluable. I enjoyed it; I mean, I did some dumb things.

I remember on the Portland--I think we talked about this--we ate off of mess tables with crockery cups and plates; we didn't have steel mess trays. Each table had a captain of that table, mostly by seniority. Eating was not only something like a family affair, but the captain of the table kept a pretty tight rein. You didn't just do anything you wanted to.

I remember one time I got carried away by my own saltiness, and I made some joshing comment to the mess captain. I think he was a leading seaman, as a matter of fact. Whatever I said got under his skin, and he just brought me up short and said, in effect, "You sound like a wise guy, and we don't like wise guys at this table." I realized as soon as he opened his mouth that I was way off base, way off base. That quickly cured a little bit of the saltiness I had inherited all of a sudden.

Q: In today's electronic and technical Navy the leading seaman doesn't have the stature he used to.

Mr. King: Oh, my goodness, no. I would have no more idea on board ship today, no matter what I did, of having anything at all to do with radar or any of the technical aspects of it. It's just another world, and that's not too good, to have that kind of compartmentalization. I don't think you any longer have this kind of general esprit de corps in the Navy. To some extent, perhaps, but the science and technology level has cut into that.

Q: Wasn't there already a specialization, at least by divisions in your time, so that groups kept pretty much to themselves rather than knowing people throughout other parts of the ship?

Mr. King: Very much indeed. The deck force was exactly that. There was a good deal of joshing around between the engineers and the deck force. They went around in dungarees, and we had to have on our undress blues and that sort of thing. There was friendly rivalry, you might say. But there was very definitely a division between the deck force and the engineers. There were relatively few married men in those days, and so when you hit the beach, that was indeed a kind of a melding of the ship's company. So nowadays where kids wear civilian clothes ashore and so many of them are married, they don't have the chance and the privilege of that kind of fraternization that we used to have, which may or may not be good.

Q: What do you recall about loyalty to one's own ship?

Mr. King: Oh, that was a given in those days. I think I made the point before that every ship I was ever on, just about, I thought was the best damn ship in the Navy. And there was some good-natured rivalry, particularly in the destroyer Navy between ships, because I think that ship loyalty was more pronounced in smaller ships. So when we would be ashore, when I was on the _Davis_, for example, in our squadron--or in our division was the _Jouett_ and the _Somers_ and the _Sampson_, I think. When we bumped into them on the shore, it was not necessarily a negative or a hostile situation, but on the other hand, that was their ship and we were on the _Davis_, and they were on the _Somers_, and so we didn't do a whole lot of palling around together on the beach.

Q: Well, and also, there was the feeling that you were entitled to criticize your own ship but nobody else was.

Mr. King: I've seen some fistfights over that, more than I have over the ladies or anything else. That was a sensitive thing. You don't allow folks to talk about your own ship. Even if your ship, like the _Davis_, was really one of the hottest ships in the Navy, you didn't take kindly to criticism from other ships.

Q: How would you describe the way that sailors were received and perceived by the civilian community in the late Thirties?

Mr. King: Oh, in the late Thirties, the Navy towns, if

that's the right word, that we were accustomed to--Norfolk, San Diego, and that sort of thing--I don't ever recall having much socialization with the civilian population. It was really almost an inbred situation. When you went ashore, you were in uniform. There was no such thing as civilian clothes in those days. You were in uniform and you felt, I guess, more at ease with other uniforms. It was really, I'd say, a fairly wide gap. I don't ever recall much socialization at all with civilians per se. It was a 100% Navy situation.

Q: Well, the girls, I would say, were all civilians. Did they view sailors as second-class citizens, or were they receptive?

Mr. King: Well, my experience and my memories are that the girls that we met and saw, for the most part, were not necessarily second- or third-class citizens. For whatever reason, people had a feeling for the Navy. It doesn't take a brick wall to fall on you to realize when you're with friends and when you're not. So most of the experiences we had--and this covered a whole gamut of the social structure, you might say--we were generally pretty well received by the ladies, God bless them. Heck, that's the main thing about the Navy you like--your liberties and seeing new ports from time to time.

C. S. King #4 - 359

Q: Well, there's also the camaraderie with your male shipmates. That's a very positive thing too.

Mr. King: It is, it is. I was always kind of struck by-- like on a destroyer, if you spend the whole damn day working side by side with some shipmate on whatever you did, and you'd see two guys doing that during the day and they'd go ashore at night and bump into each other, you'd think they hadn't seen each other in ten years. "Why, you old son of a gun. I'll be damned, there he is, old So-and-so." I thought that was a great thing; I liked that.

You always were so glad to see somebody from your own ship.

Q: And that's the kind of thing you're saying that the Navy has probably gotten away from to a large extent now.

Mr. King: I feel like we have. The last ship that I was on, of course, was in '57--the FDR. I was a warrant officer and socialized with the other warrants. But because I was in personnel, I had a pretty good feeling for the crew and what they did ashore. I had the feeling then that there was quite a difference between those days and the earlier days. Of course, I guess everybody in the world thinks that the good old days are the good old days. But I think there's some degree of truth in that.

Q: The story is that when the second Marine joined the first Marine on board ship, the first one said, "Well, you should have been here in the old Corps."

Mr. King: Yes. Also, speaking of Marines, there was some good-natured--generally good-natured--sort of a rivalry. On board ship, there was kind of a clear-cut division there between the Marines and the sailors. They didn't go ashore together, and they didn't hang around too much together. If a sailor was going to go through a hatch, say, and there was some other guy blocking the hatch, he'd say, "What are you? A damn Marine? Gangway. Get out of the way."

So there was some rivalry between the Marines and sailors. In fact, there's the old two-liner about it, a little verse, "One sickly gob lay down his swab to lick 10,000 Marines; 10,000 more stood by and swore it was the best fight they'd ever seen." Or you could turn it around: "10,000 gobs . . ." But it was that kind of thing.

Q: Going back to these times you were in the cruiser, the destroyer, Coco Solo--what was the perception of Japan and the likelihood of a war with Japan?

Mr. King: The first time period that I can associate that

with some definite feelings was, in a general sense, the Panay incident. The Panay incident kind of crystallized it as far as the sailors were concerned back in the States. Of course, out on the China Station I guess it was different. But when the Panay was sunk, that really made a very--quite an impression on me because, you know, sinking a ship is--no matter how small the ship is, that makes an impression on you.

Q: Up to then, would you say there was a feeling of invincibility about the U.S. Navy?

Mr. King: Oh, the feeling of invincibility, I guess, maybe I had that right up until December 8, 1941, and even after that a little bit. I had trouble giving that up because that was an integral part of my feeling about the Navy and why I shipped over. I just felt that it was invincible, that we could do anything. I guess I was a gung-ho Navy kid. But I really was, and I didn't give it up until it was kind of taken away from me out in the Philippines.

Q: That time on board the Peary must have reinforced that feeling.

Mr. King: You mean on the Peary, when we were getting out of the Philippines?

Q: When you were escaping, yes.

Mr. King: Yes, that really brought it home. I may not be able to explain it--but even then, the thing that was strongest in my mind was that, "We're going to get those guys, and it won't be too damn longer either." I really felt that strongly. And on the _Peary_, which was a lonesome polecat run--I mean, we didn't see any friends for a long time there, and we got kicked around pretty well. But at the same time I always felt like, "This is not the end; we're going to come back." I felt that very strongly; I never did lose that for whatever reason.

Q: You had the case where had you not been evacuated from _Houston_, say, you might have lost your life. Certainly, there were some tenuous times there. Have you reflected on what you've been able to accomplish in this added span of years you've been given?

Mr. King: That's an interesting question, Paul.

From time to time, a person does kind of philosophize in their own mind. For a while, when we finally got to Australia, I would, from time to time, reflect on the fact that that period from December the eighth until we got to Australia, was a period in which there wasn't a day went by but almost all of us made some decision that was vital to our living or dying; and we did that damn near every day.

We weren't conscious of it at the time we were doing it so much as mostly reacting. We just reacted, but you had to go one way or the other--take one fork of the road or the other. And, you know, particularly in Java, when, again, we went through the same damn thing as the Philippines. I was more conscious at the time of making decisions--not planning them out so much, but in realizing at the time, and shortly after the fact, that, "Boy, if I hadn't done so-and-so and so-and-so, I'd be a gone duck right now."

I can't really say there's a precise cause-and-effect relationship, but I've been involved in a number of things-- and in fairly recent years, 20 or 30 years, in which I kind of felt like it was kind of a payback. I've been pretty heavily involved in quote good works unquote such as the Cancer Society and in the community here, in the church and all. I was elected president of the Glen Carlyn Civic Association a few years ago, and I have been senior warden of St. John's Episcopal Church here in the village for about the last 20 or so years.

I've been sort of more conscious on a day-by-day basis that I'm pretty damn lucky to be here. Any dues that I pay now would not be wasted. Of course, my wife sometimes feels like I spend too much time with the Cancer Society and other aspects of it. I hadn't realized until almost right this second, Paul, there's not a specific relationship, but I'm sort of aware--and have been aware for a long time--that I'm a lucky son of a gun. If I want to get reminded of it, I go upstairs and read my obituary again.*

A guy called me up last night from the West Coast--a high school classmate of mine--and we stay in touch. He said, "By the way, I was looking over some old reunion literature the other day. I remember seeing that you were deceased." At one reunion they had me listed in all the paperwork as "Cecil King, deceased."

Q: Maybe this payback thing has been a subconscious thing with you, but very real, nonetheless.

Mr. King: I think that's exactly right. It is, because I don't think I've done anything in the Cancer Society, or church, or whatever, that was a conscious effort to pay back. But there's been maybe a need on my part to pay back a little bit, and I'm very happy about that.

Q: What other themes do you have in your notes?

Mr. King: One incident that I wanted to maybe cover again a little bit was the time when I phoned back home from Java,

---

*Mr. King's obituary was published in a newspaper in 1942 after the <u>Houston</u> was sunk and he was erroneously reported as being missing and presumed dead.

and at the time when I was supposed to have been dead. My mother--like all mothers, I suppose, to some extent--was very much uptight when the war started with three of her sons in the Philippines and all the stuff going on. Dad told me later on that she just really wasn't much good at anything at that time.

So when I was reported killed, I guess this just kind of confirmed what she had been feeling. And so when I called back--and I had no reason to call back, except I got this availability on the phone, and at the time I found out from the operator back home that Dad had taken my mother to Mexico, because she just needed to get away from things. So they finally were able to locate her. I guess the impression that I had was that when I was reported killed, that she just really knew that in advance. It didn't come as that much of a surprise.

My mother was always a person who, to some extent, was inclined to make something out of a situation that was not really there, in terms of the effect it had on her. What I'm trying to say is that, for example, when I was killed, right away she got a "gold-star-mother" placard to put in the window.* My dad is exactly the opposite. He was sort of taciturn and very much introverted type of person. He kept his emotions to himself, and my mother didn't.

---

*During World War II, families of servicemen hung a blue star in the front window for each son on active duty. If a son was killed, a gold star was substituted for the blue.

So I felt at the time, when I called up and realized that I was supposed to have been dead--I felt then a kind of sensation myself of--it put a kind of dream-like quality over the experiences of those past several months as if I-- maybe I was dead, that sort of thing. It was kind of strange to try to put it in words, but it gave me a very strange feeling, which I had for some little time, which sometimes was sort of saying, "Am I alive or dead?"

Q: It would have been interesting to read her thoughts when she took down that gold star and put a blue one back up.

Mr. King: Yes.

Also, they had a kind of wake of all my high school class during that period of time when I was reported killed. My mother got one of these memory books, like an autograph book. Each kid in the class would write down I was a good guy, or whatever, and that sort of thing. She kept that over the years. In fact, I don't know whatever happened to it, to tell you the truth. But she was very much aware of the fact that this was kind of a distinction--a melancholy distinction--to have a son who had given his life for his country.

Q: Your mother's reaction really sounds the opposite of what I've heard in so many cases of that--denial. The report comes in of a death of a son and a mother just refuses to believe it.

Mr. King: She kind of went in the opposite direction for whatever strange psychological reason, and that was unusual.

Q: Did you find that your relationship with her had changed after you came back from the dead?

Mr. King: Well, I don't know. I was not that close. After I joined the Navy, I kind of cut the umbilical--not in a hostile or negative sense. I really had a new family in the Navy, although I didn't cast my old one aside there. Far from it. But there was a definite change in my relationship with my family. Not my brothers so much, because they were a part of the Navy too, but my mother and dad. I have to stress the fact that it wasn't hostile or negative, but there was a different relationship, and I noticed that more and more over the years.

Q: I saw an interesting letter in one of the advice columns in a newspaper recently: "Parents, don't complain if your children don't call or write frequently. You've made them self-sufficient, as you tried to do."

Mr. King: I can understand that.

We four boys were home at one time after the war--or maybe it was before, I've lost track of time. My dad was just busting proud of these four sons of his. When we were home and all at one time, all four of us--he had to have some coffee. In Texas, coffee's kind of a ritual, and that's where you go on any occasion, go down and have a cup of coffee at the cafe. So we had to go down and get a cup of coffee, and my dad was going down the street here with his four boys in behind him, all in uniform, and he would wave to this guy and wave to that guy. He was a very undemonstrative person, but he was really enjoying that moment.

Q: This is an exception.

Mr. King: It was an exception, very much so.

Q: Well, as you sort of pointed out in your preface, there was an ability to have emotional satisfaction then that wasn't possible for Korea or Vietnam, when we hadn't won the victory.

Mr. King: Yes, that is something that in recent years I think more and more of. We in the service enjoyed a tremendous benefit, because we really felt like the whole country was just 100% in behind us. The patriotic songs:

"Praise the Lord and Pass the Ammunition," and "Rosie the Riveter," and all of these things that went on were sort of continuing support mechanisms. I was very much aware of that, and I thought that confirmed everything that I had ever thought about the service: "Okay, now here we are in the war. We're the boys in blue, and the civilian population is behind us 100%." They were buying war bonds--all that sort of thing. I just thought that was wonderful.

Q: Was there any sense of letdown when you had to get back to the more mundane tasks and some of this patriotic fervor wore off?

Mr. King: Well, you know, that's another difference between Vietnam, for example, and World War II, where there was actually some hostility at that time between the population and the Navy. You know, kids going to Canada, and all that sort of thing, which is foreign to me; I never could understand that sort of thing. I guess I was a product of my times. But when I got back and the war was over, I never felt like I was owed anything--far from it.

I mean, I felt like we had a chance to pay our dues to Uncle Sam, and that was great. I suppose there were World War II veterans, after the fact, who felt like their country owed them more than they were getting, and that sort of thing. But I sure never felt that way. I think that's a mark of the career service person. I think that really is, just kind of comes with the territory, so to speak.

Q: Well, you'd had this great motivation to beat the enemy. How do you keep yourself motivated when that threat is no longer there?

Mr. King: Oh, I think at one time after the war was over--I must have had around 12 years' service in by that time--I toyed with the idea of leaving the service, but I was never serious about it. I think that was just talk. I knew at the time that I wasn't really serious about it. But I put on a pretty good front, you know: "People make money on the outside now, and here we are working for peanuts. I'm going to go out and get a job." I didn't really mean it--not for a second.

Q: You passed a threshold at some point, without even realizing it. You said when you went to the Portland, it was this strange new world. After a while the outside gets to be the strange different world.

Mr. King: That's right, that's right. It does indeed. I passed a demarcation line there some time after the war in which all of a sudden I realized in my own mind that I was career Navy for better or for worse. I enjoyed it, and I just all of a sudden accepted the fact that I was in, that that was it, no question about it. And I felt good about that. Everything just kind of fell into place.

Not that I wasn't a gung-ho sailor up till that time, but I guess you pass a point there when you hit around 10, 12 years in the service where you go through some kind of stage in your own mind and you realize and accept it. You're either glad about it, or else you go around feeling sorry for yourself all the time. But I felt very glad about it. In fact, I would never have left the Navy if it hadn't been for my wife, because I really enjoyed every bit of it. But I knew that she was right. In raising our kids, we had to have some more income.

Q: There's a story about the chief that encounters some griping sailor on the fantail, and he says, "Kid, if you don't like the Navy, just do your 20 years and get out."

Mr. King: [Laughter] Yes. Well, that's a good point. I remember, also, during the war we would talk about this, that one of these days the lights are going to go on. They're going to go on again all over the world and it'll be a great big, beautiful world. There won't be any problems, and that sort of thing. I never felt bitterly disappointed. I mean, because I think any person with a practical turn of mind has to realize that the world's going to go on, war or no war, and there will be world wars and other conflicts.

The other thing that came to mind when I was reviewing the transcripts was that I think that what I said about Admiral Tom Moorer could have been misconstrued. I think he was the pilot in that PBY that spotted us when we were going into Celebes. And at that time the _Peary_ had a jury bow. I think 20 or 30 feet of the bow had been cut off in collision with the _Pillsbury_ just before the war.

This jury bow changed her silhouette. And, also, we consciously added to that, when we made the suicide run out of Corregidor by stringing canvas between the stacks, to break up that four-stacker silhouette. With palm leaves all over the topside, we were hardly recognizable as a Navy destroyer. And from whatever distance Admiral Moorer--if that really was him--to see us going into a port that was on fire at the time and being invaded by the Japanese, I think that would be a natural reaction to have a little problem identifying us. So I would not want these pages to reflect that I had any kind of a negative feeling about Admiral Moorer, because I think he is just one of the greatest admirals in his own way. He's not, maybe, as famous as a Mitscher, or a McCain, or a Halsey, but at the same time, I think just as a solid Navy admiral, he's a great man. So I wouldn't want anybody to think that what I said about his spotting us and maybe reporting us as a Japanese--some kind of a Japanese craft was a thing that I felt bad about.

Q: Would you assign any degree of probability or certainty to the fact that it was he?

Mr. King: I read that it was he in one of these Navy magazines.* A lot of it had to do with Admiral Moorer and when he was in Patrol Wing Ten--Wagner's outfit out in the Philippines and flying PBYs.** But I got the impression then that it was Admiral Moorer who was the one that spotted us. Also, it's my impression that when we were on that island of Ternate, where we spent a couple days, that he was the pilot that flew in and brought us some critical supplies for patching up the Peary--some rudder cables and stuff like that.

I've seen Admiral Moorer once or twice or maybe more over the years when I was in the Pentagon. It was my impression then, as it is now, that he also had that mystical feeling about those days in the Asiatic Fleet. He probably remembers them with much affection, as most of us do who went through them.

Q: Did you have occasion to talk with him then?

---

*The article cited by Mr. King was Clarke Van Vleet, "South Pacific Saga," Naval Aviation News, February 1977, pages 32-37. It indicates Lieutenant Moorer was then flying a PBY in Patrol Wing Ten but does not specify that he made an attack on King's ship.
**Captain Frank D. Wagner, USN, Commander Patrol Wing Ten.

Mr. King: I've talked to him briefly once or twice, not nearly as much as I'd like to, because I guess I never had the chance to tell him to his face. I wrote him a couple letters at different times, when he made decisions on the Joint Chiefs of Staff--I'm a great letter writer. But I wrote him a couple times, as I have done Senator McCain, because I worked for Senator McCain's grandfather, J. S. McCain, down at Coco Solo in the Thirties.* And then when I was in the Pentagon, his dad was Chinfo, and I used to talk to him from time to time.** I'd bump into him around the building, and we would tell grandfather stories about his grandfather. He loved to do that. And then his son, Senator McCain, was captured in Vietnam. I've written him a couple of times about his dad and his grandfather.

Q: What are your impressions of his dad, the Chinfo admiral?

Mr. King: I don't have the impression of him that I had of his father. In talking to him, he seemed to be a guy of some substance, but he just seemed to have a quieter nature than his dad did. He was sort of soft-spoken, and I had a

---
*Captain John S. McCain III, USN (Ret.), became a U.S. senator from Arizona in 1987.
**Rear Admiral John S. McCain, Jr., USN, served as the Navy's Chief of Information (Chinfo) in 1962-63. He eventually retired as a four-star admiral.

very favorable impression of him. He seemed to be a man of self-possession in a quiet way, kind of understated, if you know what I mean. But I never had much feeling for him in the factual sense of his performance. I mean, I never did know that, you know, that he was the greatest Chinfo, or whatever. I just didn't have that kind of feeling for the guy.

Q: Well, he has the reputation of being a great exponent of sea power, giving a lot of presentations and talking for hours at the drop of a hat, which sort of is at variance with your impressions of him.

Mr. King: Well, I guess, maybe on the podium it might be one thing, and then over a cup of coffee, it might be something else again.

Q: I see.

Mr. King: Well, no, he was not an Arleigh Burke. I mean, there was never any doubt around Arleigh Burke how he stood on anything.

Q: That's for sure.
What other items do you have in your notes?

Mr. King: I guess, again, in reading through them, it's a kind of feeling where I could take any point, or any incident, and dwell on it, but I did not feel in reflection, in going over the three sets of documents, that there was anything of substance left out. There are many areas where I could expound on this, that, and the other, and probably tell a few sea stories. And, I guess, that's really what I probably should be doing instead of the kind of reflection that I'm doing right now.

But I do feel like it does represent a fairly complete broad-brush picture of those years that I lived through in the Navy.

Q: Well, if there are any revealing sea stories that occur to you now, this is certainly the opportunity to include them.

Mr. King: I don't think I saw in the transcript anything about our robbery on the <u>Midway</u>, where the crap game was held up.

Q: I don't recall that.

Mr. King: It caused quite a bit of talk at the time.

We were at sea in the Med and were going into port the next morning. It was a payday, and on paydays on most large ships--on the _Midway_, for example--there'd be nickel-and-dime crap games and card games around the ship during the day. The winners of a group would get together and play each other. That night there'd be one game going on, and that's where the big money was.

So there was a crap game going on up in the 02 level somewhere. Not every guy on board ship gambles. So the high rollers were in this one crap game, which was at the very height. A young sailor--appeared to be young--with a neckerchief across his face and a white hat pulled over his eyes and with a Beretta pistol in his hand, gave the secret knock, and so they let him in. He came in with this gun and said, "I want it all."

At first they thought he was kidding, but then they quickly realized--he was nervous and his hand was shaking with the gun, and that scared the bejesus out of some of these guys. You know, if you want to be held up, you want to be held up by somebody that knows what they're doing and not scared to death. He had a bag of some kind, a soft bag, and he just went around taking the money from people and putting it in the bag. The guy completed the robbery, and then he said, "If anybody moves or comes out the hatch, I'm going to shoot them," and he left. They did wait for a couple minutes, and then all hell broke loose, and they all went out looking for the guy and calling for the chief master-at-arms.

There was a sidelight to the incident where one of our warrant officer's mess stewards was owed about a hundred dollars by a guy who was involved in the game, and, as a matter of fact, was way ahead at the time of the robbery. Our steward got the word that this other guy was holding a bundle and went up to collect. Sure enough, when he got to the game, his friend was rolling in it and had tens and twenties between the fingers of both hands. It was like "when you're hot, you're hot." Our steward went up and braced him for his debt and the guy counted it out and handed it right over. Our steward was just recounting it when the robber came in and took the whole works, including our fellow's hundred.

Our guy was not too happy about this, as you can imagine, and the next day he came to me in the warrant officers' mess to complain about the turn of events, but about all I could tell him was, "When you're not, you're not." He said, "I had the money, but now I don't have it. What can I do?"

I said, "There's not a damn thing you can do. I'm sorry about that, but you were paid off fair and square."

This was out at sea, and you would think that a robbery conducted on board a naval ship out at sea would be fairly easy to solve. But they never did get this guy, never did. The next day when we hit the beach, they held up liberty for a while, and then some ONI people came aboard--civilians--

and we had really a substantial investigation under way.* I was personnel officer at the time; I was involved in it. There was some speculation as to who the guy was, but he got away clean.

ComSixthFlt was some kind of upset.** He sent us a real snotty dispatch of some kind--remarked on the fact that if we get too busy getting robbed or robbing each other, why not think about acting more like a carrier or something like that. It was really a sarcastic dispatch.

Q: I'm sort of amused that the command--and higher than the command obviously--would take such an interest in it. Some might feel, well, these gamblers got what they deserved, because what they were doing was illegal.

Mr. King: That was not a hidden emotion. But, I guess, to the authority you don't have a robbery on board ship. But there was some feeling that these guys that were shooting craps did get what they had coming to them.

Q: Would you remember about when that happened?

Mr. King: Let's see, that was on the Midway. It was somewhere in the early 1950s. I suppose there's a rather substantial record of it somewhere.

---
*ONI--Office of Naval Intelligence.
**ComSixthFlt--Commander Sixth Fleet.

We had this exec, Carlyle Ingram--we called him the "Red Raider"--and that was his moment of glory.* He was going to solve it, no matter what, and so he got me to work with him, and we would interview people and that sort of thing. We got the chief master-at-arms involved in it. The exec thought that that kind of investigation would be fruitful, whereas the ONI people didn't know what they were doing. But we didn't really make much headway out of it.

Q: Well, that's a good story. Have you more?

Mr. King: Well, let's see, this chief master-at-arms named Harris was quite a character. We called him sheriff, as most chief masters-at-arms are called. He was a little guy, physically--very small guy, but he was one of the most powerful men that I ever ran into in carrying out his job. One time he got wind that some sailor on the ship had a Beretta pistol in his locker. So the sheriff went to him and took him back to the sheriff's room and said, "I know what you've got in your locker, and I want to give you a chance to get rid of it without any trouble. So let's you and I go down to your locker, and you get that stuff out of there, and then we'll go up topside and throw it over the side."

He had this capacity for being totally credible. He

---
*Commander Carlyle Ingram, USN.

and the sailor went to the guy's locker. The sheriff said, "I'm going to turn my head while you do this, but you get that stuff out of your locker." So he turned around and this fellow then took a couple of seconds or whatever, and then the sheriff took him up topside and he said, "Now throw it over the side." The sheriff told me it rained pistols for about the next two minutes. The guy must have had an arsenal in his locker. He said he threw pistols over--pistols and pistols.

Q: Wonder what he had in mind with all that.

Mr. King: I don't know, probably buying and selling.

Q: There could be an argument made that that system of discipline was more effective than the one with all the lawyers involved.

Mr. King: Oh, it worked with him.

Another incident that I remembered--we had a case where there was a fellow who would go around at night, taking money out of guys' clothes. A lot of sailors would, when they'd go to bed at night, just get in the old rack and hang their clothes up. So this guy was taking easy money. The ONI was called in and they got this fluorescent powder, that fluoresces under ultraviolet light.

They took a guy who agreed to do this--sort of a shill--and he came back and he acted drunk, and he was singing and staggering, and finally got in his bunk and dropped his wallet on the floor, and picked it up and counted the money very loudly. He stuck it back in his pocket and took off his clothes, and made a lot of commotion.

So, sure enough, this guy came tiptoeing down the passageway and got the wallet, looked in it, and put it back in his pocket and went on off. As soon as he got about 30 feet away, they broke out this ultraviolet light, and, gosh, I mean that stuff just really turned to fire under ultraviolet light. So they quickly caught up with this guy and he was just covered with it, because that powder just gets all over you. So they just put this light on him, and he just turned to flame and there wasn't a damn thing he could do. So that solved that case very quickly.

Q: One of the other disciplinary situations that comes up is the presence on board ships of homosexuals. How much were you aware of that as personnel officer?

Mr. King: We had a couple of cases on the <u>Hornet</u>. There was a mess cook in the chiefs' mess, but no one really knew whether he was putting on an act or not. But he acted very feminine, and would go down to the rag locker and find women's underwear and put them on and go around the ship. He was kind of a comedian, but, nonetheless, he was definitely homosexual. He was caught in the act, and they just transferred him off the ship, because that was on the <u>Hornet</u> during wartime.

We knew there were homosexuals on board ship, but I don't ever recall a situation where it got aggravated. I mean, it was kind of a live-and-let-live situation. There wasn't that many of them that it was a problem. If there were one or two of them around, I guess whatever they did was not accepted, but the command didn't make a federal rap of it, you might say.

Q: It sounds as if they were discreet.

Mr. King: I think they were discreet, and I think it was not the kind of a situation where people felt it had a terribly high priority at that time because I think in combat you may tolerate things like that.

I remember a homosexual case when I was in Panama in 1937 or '38. That caused a tremendous amount of publicity down there. It was a first class aviation metalsmith. He was given a general court-martial on the scene and reduced to apprentice seaman and sent to the naval prison at Portsmouth, New Hampshire. That just caused a sensation.

Q: That's a pretty severe reaction, certainly in light of what we hear about today.

Mr. King: That was a terribly severe reaction. I think that on just about every ship I was ever on, there was probably knowledge--maybe not specific in every case--but there was knowledge that there were queers in the Navy. But it was never anything that I ever felt was really a problem in the numerical sense. What they did after hours that didn't cause any problems, you know, live and let live, I suppose.

Q: Probably the source of a fair amount of joking.

Mr. King: Oh, yes. That was the kind of a situation where it was really a pragmatic approach to life, where you didn't approve of it or condone it necessarily, but you didn't get terribly upset about the idea.

Q: I remember an interview I had with an officer who served in a battleship in the Thirties. After I had asked all my questions, I said, "What question haven't I asked that I should have?"

He said, "You haven't asked me how 1,000 people could live together in a space about 600 feet long." He said, "Everybody knew his own place in the hierarchy, and he didn't pay attention to things that he shouldn't."

Mr. King: [Laughter] That's a good way to put it.

There was a fair amount of humor about the situation. For example, a guy would say in a joking way to a shipmate, "You'd be safe in the chiefs' quarters of a Turkish battleship." You know, that kind of thing. But the people just sort of, as I said, just let it go. I never knew of any overt hostility, where anyone would get beat up for that reason.

Q: But, certainly, there were cases of that in the civilian world.

Mr. King: Oh, yes, even today you read about things like these so-called skinheads that go around bashing homosexuals. But it's a far cry from today's social world than it was to the military life back in the Thirties and Forties and Fifties.

Q: Going back to a topic we raised before the tape started, what are your recollections of the racial situation throughout your naval career?

Mr. King: In the Thirties and on through the war, to some extent, there was not a racial problem in a sense that it was a high-visibility, or high-profile, problem. In the Thirties every colored person that I knew in the Navy was either mess attendant or steward.

Then during the war, of course, this gradually began to crumble, and we saw more and more of the racial problem--not being a problem per se, but just being sort of fading back. I knew of individuals who were reluctant to accept this.

But in retrospect, I don't recall any real situation where it got to be a problem per se. It was just a gradual acceptance of the facts of life. And then after the war--by that time, we were moving pretty rapidly in the opposite direction. But I really don't recall a single case of overt racism, as such. The Navy's always been to some extent a kind of live-and-let-live situation, I mean to accept the inevitable. If a guy did feel negative, I don't know what you're going to do.

Q: Well, the Navy has been slower than the other services in integrating.

Another aspect of that, say, in the Thirties, the early Forties, you saw black individuals who just didn't have a very wide span of opportunity, not because of ability but simply skin color. Was that a thing you even reflected on or even thought about?

Mr. King: No--I'm being personal now--I never reflected too

much on that problem. Being involved in personnel in all those years, I was aware of the fact that we were seeing sort of a sea change in the Navy. But it was something that I, myself, personally, had no strong feelings about. I mean, I was raised in Texas, where we had a color line. It was probably more Hispanic than black, but there was definitely a line. Boy, in the part of Texas where I was raised up, there was no question about it. But I guess my own personal philosophy, there was never a problem in accepting the inevitable. I've always been able to accept the inevitable.

I don't ever recall a problem connected with my duties in which that was a problem. I don't ever recall any sense of frustration or having any kind of a problem in my work, that that was a part of. It just gradually began to be a fact of life.

Q: It sounds as if you accepted both the segregation, and then when it came, you accepted the integration.

Mr. King: I guess, in the same sense, I did, yes. In reflection, right now I can think that to some extent I realize the injustice of it when it was going on. But at the same time I think I, having been a product of that period of time, that I also realize there wasn't a hell of a lot that I could do about it. That's the way it was then.

Q: You accepted that, probably, just the same way you accepted that boatswain's mates are the guys that handle the lines and blow the boatswain's call.

Mr. King: All a part of the game, yes, all a part of the game.

So, no, I guess that's something that I haven't looked back on in retrospect up until this very moment, in terms of an objective look at it. It was never a real problem to me.

Q: What other topics do you have from your notes?

Mr. King: You asked a while ago about the CNOs that I worked for starting out with, I guess, Fechteler and then Carney and then Burke.

These were, like in so many cases, three different men entirely in their modus operandi, in their personality, and that sort of business. But I don't recall anything that would be suitable material for an authoritative biography of these three guys. I just recall working for them at the time, and being exposed to them in the sense that I was, which was not a direct relationship. I guess it was more with Admiral Burke than with Carney or Fechteler.

Fechteler was not a distant man, but in my relationship with the three of them, I felt like Carney was more of the human being. There was absolutely no question about Burke. I mean, when you worked for Arleigh Burke, he removed all doubt.

But Carney, I felt, had more of a personal ego--a sense of himself. Fechteler was more of an objective guy. But Carney came across to me as more of a human being. He had this guy Herb Carroll who'd been with him since the year one. Herb was really his window to the outside world in a personal sense. Herb did all of his personal work and that sort of thing. Any intercourse that I had with Admiral Carney, in any kind of an official sense, went through Herb Carroll, which was all right, because Herb was a nice guy; I liked Herb, got along fine with him.

Q: The problem that I could see with that from Admiral Carney's standpoint is that you get yourself relying on this one limited source of information. There may be other things that you should be hearing that don't come through that conduit.

Mr. King: Exactly. But he really trusted Herb implicitly, and if anything came up that there was the slightest doubt about, well, Herb's view was the one that he listened to. I don't mean in terms of moving fleets around or that sort of thing; I just mean in the day-to-day activities of the office, that sort of thing.

Q: He sounds like a useful sounding board for Admiral Carney, to try out his ideas on somebody he can trust.

Mr. King: Or maybe some guy that maybe Carney didn't know all that well down in OP--whatever it was, he might say to Herb, "What about So-and-so down there? What's the word up and down the passageways?" and that kind of thing.

Q: Did you at any time serve as this sort of sounding board in the front office? Did you get asked, say, what would be an enlisted perspective on this issue?

Mr. King: I guess not. That wasn't part of my makeup. There are standards, and I would not, I don't think, under any circumstances, prattle about things to a senior officer who might have a direct interest in them. I just wouldn't do it, and I guess that might come through in an evaluation of my personality.

Q: Well, you would if you were asked. Are you saying that you weren't asked?

Mr. King: I guess I would if asked, but at the same time, I'm not sure how complete an answer I would give. I don't believe that most of the senior officers that I knew fairly well and respected would ask that kind of a question, if you know what I'm trying to say. I don't think they would ask that kind of question.

On the other hand, I was always astonished--right up to the day I left the Navy, I was always astonished at how much they really knew. How they came by that, I don't know. But I was always astonished that they knew of things that I thought were pretty well kept under the covers.

Q: Do you have an example?

Mr. King: Well, I guess it was in personnel work where a case might arise to where an individual is involved in something that maybe is not necessarily shady per se, but brings a certain amount of attention. If this came up in a mast situation, and I might in a perfectly straightforward evaluation say so and so now--"this guy's been known to"--then the exec I was talking to might expound on that: "Yes, not only that but"--you know. So somehow, by osmosis or whatever, most good senior officers really have a feel for what's going on in their command, a lot more so than the rank and file would believe. Where they get that, I don't know. Whether it's just their own perspicacity or their own sensitivity or their own--or maybe the wardroom talk is such that that stuff does get around more than we would think it does, that kind of thing.

Q: Did you ever encounter some senior officer who was so obtuse that he thought he knew it all, when, in fact, there were many things he didn't know but should have?

Mr. King: That sounds like a familiar pattern, but I'm trying to think of an example.

I don't guess I recall a specific example at the flag level. I've known a couple of senior officers at flag level or chief of staff four-striper, or something like that, who let their own ego get in the way of knowledge. I think I can remember cases where they wouldn't pick up on something just simply because of their lack of sensitivity to all aspects of the situation. And it seems to me my feeling about that is that it came up in kind of an ego sense of the word. They felt like, "Well, they can't pull the wool over my eyes," or something like that.

So I was more sensitive to the cases where I felt like, "Boy, that guy really knows what's going on," than realizing that some guy was kind of a dunderhead really and wondered how the hell he ever made flag rank in the first place.

Q: Well, it speaks well of the officer corps of that period that you did form that impression, that they did know their business very well.

Mr. King: Yes. I guess that to some degree is a function of the times, of that period of time and the size of the Navy. You know, I think the smaller the Navy, the more intense the relationship gets in that sort of situation to where there's more reliance on the individual, on a smaller ship with a smaller crew. On a destroyer, for example, there are no strangers. Not only the skipper and the exec and everybody else, but there are no real secrets on a destroyer. On the other hand, on a carrier, on a big carrier like the Midway or FDR, hell, some of them might as well be Eskimos as far as really knowing the rank and file of the crew. But, again, at the same time, it must be pointed out that on a 3,000-man ship, there's probably less than 50 people who go to mast all the time.

Q: I think you made that point before.

Mr. King: Yes. The vast majority maybe are not all great human beings or models of behavior, but the people that get in trouble are the same ones that get in trouble over and over again. The people that are inclined to mess up, mess up over and over again, and they get to be known.

Q: I think if we were drawing a comparison between today's Navy and the one that you joined 50-some years ago, in that time there was much less inclination for people to challenge authority than there is now.

Mr. King: There was not only no inclination, there was no opportunity. I accepted the Navy in its totality. I mean, I was in the military, and every officer got the old salute, and that was just the way it was. I accepted it, not in an obsequious sense or anything, but I realized that I was in a military outfit, and we had guns on the ship and we used them. I really felt strongly about that. I would no more have challenged the authority of an officer than I would have flown to the moon. I was a gung-ho sailor.

Q: One officer who has gotten notice as being something less than completely pragmatic was the first skipper of the Hornet, Miles Browning. Did you have any dealings with him?

Mr. King: I had dealings with him in the sense of his being the skipper of the Hornet, and that being a period in which we were going to take the Hornet to sea and to combat. As such, I think you pay more attention to your skipper than you do in peacetime. But Miles Browning was sort of a spectacular individual. He created a tension, and--for better or for worse--he was the captain of the Hornet.

I guess it was when we actually left the West Coast headed for the combat zone that I began to have the feeling about Browning that he might be too much of a good thing. I just began to get the feeling that he would do anything in the world that he wanted to without regard to the outside world. While I was as anxious to win the war as anybody, and I didn't have any real misgivings about the guy, you never knew from one day to the next what kind of an order he might put out.

Q: Did the crew, in your recollection, have a sense of relief when he was taken off the ship?

Mr. King: I think that probably was the case, Paul. I get the feeling that it was an accepted thing that he wouldn't last all that long. When he left it didn't surprise many people, I guess. The skippers we had after him--Sample, for example--were so different in their personalities, and the Hornet was so involved. I mean, we were really a combat ship. We were at GQ more than we were not. So I think a little easier hand on the reins was probably accepted pretty well by the ship. Because on a carrier in combat, you're pretty close to the core. So I think a little easier hand on the helm is accepted a lot better rather than all these gyrations.

Q: Practically any hand would have been easier at that point.

Mr. King: Yes. He was a definite personality.

Also, I'm not sure about how much coloration he carried over from Halsey was actually the case or not. I mean, he kind of rode along on the fact that he was his chief of staff and everything; ergo, he could do no wrong at anything, and that sort of business.

Q: I think he had that sort of personality even before he had encountered Halsey, at least to my knowledge.

Mr. King: Yes, but another thing is that, given the situation, given the combat, given all the other wartime--the aspects of wartime life--you don't spend that much time worrying about your skipper's personality. At least, I didn't. I guess it's factual to say that there was a problem, but given everything else going on, okay.

Q: Well, it would have a different impact at different levels. If the air group commander and three or four squadron commanders got fired, they'd definitely have a problem with that sort of personality.

Mr. King: Oh, yes. And the closer you got to the boiler, the more heat you felt, sure. My role on the Hornet as regards to the skipper was such that I didn't have that much necessity for being involved with him. You know, the personnel officer is the exec--that's the guy that I worked with. Also, we spent so damn much time in GQ or I-A or whatever, that there was really not that much time--I mean there were priorities that took place. You know, if you're out in GQ with a combat situation and an actual battle going on around you, you don't spend a heck of a lot of time on abstract problems of the ship. At least I didn't.

Q: Going to another philosophical area, what are your feelings about just the business of going to sea?

Mr. King: Well, you know, Paul, I guess I had more time at sea than most any other chief yeoman in the Navy. That was really because I enjoyed every damn day that I was ever at sea--not enjoyed it in the sense that it was an obsession or anything. But I just felt comfortable on board a ship. I did when I went into the Navy. The ratio for shore duty to sea duty would be, in the case of a boilerman or something like that, maybe six years at sea for two years ashore. It varied with every rate. For yeomen, it was more like two and three--two at sea and three ashore. Something like that for the Navy sea-shore rotation. And at that time foreign duty counted as sea duty for purposes of rotation, but, anyway, the first shore duty that I had as shore duty was Naval Air Station Minneapolis, something like ten years after I shipped into the Navy in '34.

C. S. King #4 - 398

But I figured I was in the Navy to go to sea, and that's where I belonged. My personal feeling was that I loved sea duty.

Q: Was there an esthetic quality of it that appealed to you?

Mr. King: Oh, as we were getting under way, I used to find I would get a big bang out of hearing the boatswain's mate say, "Okay, fellows, let's get out of here and get some land stink blown off of us." That was the Navy to me.

Also, on a destroyer, to go back to the fantail off watch and just sit around with a cup of coffee and watch the water go by. I could do that by the hour, just like watching TV, I suppose, today. I just felt at home on the sea. I really did. I felt like that's what the Navy's all about. It's not that I didn't enjoy liberty or anything like that. On the contrary. I guess nobody ever hit the Navy that enjoyed liberty as much as I did. But I just felt like the Navy was sea duty, and that's where I belonged.

Q: My favorite time of day on board ship was in the evening as the sun was going down.

Mr. King: Yes.

Q: I enjoyed being out on deck, and I just don't have that feeling on land.

Mr. King: Yes. Then you know exactly what I'm saying. And on carriers like--well, the Hornet, the Princeton--all of them, I was many times just wandering around the ship, particularly in late afternoon, just enjoying being there. Go over to the deck edge elevator and stand there and watch the ocean going by. Also, I enjoyed very much going to different parts of the ship to see how they did things. I liked to go up on the bow and watch them drop anchor, or take it up, that sort of thing. That's impressive to lift the damn anchor--the size of that thing. I had a battle station on one destroyer, main engine control on the Davis when I was in the logroom.

I always liked to wander around the ship and see what's going on. I felt good about that.

Q: What can you say about the times in which you lived and served in the Navy?

Mr. King: Well, I thought about that, Paul; I thought about it recently, because in April this year I had a malignant tumor of the colon removed. When this kind of thing happens, it brings out your philosophical side of you. I mean, you reflect about things like that. Next month I'm going to have another bout of surgery--not that problem, but it's an aneurism of the aorta. While that's not necessarily life-threatening, it does put you in a philosophical mood, if you know what I'm trying to say.

So, against that background, I feel like I'm probably one of the luckiest people in the entire world. First, for having been born in the year that I was, so I was at the proper age to be able to fight for my country in World War II; and secondly, this whole era that I've lived through is something that I just feel real privileged to have gone through, and having been involved in it to the extent that I was--in the Navy and in the Atomic Energy Commission and so on, and in the Cancer Society.

And also, to some extent, World War II was a kind of justification of my feelings. That is to say, I always felt that the United States Navy was the greatest outfit in the world--all these corny things. I really felt it deeply, and I don't ever recall a twinge of fear in the Asiatic Fleet as the war got closer or when it actually happened. And that might have been maybe even bordering on stupid in some ways, but that's just the way that I am.

So I felt after the war started like there was only one outcome possible: we were going to beat the living bejesus out of the Japs. I just knew that in my heart and soul. During all the ups and downs of the first days of the war and the <u>Peary</u> and getting out of Java and all that stuff,

C. S. King #4 - 401

the main thing in my mind was, "We're going to get those bastards one of these days, and we're going to get them good." I accepted that like I accept Notre Dame and the New York Yankees and things like that. I mean, that's a given.

So later on, when I was on the Hornet, and we were doing exactly that, that didn't necessarily surprise me. I just felt good about it. I thought, "All right, I knew we were going to do it, and by God, we're going to do it; we're going to beat their tails off." A lot of people aren't that lucky to have this kind of a feeling come true. I mean, a lot of people have their worst fears confirmed some day. But for a person to feel as strongly as I did and do about the United States Navy, and had it come out this way, is just like Hollywood and the Marines come up over the horizon in the last reel. That's what I really feel good about.

So, all in all, it just sounds like a recruiting poster or something, but that's the way I feel and I've enjoyed very much putting these few words down with your help. It's been something that I had wanted to do in my own mind, but I never would have done it. Oh, my son and my wife keep on me, but I mean, now I've done it and I feel awfully good about that. I owe you a big vote of thanks, Paul, for your help in this because you certainly have been able to prod me on. But, anyway, I guess my benediction words would be, "I've been a lucky guy."

Q: Well, it's a privilege for me to meet somebody with such an outlook on life; just to illustrate, you sent me a note after you had the cancer surgery. You said you no longer had a colon, you had a semicolon, so you find the humor in anything. Also, just to comment on the payback business. You said that maybe the work with the Cancer Society and so forth was a payback for the fact that you'd been given more years. Well, maybe there's a payback in the other way in that you've survived this thing because you gave some effort yourself to the cause.

I have enjoyed this. On behalf of the Naval Institute, I'm grateful for the effort you've put into this, because this will be a legacy for the future.

Mr. King: Well, I thank you.

Appendix

U.S.S. BOISE

January 10, 1942.

C-O-N-F-I-D-E-N-T-I-A-L

MEMORANDUM FOR: Commander in Chief, U.S. ASIATIC FLEET.

Subject: Narrative of Events.

1. The following narrative of events is submitted for whatever it may be worth. The information is not guaranteed to be accurate in every detail, but is based on my own observation and from reports which are believed to be fairly reliable. I shall attempt to give a chronological record of events which have occurred from the time I left you until the present.

December 25, 1941.

The Flag personnel who were on the Torpedo Boat when you left went to Corregidor. Arrival was after dark. Men were assigned to tunnels in which to sleep.

December 26, 1941.

I reported to Tunnel QUEEN and made preliminary assignment of personnel to the various activities as directed by the Commandant and other competent authority. Word was received from Commander Dennison that Admiral Rockwell intended to release one Destroyer, and possibly two, for transportation south. PEARY was designated and I was directed to submit the names of enlisted men to make the trip. KING, Y1c, and myself were selected to go plus five radiomen who were to be volunteers. Upon muster, it was found that all were volunteers so the "name in the hat" system was used to designate the remainder of the contingent. It developed that the men would be: Ensigns GILLILAND and HIRST, U.S.N.R., BOAZ, CY, KING, Y1c, DOE, STEVENSON and CAPPS, all RM1c, CORKERN and SHIELDS, both RM2c. Also to be taken aboard were four bags of Officer Messenger mail, certain cryptographic aids and a radio receiver. A matter of moments before we left, it was learned that PILLSBURY was also leaving and would take another group of men. Upon boarding the PEARY in mid-afternoon, it was learned that she had been bombed several times that morning in the waters off Corregidor but had received no hits. Underway before dark, watches were stationed and our men were given battle lookout stations. The Commanding Officer informed me that my responsibility was to account for our men and, when informed that I was familiar with the cryptographic aids, to assist Ensign

C-O-N-F-I-D-E-N-T-I-A-L   January 10, 1942.

GILLILAND in that capacity; the latter having been assigned duty as Communication Officer. We were informed that enemy opposition was likely to occur and that our own protection was in six torpedoes, a 4" battery and .50 and .30 caliber machine guns. During the early part of the night, all hands who were not on watch participated in a "camouflage ship" operation consisting of the use of green paint, as it was intended to take advantage of island protection during the daytime. After dark, the Commanding Officer told us to go through his safe and to destroy anything which would not be needed on this one trip, the remainder to be suitably prepared for immediate destruction in case of attack which might lead to possible compromise of classified documents. All documents for immediate destruction were properly bagged, weighted and thrown overboard. This included the Electric Coding Machine, which was inoperative due to rupture by a shrapnel fragment. This operation was completed about midnight.

December 27, 1941.

Shortly after midnight, we suddenly seemed to have fallen with an enemy force consisting of ten or more ships. Of course, we were completely darkened and strange signals were seen being exchanged between the ships. By some turn of luck, none were directed at us and we managed to fall out of their most unwelcome company. Near sunrise, while in the process of entering a sheltered cove and while having practically no headway, five four-motored bombers were sighted. They were not very high but, due to our camouflage, it was thought that we were not spotted by then. Proceeded to a small cove at the tip of the island of Negros. Bancas came out to the ship and informed us that three ships (supposedly Jap) had left a short time before we arrived. Stayed pretty much under cover all day. Underway at dusk. During the night, we passed within close proximity to a ship. From observation possible, it looked as though it might have been a Cruiser.

December 28, 1941.

Kept underway. At about 8:00, one heavy bomber appeared in the distance and continued to keep very far distant. It would circle us at intervals, but for the most part kept on our port side. Attempt was made to exchange ANDUSREC signals with it, but no results were obtained. It was then considered to be a Jap bomber. During all this time, radio signals of MPO (Corregidor) were fair to good. Shortly before noon, the plane was joined by another. We received a message (from Comtaskfor-5, I believe) addressed to PEARY and PILLSBURY, but it was encrypted in a system which we did not hold. We then sent a

C-O-N-F-I-D-E-N-T-I-A-L   January 10, 1942.

message asking for a repeat in a system which we did hold (which were two) making PILLSBURY an information addressee. Getting no response, I took the message which we had sent down to the cabin in which we had our classified material and started to decode it, just to make sure there had been no error in it. Just as I had started to break it, word was passed "AIR ATTACK". Seemingly in a matter of seconds, the ship was attacked. My first reaction was in regard to the cipher which I was using and what other classified publications which we had. I emptied a handbag of clothes on the deck and packed the publications in it. During this time our machine guns were in action and I could hear the explosion of bombs fairly close. I started for the topside with the bag but, while passing through the wardroom, changed my mind as the planes were machine gunning us. I knew that we had not been hit by the bombs and figured it was safer below decks than it was on top side. I returned to the cabin and took shelter where I thought the most protection was afforded. Ensign GILLILAND's thoughts must also have been in regard to the safety of our publications, because he came down to do the same thing as I had done. This seemed to be the end of the attack, so we went on top side to the C.O.C. where our O.M. mail was stowed. During this attack, eight bombs were dropped, not believed to have been very heavy ones. The bombers were thought to have carried false insignias. No hits on the ship and no casualties to the crew.

Sometime near 1400, "AIR ATTACK" was called out again. Three planes had been sighted and were preparing for an attack on us. We figured that the next few moments might be pretty hot, so Ensign GILLILAND directed that the O.M. mail bags go over the side. This was done. Of this group, one was a bomber and two were torpedo planes. Machine gun fire was opened by PEARY and the Commanding Officer ordered the 4" battery manned and put in action. Mechanical operation of machine guns was excellent. The bomber dropped two bombs and the torpedo planes dropped two torpedoes each. They returned to machine gun us. The planes departed, evidently thinking that one of their bombs had hit us near the bow. No hits on the ship and no casualties to the crew.

At approximately 1630, when entering Makassar Strait parallel to Celebes Island and near the town of Menado (which was burning), three twin motored dive bombers were observed to be approaching us from the stern. "AIR ATTACK" was again called out and battle stations manned. Fire was opened on them. As they separated, preparatory to coming in on us from three directions, the British insignia was observed on the wings which left minds confused as to "what do now". Order was given to

C-O-N-F-I-D-E-N-T-I-A-L   January 10, 1942.

hold fire. However, one plane dived on us from astern, dropping two bombs approximately fifty yards behind us. Then there was only one alternative - to drive them off with all means at our disposal. Another plane dived on us from the port beam, dropping two bombs which landed near our port bow. The third plane dived on us from the starboard beam, dropping two bombs which landed near the port propeller guard rail. This came near to being a direct hit as it severed the wheel ropes, split open two depth charges and wounded several men aft. Hand steering was used and ship was only able to make eighteen knots. "MAN OVERBOARD" was called out. GREEN, Sealc, was overboard. It seems as though he lost his balance and fell overboard or was knocked overboard by the recoil of a 4" gun. He was a lookout on the after deck house. There was neither time nor opportunity to attempt a recovery. He was wearing a life jacket and was thrown a life ring by DOE, RM1c, (one of our men, who was also stationed as a lookout on the other deck house. When last seen, GREEN was swimming for the shore, which was about a half mile away. Natives in bancas were seen on the beach and there is every reason to believe he reached shore safely. At this same time DOE was hit in numerous places by flying shrapnel. An incision was made across his right temple, shrapnel in both buttocks and numerous minor wounds in back and legs. First aid to the temple wound was rendered by the ship's pharmacist's made and he was carried to the C.O.C. He laid him on a mattress and I examined him for other possible serious wounds. Applied bandage to what appeared to be a chin wound, using a first aid pack which was attached to my gun belt. Shrapnel seemed to be imbedded in the other places, so I did not bother it. No serious bleeding. On the flying bridge, QUENEAUX, Sealc (later found to be French-Canadian by birth), was struck in the head by a shrapnel fragment and killed instantly. As lookout, he, King, Y1c, and CAPPS, RM1c, (the latter two being our men), had been ordered to take over behind a pile of sand bags on the flying bridge. CAPPS received minor shrapnel cuts, while KING was uninjured. When the wheel ropes had been severed, the ship took hard left rudder and began to spin in a tight circle in the middle of the channel. Control was gained by means of hand steering. Then the rudder was completely dead, but was repaired in about ten minutes. While the above was going on, word was passed for a relief for QUENEAUX. Everyone else was busier than I, so I left DOE and went to the flying bridge and took station. By this time, the attack seemed to be over. It later developed that a Signalman, second class, had been hit by flying shrapnel just above the ankle, penetrating downward. Six bombs had been dropped during this attack, in addition to attack by machine gun fire. Holes had been made in the stern of the ship and she had begun to take

C-O-N-F-I-D-E-N-T-I-A-L   January 10, 1942.

some water. Her speed had been reduced to eighteen knots. Something went wrong with one of the thrust bearings. I seem to remember someone saying that the throttle to one engine had stuck on "FULL ASTERN" for a time. Steering cable was repaired and engine made operative again. Underway again and hoping for darkness to come because it was felt that the ship had taken about all she could for one day.

The preceeding paragraph is rather lengthy, when actually the elapsed time from start to finish was not very long.

About this time., we received a message (either from Comtaskfor-5 or CINCAF) which was a paraphrase of the one received earlier. When decoded, it informed us that a substantial Jap force was operating in our path down Makassar Straits. The ship's course was immediately altered and headed for the Molukka Passage, with the idea of beaching the ship when a suitable spot was found. This was found in the Halmahera Group. The exact spot was Malati Island, a small island between Ternate and Tedori Islands. We arrived at approximately midnight.

December 29, 1941.

The ship was brought up alongside the beach until she was on near bottom. The water was clear and bottom could easily be seen. Bow and stern lines were swam ashore and secured to coconut trees. Landing force equipment was assembled. As soon as it was light enough life rafts were used to carry coconut tree branches from the beach to the ship. Canvas painted green and coconut tree branches were used to camouflage the ship as completely as possible. The crew then moved ashore, locating our camp site approximately a quarter of a mile up the beach from the ship. Several natives were on hand. They were very friendly and anxious to help us in any way possible. Language spoken was Indonesian, but several could speak a little English. In fact, one fellow was very much interested in Hollywood. While looking through an Esquire magazine which someone happened to bring along, he would compare the Petty drawings to certain of the movie stars - naming them by name. .30 caliber machine guns, B.A.R.'s and all small arms were taken with us. Prior to leaving the ship, we sent a message telling where we were. We took a receiver and the necessary equipment ashore with us and set up a portable radio station near the top of a hill. Reception was good. Having had nearly no sleep or rest since leaving Corregidor, the Captain told all hands to turn in and sleep. Most everyone was up again about noon, so breakfast was served. Scrubbed out coconut hulls

C-O-N-F-I-D-E-N-T-I-A-L   January 10, 1942.

were used for plates. After breakfast, .30 caliber machine guns were dismantled and cleaned and ammunition belted. Earlier in the morning, the Captain visited Ternate, which seemed to be the capital, and contacted a Dutch Army official. Our wounded were also taken and given medical attention in their hospital. It was reported that the place had been bombed by the Caps about ten days previous, four bombs having been dropped. Women and children had been evacuated to Tedori. In the afternoon, two planes were sighted and all hands abandoned camp. An expression of relief was felt when it was found that they were our own PBY's. Heretofore, every plane we had seen had tried to blast us out of the water. The Captain went out and talked to the pilots. Upon his return, quarters were held and it was announced that, provided the ship was found seaworthy and fuel enough remained, we would depart the next day for Ambon Island. We were also informed that our supposition as to the identity of the aircraft in our last attack was correct - that they were Australian planes who were bombing what they thought was a Japanese Cruiser. They had been advised that no Allied ships were supposed to be in the vicinity. Previously, the Japs had bombed the village which we had seen burning and the usual procedure for them to follow was to bomb a place and follow it up with a landing party. It seemed quite natural to the R.A.A.F. that we were the expected landing party. The Captain told use that the preceeding was for our own information only and under no circumstances was it to be mentioned ashore. It later developed that each place we visited knew as much about it as we, if not more.

At about dusk, quarters were held and the body of QUENEAUX was brought from the ship. The Captain made one of the finest speeches in tribute of QUENEAUX that I have ever heard. All hands remained at "ATTENTION" while the Captain and a firing squad embarked in the boat and headed for the mouth of the channel toward the open sea. QUENEAUX's body was entrusted to the sea in a simple and sailorman's custom.

Engineer and fireroom personnel returned to the ship and worked all night patching holes and repairing the engines. After sundown, the remainder of the crew were allowed to take a bath and scrub clothes in the ocean. No potable water was found on our island. Mosquito nets were necessary, due to the presence of extremely large ants which became almost unbearable.

December 30, 1941.

Early reveille. .30 caliber machine guns were

C-O-N-F-I-D-E-N-T-I-A-L   January 10, 1942.

brought ashore and cleaned up. Ammunition was belted. During the morning, two PBY's came in to check up on us. We were informed that they would give us an air escort the following day. Also reported that our camouflage was very effective from the air. We moved back aboard during the afternoon. Underway at 1800 for Ambon with water only for drinking purposes and just enough fuel for the trip.

December 31, 1941.

Patrol planes picked us up and gave us air escort into Ambon. Arrived in mid afternoon. We were met by a Dutch tug which led us through the mine fields. Captain went over to the CHILDS and also contacted Compatwing-10. Their Doctor came aboard and examined the wounded. Water barge came alongside and gave us water. At 1600, we went alongside a dock and took on oil. Liberty was granted from 1800 to 2100. Ambon is a very small place with practically no activity at night. Water is not recommended for drinking. No place to eat ashore under favorable circumstances. There seemed to be an abundance of native troops stationed there and also a contingent of Australian soldiers. I contacted an Australian soldier ashore who was a chemist. He was buying up all available camera film. The purpose therefor was to extract the nitrate from the film in order to make flares. Their supply of flares had been exhausted. Ambon seems to have a great amount of Chinese inhabitants. The town has one American family. He is an ex-Seattle banker who is now a missionary. This family has been in Ambon for four years.

January 1, 1942.

Finished fueling and taking on water. A small Dutch Submarine stood out. The story was circulated that she originally had six torpedoes. She went out on a mission and sank two enemy ships and was now underway to sink four more - even if she had to go to the Philippines to do it. PEARY underway at 0900 for Port Darwin, Australia. We were escorted out by two of the same three planes which had bombed us on the 28th. The R.A.A.F. was very apologetic for their error and couldn't say or do enough for us to make up for their attack on us. It seems as though we were successful in registering several hits on one of their planes. At about 1600, a large four-motored transport plane passed over us. Deduced as Dutch. Our air escort left us at 1800.

January 2, 1942.

Sent a dispatch to Comtaskfor-5 stating that we had no charts or instructions on board for entering Port

C-O-N-F-I-D-E-N-T-I-A-L					January 10, 1942.

Darwin. Also, did not know whether or not the entrance was mined. Comtaskfor-5 readdressed it to GOLD STAR for action, by which we surmised that GOLD STAR must be in Port Darwin. When about fifteen miles out, we still have no instructions. We tried to contact GOLD STAR and Radio Coomawarra (Darwin), but with no results. Anchored for the night.

January 3, 1942.

PARROTT came out and brought us in. Upon anchoring, an officer who came aboard informed us that Commander Jeffs and Lieutenant Commander Linaweaver were based ashore in Darwin. Ensign Gilliland and I went ashore and contacted Lieutenant Commander Linaweaver. I requested that we go to some ship where medical attention could be rendered and where we could get some clean clothes. LANGLEY was suggested as it was acting as a communication center and most of our men were Radiomen. Ensign Hirst wished to stay in PEARY for duty as Communication Officer and his request was authorized. Remainder of Flag personnel shifted to LANGLEY.

January 4, 5, 6, 1942.

Lieutenant Commander Linaweaver came aboard LANGLEY and told King and I that we were required ashore to establish Headquarters, U.S. Navy, Port Darwin. We received orders from LANGLEY to report to ALUSNOB, Port Darwin, for temporary duty. We went ashore and established an office in a building formerly occupied by the Chief of Police. It is just at the rear of the Observer's office. Work consisted mainly of cryptographic work between Opnav, War Department, ALUSNOB and U.S. Army forces in Australia. In fact, I believe we were handling all of the Army's traffic, that is, the encoding and decoding of their traffic. Navy traffic is being handled through LANGLEY due to the fact that her equipment is the most powerful in the harbor. Lieutenant Commander Linaweaver is very busy as general co-ordinator between ship and shore, but seems to have no definite status. He would like to have clarification on that point. GOLD STAR is acting as general Station Ship. HOLLAND is Administrative SOPA. Lieutenant Commander Linaweaver intends to set up communications ashore but lack of equipment is a major obstacle. PENSACOLA dropped off nothing in the way of transmitters, etc., as was expected she would. Believe some steps have been taken to secure certain equipment from Adelade, Australia. He hopes to install an E.C.M. ashore and then tell Washington to use that system for traffic to the Army. An Issuing Officer is needed badly. He suggests that either Lieutenant Roeder come to Darwin

C-O-N-F-I-D-E-N-T-I-A-L				January 10, 1942.

or that Lieutenant Fahy, now in BLACK HAWK, be designated as Issuing Officer. A fleet Personnel Officer is needed - one who has records of what each has and who they are. He recommended that Lieutenant Commander McDill and Hartwich come down. Headquarters, U.S. Army Forces in Australia, is now located in Darwin.

      Port Darwin itself is somewhat of a non-descript place. Tide variation is about twenty eight feet I believe. Usually rains in the afternoon or night. The rainy season has just started. Mosquitos and other insects are very prevalent, especially at night, and they are Dengue Fever carriers. There is a movie house which, I believe, shows American movies. Usually full of Australian soldiers. A biweekly paper is published. There is an Australian Navy signal tower located on the landing. U.S. Navy Signalmen have been assigned to assist. Telephone service is available and orders have been issued that they be used as little as possible for personal calls. No taxiis are available. Two cars and two station wagons are assigned to naval activities ashore. Hotel Darwin, Ltd., is a one story wooden affair. As far as can be determined, the name "Hotel" is misleading. It mainly consists of a barber shop, pool tables and a good sized bar. It is open to the public and is thoroughly crowded each day with Australian soldiers until the beer supply for the day is exhausted. On the corner of the same block is the New Hotel Darwin which is a modern two story building. ALUSNOB is located here. Meals are available to persons living in the hotel or connected with Navy or Army activities ashore. It has two dining rooms - first and second class. Meals are satisfactory with the exception of coffee, which is terrible. Several heavy anti-aircraft batteries and an Australian Army contingent are located in close proximity. Blackout precautions at night are about the same as none at all. Auto headlights are somewhat dimmed, but not nearly as effective as was the case in the Philippines. Civil Defense Measures have been issued, seemingly effective upon the appearance of enemy action. The soldiers stationed here have seen no action as far as I could determine and do not seem particularly interested in the war. Several cases of criticism were heard in regard to England and her attitude toward her Dominion Possessions. The relieving of command of Chief Air Marshal Brooke-Popham seemed to be welcomed. His successor is held in high esteem. The news of the appointment of yourself as Commander in Chief of the Allied Naval Forces in the far East was received with enthusiasm. U.S. currency cannot be used for transactions ashore, but must be exchanged for local currency. This is possible at the Commonwealth Bank and at certain other private establishments. The exchange rate is $3.2484 for one Pound.

C-O-N-F-I-D-E-N-T-I-A-L				January 10, 1942.

January 7, 1942.

    Word was received that King and I were to report to BOISE for transportation. I made a circuit of the harbor to collect mail of all classifications for CINCAF and other units surmised to be in company. Received three bags of registered and ordinary mail from GOLD STAR. CHAUMONT had a large amount of mail in her holds which could not be reached until troops were disembarked and cargo cleared. Her Communication Officer has in his custody three bags of O.M. mail which is consigned to the Issueing Officer, 16th Naval District. I was advised that it should remain in Darwin until proper disposition was directed. I was also told that she carries a certain amount of mail for the U.S. Army Forces in the Philippines and for the city of Manila. King and I reported to the BOISE. Remainder of Flag personnel is in LANGLEY, with the exception of Capps, RM1c, who is ashore for duty in connection with the establishment of radio facilities. Ensign Gilliland is in LANGLEY in connection with communication duties. Ensign Hirst is in PEARY. When we departed, PEARY was alongside BLACK HAWK.

    A report on the equipment in the Flag Office of BOISE is handled in separate correspondence.

    2.   The foregoing is written from my own standpoint and views. The part concerning our engagement with the enemy while in PEARY is, naturally, written in the first person. During the complete voyage, the other men in my charge were standing lookout watches of a more or less continuous nature. They did it willingly and well.

    For the Commanding Officer, Officers and Crew of the PEARY, I have the highest admiration and deepest respect. There was perfect co-operation and co-ordination at all times. Their only thought was in saving the ship and wishing for more means at their disposal with which to meet the enemy.

                                     Respectfully submitted,

                                        H. B. BOAZ,
                             Chief Yeoman, U. S. Navy.

U.S.S. BOISE,
January 10, 1942.

Index to
Reminiscences of CWO Cecil S. King, Jr.

ABDA Afloat
  The remnants of the U.S. Asiatic Fleet staff set up shop under Admiral Thomas C. Hart as ABDA Afloat in Surabaya, Java, early in 1942, 193-195; comfortable living conditions ashore for staff members, 195

Accidents
  Lieutenant Commander Frank C. Fake crashed a glider while attempting to land at Coco Solo Fleet Air Base in Panama in the late 1930s, 61-62; King served as reporter for a court of inquiry following the crash of a Pan American plane in Panama in the late 1930s, 63-64; an experimental XP3D seaplane crashed in Acapulco, Mexico, in early 1937 with Rear Admiral Ernest J. King on board, 81-82; flight deck mishaps on board the carrier Hornet (CV-12) in 1943-44, 216-218; hangar deck accidents in the Hornet, 231-232

Advancement in Rating
  Because of the slow rate of advancement for enlisted men in the 1930s, it took King a considerable time to become a petty officer while stationed in Panama, 65-68, 77-78; advancement to chief petty officer at the beginning of World War II did not follow the prewar routine, 206; Radioman First Class George Tweed was advanced to chief radioman after the carrier Hornet (CV-12) recovered him from Guam in 1944, 234-236, 238; while serving in the yacht Sequoia (AG-23) in the 1930s, a yeoman advanced a coxswain to first class petty officer on the say-so of President Franklin D. Roosevelt, 236-238

Air Force, U.S.
  Vice Admiral John W. Reeves issued a good deal of paperwork in the late 1940s to make the Navy's case against the Air Force, 272-275

Alaska
  The heavy cruiser Portland (CA-33) fired her guns at the Columbia glacier during operations around Alaska in the mid-1930s, 48

Alcohol
  Navy recruits on liberty in San Diego in 1934 liked to pretend that they had drunk more than they actually had, 14-15; an officer in the heavy cruiser Portland (CA-33) in the mid-1930s was put in hack because of his liquor problem, 36; served as a center of gravity for liberty in Long Beach in the mid-1930s, 44; King had to serve as reporter for a court-material in Panama in the late 1930s because the regular yeoman he worked with had a drinking problem, 64-65; while serving in the destroyer Davis (DD-395) in the late 1930s, King bought some liqueur-filled candy for the ship's store, 102-103; King and a shipmate found liquor to be readily available at low prices in 1940-41 in Shanghai, China, 148-149; men on board the destroyer Peary (DD-226) greatly enjoyed quarts of Dutch

1

beer at Halmahera in December 1941, 191; the storeroom for beer on board the carrier Hornet (CV-12) in World War II had to be welded shut to prevent theft, 233-234; chief petty officers of the Hornet had several drinks to celebrate victory in the Battle of the Philippine Sea in June 1944, 240; Guantanamo Bay, Cuba, was a source of rum for warrant officers in the carrier Midway (CVB-41) in the early 1950s, 306

American Cancer Society
King worked as a volunteer fund-raiser in the 1970s and 1980s, 347, 349, 363-364

Anacostia (District of Columbia) Naval Station
Struck King as a dead-end sort of place when he served there briefly in the summer of 1952, 306-308

Antiair Warfare
Antiaircraft practice with the 5-inch guns of the cruiser Houston (CA-30) in 1941, 156-157; intense antiaircraft fire by U.S. warships in the Central Pacific in 1944, 227-228; a yeoman striker was killed on board the carrier Hornet (CV-12) in 1944 soon after moving to a 40-millimeter gun mount, 242-244

Antisubmarine Warfare
Several U.S. destroyers endured miserable weather while looking for German submarines in the Atlantic as part of the Grand Banks Patrol in 1939, 97

Argonne, USS (AS-10)
As flagship for Commander Base Force in 1940, her staff personnel office arranged inter-ship transfers for men, 112-115

Army, U.S.
Soldiers began arriving in the Philippines in late 1941 but did not inspire a great deal of confidence, 170-171; military policemen did not treat Navy men kindly on a cross-country train in the spring of 1943, 209

Asheville, North Carolina
Commander Frederick L. Ashworth provided King with rides home to Asheville, North Carolina, during proficiency flying time in the early 1950s, 298

Ashworth, Captain Frederick L., USN (USNA, 1933)
As executive officer of the carrier Midway (CVB-41) in the early 1950s, administration of personnel matters was included in his duties, 281-283; provided King with rides home to Asheville, North Carolina, during proficiency flying time, 298; viewed as a real gentleman, 299

Asiatic Fleet, U.S.
In the late 1930s, enlisted men with families sought to avoid overseas duty with the Asiatic Fleet, 100, 134; a

senior petty officer's voluntary request for transfer to the Asiatic Fleet was rare around 1940, 112-115; the fleet had a romantic, mystic air to it that attracted young sailors, 117-118, 134-135, 151-152; Chinese served as mess boys in Asiatic Fleet ships in 1940, even though they weren't officially part of the U.S. Navy, 121-122; enlisted men who retired from Asiatic Fleet duty often stayed on in the Far East as "bamboo Americans," 120, 123; work of the fleet staff on board the flagship in 1940-41, 124-130, 161-166, 171-173; conditions on board the Augusta (CA-31) and Houston (CA-30) as a result of being the fleet flagships, 131-134, 154-155; pride in being part of the fleet, 136-139, 144; oriental attractions for sailors on liberty around 1940, 142-144; the flag lieutenant for the fleet commander in chief cautioned new members of the staff to avoid contacts with Japanese while on liberty, 150-151; the pattern of operations for the fleet became more intense as war approached in 1941, 156-158; Chief Sid Zeramby was the colorful leader of the fleet band around 1940, 158-159; in 1941 King put together daily reports on the movements of fleet ships, 159-160; in 1941 members of the fleet staff were not formally given security clearances but got access to material by virtue of their jobs, 161; communications were upgraded in 1941, 161-162; in June 1941, the fleet staff moved ashore to the Marsman Building in Manila and encountered the Japanese frequently, 168-170; the staff went through pandemonium when war broke out in December 1941, then settled into a wartime routine, 173-174, 176-177; the remnants of the staff set up shop as ABDA Afloat in Surabaya, Java, early in 1942, 193-195

Athletics
　The heavy cruiser Houston (CA-30) was given preference when athletes were assigned to various warships in the mid-1930s, 24-25

Atomic Energy Commission
　Captain Frederick L. Ashworth was instrumental in getting King a job with the AEC in 1957, 299; impressed King as a hard-driving, mission-oriented outfit when he went to work there, 338-339; John McCone was an energetic chairman of the AEC from 1958 to 1961, 339-344; methodical Glenn T. Seaborg was chairman from 1961 to 1971, 343-345

Augusta, USS (CA-31)
　Heavy cruiser that had a variety of colorful characters on board while serving as flagship of the Asiatic Fleet in 1940-41, 118-122; Chinese served as mess boys in the ship in 1940, even though they weren't officially part of the U.S. Navy, 121-122; conditions on board as a result of being the fleet flagship, 131-134; comparison with the USS Houston (CA-30), which became fleet flagship in 1940, 154-155

Australia
   Crew members of the destroyer Peary (DD-226) arrived at Port Darwin in January 1942 and encountered an invasion of flying termites, 191-192; shore duty was quite pleasant for American Navy men in Perth in 1942, 198; the U.S. Navy's registered publications issuing office moved from Perth to Melbourne in the spring of 1942, 200-203; a Navy captain made contact with aborigines during a trip across country in 1942, 201

Aviation Maintenance
   The Douglas P2D patrol plane required carpenter's mates for maintenance at Coco Solo, Panama, in the late 1930s, 59

Ayrault, Lieutenant Arthur D., Jr., USN (USNA, 1921)
   Aristocratic officer who served as ship's secretary on board the heavy cruiser Portland (CA-33) in the mid-1930s, 35-36

Baker, Chief Boatswain Albert E., USN
   Pilot of an experimental XP3D seaplane that crashed in Acapulco, Mexico, in early 1937 with Rear Admiral Ernest J. King on board, 81-82

Battle Reports
   King served as stenographer during after-action debriefings of squadron pilots on board the carrier Hornet (CV-12) during World War II, 218, 241

Bermingham, Lieutenant Commander John M., USN (USNA, 1929)
   Commanded the destroyer Peary (DD-226) as she fled south from the Philippines in December 1941, 184-185; gave a moving tribute to an enlisted crew member killed in action, 191

Bermuda
   King met his future wife as the result of a foolish bet while he was on liberty in Bermuda in 1939, 93-94

Blacks
   Served only as mess attendants and stewards in the Navy of the 1930s but gradually came more and more into the mainstream of the service following World War II, 384-388

Boaz, Chief Yeoman Harold B., USN
   Served as admiral's writer for Admiral Thomas C. Hart, who was Commander in Chief Asiatic Fleet at the beginning of World War II, 129, 165; escaped to Australia on board the destroyer Peary (DD-226) in January 1942 to reconstitute part of the fleet staff as ABDA Afloat, 191-194

Boise, USS (CL-47)
   Had the nickname of "Reluctant Dragon" while transporting

former Asiatic Fleet staff members to Surabaya, Java, in early 1942, 193

Bombing
American Lockheed Hudsons mistakenly attacked the U.S. destroyer Peary (DD-226) while she approached Celebes in December 1941, 188-189

Bombs
A bomb cartwheeled down the deck of the carrier Hornet (CV-12) in World War II and caused a number of casualties, 217-218

Boston, Massachusetts
In 1939 a reporter for a Boston newspaper promoted a romance between King and a girl he had met on liberty in Bermuda, 95-97

Bradbury, Norris E.
Physicist from the Los Alamos laboratory who crossed the equator on board the carrier Franklin D. Roosevelt (CVA-42) in 1956, 332

Browning, Captain Miles R., USN (USNA, 1918)
Was dedicated and hard-driving as the first commanding officer of the carrier Hornet (CV-12) in 1943-44, 212, 219-220, 394-397; relieved of command in 1944, 229-231

Bruner, Commander Roy W., USN
Grandfatherly officer who was the Asiatic Fleet staff engineer at the outset of World War II, 163

Burke, Admiral Arleigh A., USN (USNA, 1925)
As Chief of Naval Operations in the mid-1950s, expected his enlisted administrative staff members to put in long hours on the job, 311-312, 321; offered King advice about asking for things, 313-314; issues dealt with as CNO, 320; had high regard for VCNO Donald Duncan, 322; working style as CNO, 322-325; made a point of seeing King while visiting the aircraft carrier Franklin D. Roosevelt (CVA-42) in 1956, 329-330

Camouflage
The four-stack destroyer Peary (DD-226) was covered with foliage and paint in December 1941 to try to keep her from being spotted by the Japanese as she fled from the Philippines to the Dutch East Indies, 182-183

Cannes, France
A warrant officer from the carrier Midway (CVB-41) had difficulties with a customs official in Cannes in the early 1950s, 295-296

Cape Horn
Site of stormy weather when the carrier Franklin D. Roosevelt (CVA-42) rounded the tip of South America in

1956, 332-333

Carnegie, USS (CVE-38)
Escort aircraft carrier commissioned in August 1943 at Tacoma, Washington, and soon turned over to the Royal Navy, 206-207

Carney, Admiral Robert B., USN (USNA, 1916)
Working style as Chief of Naval Operations in the early 1950s, 316-319, 389-390

Carr, Lieutenant Commander T. De Witt, USN (USNA, 1916)
As commanding officer of the destroyer Davis (DD-395) in the late 1930s, dispensed discipline in harsh, sometimes bizarre fashion, 90-91, 96, 107-109, 111; tried to make a good impression on Captain Louis E. Denfeld, the embarked commander, 109-110

Carroll, Lieutenant Herbert C., USN
Provided outstanding service as an assistant to Chief of Naval Operations Robert B. Carney in the early 1950s, 317-318, 389-390

Casualties of War
A number of Navy personnel were killed or wounded when the Japanese attacked Cavite on 10 December 1941, 163, 174-175; a USS Peary (DD-226) crew member was killed when the ship was mistakenly attacked by Lockheed Hudsons in December 1941, 188, 190-191; a bomb cartwheeled down the deck of the carrier Hornet (CV-12) in World War II and caused a number of casualties, 217-218; a yeoman striker on board the Hornet was killed in 1944 soon after he got a battle station on a 40-millimeter gun mount, 242-244

Cavite (Philippines) Navy Yard
A number of Navy personnel were killed or wounded when the Japanese attacked Cavite on 10 December 1941, 163, 174-175

Celebes
The destroyer Peary (DD-226) landed at the town of Menado while escaping from the Japanese in December 1941, 187-190

Chaplains
A chaplain at recruit training in San Diego in 1934 directed King to write home to his parents because he had been lax about doing so, 17; chaplains on board the carrier Midway (CVB-41) in the early 1950s were likely to be sympathetic to requests for emergency leave, 304-305

Chaumont, USS (AP-5)
Colorful transport that carried sailors and Marines to the Asiatic Fleet in the spring of 1940, 115-118

Chief of Naval Operations, Office of
   Administrative running of the office in the early 1950s, 308-325; Admiral Arleigh Burke expected his enlisted staff members to put in long hours on the job, 311-312

China
   Local merchants sold a variety of items to U.S. Navy men who visited various ports in this country shortly before World War II, 140-142; exotic liberty attractions in Tsingtao in 1940-41, 142-143; sailors mostly had social contacts with White Russians in Shanghai in 1940-41, 144-145; when U.S. Navy ships visited Chinwangtao shortly before World War II, sailors threw coins for the Chinese coolies to dive for, 145-146; Americans were hassled by Japanese in Shanghai in period shortly before World War II, 146-148, 150-151; King and a shipmate found liquor to be readily available at low prices in Shanghai in 1940-41, 148-149; rickshaw drivers attached themselves to American sailors who went ashore in Shanghai, 151-152; Japanese soldiers put on an impressive show when they marched in Tsingtao shortly before World War II, 169-170

Chinese
   Served as mess boys in Asiatic Fleet ships in 1940, even though they weren't officially part of the U.S. Navy, 121-122; merchants sold a variety of items to U.S. Navy men who visited various ports in China shortly before World War II, 140-142; when U.S. Navy ships visited Chinwangtao shortly before World War II, sailors threw coins for the Chinese coolies to dive for, 145-146; rickshaw drivers attached themselves to American sailors who went ashore in Shanghai, 151-152

Chinwangtao, China
   When U.S. Navy ships visited this port shortly before World War II, sailors threw coins for the Chinese coolies to dive for, 145-146

<u>Cincinnati</u>, USS (CL-6)
   King and his brother nearly tangled with crew members of this cruiser while on liberty in Manila in 1941, 137-138

Clark, Rear Admiral Joseph J., USN (USNA, 1918)
   Colorful task group commander embarked in the carrier <u>Hornet</u> (CV-12) in 1944, 220-223, 233-236

Classified Information
   In 1941 members of the Asiatic Fleet staff were not formally given security clearances but got access to material by virtue of their jobs, 161; the crew of the destroyer <u>Peary</u> (DD-226) dropped classified material overboard when attacked by the Japanese in December 1941, 186

Clement, Colonel William T., USMC
   As senior Marine officer on the Asiatic Fleet staff at

the outset of World War II, he was held in awe by those with whom he served, 163-164

Coco Solo (Panama) Fleet Air Base
Living accommodations for enlisted personnel in the late 1930s, 57-58; the base operated mostly patrol aircraft in the late 1930s, 59-60; Lieutenant Commander Frank C. Fake crashed a glider while attempting to land at the base in the late 1930s, 61-62; King and a radioman created an uproar in the late 1930s by concocting a fake news report that indicated the U.S. embassy in China had been bombed, 69-72; office routine for yeomen, 76-77; while on liberty in Panama in the late 1930s, sailors found liberty both in the town of Colon and on the fleet base at Coco Solo, 84-85; homosexual court-martialed and imprisoned in the late 1930s, 383-384

Colon, Panama Canal Zone
While on liberty in Panama in the late 1930s, sailors found liberty both in the town of Colon and on the fleet base at Coco Solo, 84-85

Columbus
German passenger liner that was scuttled by her crew in December 1939 after being pursued by U.S. and British warships, 97-98, 111

Communications
King mishandled a radio message regarding the USS Gold Star (AG-12) prior to a visit she made to Hong Kong around 1940, 125-127; security war upgraded in the Asiatic Fleet as war approached in 1941, 161-162

Continuous Service Certificates
In the late 1930s, the records of Navy enlisted men, including continuous service certificates, were maintained by yeomen, 103-105; Captain John Hoskins of the carrier Princeton (CV-37) threw away King's CSC during an unpleasant exchange in 1946, 262

Corpus Christi (Texas) Naval Air Station
An overzealous Marine guard hassled Rear Admiral Ernest W. Litch about leaving the base in the late 1940s, 268-269

Corregidor
Members of the Asiatic Fleet staff were evacuated to this island fortress in Manila Bay after Manila was declared an open city on Christmas of 1941, 181-182

Courts of Inquiry
See Investigations

Courts-Martial
King had to serve as reporter for a court-material in Panama in the late 1930s because the regular yeoman he

worked with had a drinking problem, 64-65; homosexual court-martialed and imprisoned at Coco Solo Fleet Air Base in the late 1930s, 383-384

Cuba
Guantanamo Bay was a source of rum for warrant officers in the carrier <u>Midway</u> (CVB-41) in the early 1950s, 306

Customs
A warrant officer from the carrier <u>Midway</u> (CVB-41) had difficulties with a customs official in Cannes, France, in the early 1950s, 295-296; customs officials in Norfolk, Virginia, seemed shrewd about who had what items, 296-297

Darwin, Australia
Crew members of the destroyer <u>Peary</u> (DD-226) arrived here in January 1942 and encountered an invasion of flying termites, 191-192

<u>Davis</u>, USS (DD-395)
Destroyer that went into commission in late 1938 under an eccentric commanding officer, Lieutenant Commander T. De Witt Carr, 90-91, 96, 107-111; visited Bermuda on her shakedown cruise in 1939, 93-94; served in the North Atlantic as part of the Grand Banks Patrol in 1939, 97, 109-110; King ran the small ship's store, 102-103; operation of the ship's office in the late 1930s, 103-105; comparison with cruiser duty, 105; encounters with crew members from other destroyers, 356-357

Denfeld, Captain Louis E., USN (USNA, 1912)
Proved to be capable and confident while serving as Commander Grand Banks Patrol in the USS <u>Davis</u> (DD-395) in 1939, 97, 109-110

Discipline
King learned that the Navy had a no-nonsense way of living when he went through recruit training at San Diego in 1934, 13-14; an officer in the heavy cruiser <u>Portland</u> (CA-33) in the mid-1930s was put in hack because of his liquor problem, 36; not a big problem on board the <u>Portland</u>, 54-55; as commanding officer of the destroyer <u>Davis</u> (DD-395) in the late 1930s, Lieutenant Commander T. De Witt Carr dispensed discipline in harsh, sometimes bizarre fashion, 90-91, 96, 107-109, 111; handling of captain's mast cases on board the carrier <u>Midway</u> (CVB-41) in the early 1950s, 300-303; a chief master at arms in the <u>Midway</u> compelled an enlisted man to get rid of a number of pistols stored in his locker in the early 1950s, 380-381

Dixon, Chief Ship's Clerk Joseph R. Dixon, USN
Warrant officer who helped ease King's transition to that status on board the carrier <u>Midway</u> (CVB-41) in 1950, 281-282; suggested that King relieve him in the office of the

Chief of Naval Operations in the summer of 1952, 308

Drinking
See Alcohol

Drugs
Opium and marijuana were available to sailors of the U.S. Asiatic Fleet around 1940 but were seldom purchased, 143

Duncan, Admiral Donald B., USN (USNA, 1917)
While serving as Vice Chief of Naval Operations in the mid-1950s, was held in high regard by CNO Arleigh Burke, 322

Dutch East Indies
The destroyer Peary (DD-226) landed at the town of Menado, Celebes, while escaping from the Japanese in December 1941, 187-190; the Peary beached at Halmahera for temporary repairs in December 1941 before going to Ambon and then on to Australia, 190-191; the remnants of the U.S. Asiatic Fleet staff set up shop as ABDA Afloat in Surabaya, Java, early in 1942, 193-195; comfortable living conditions ashore for staff members, 195; a group of U.S. Navy men had an all-night poker game on board the Dutch passenger ship Zandam at Tjilatjap, Java, in early 1942, 196-197

Education
Public schools in Texas in the 1920s and 1930s had a demanding curriculum, 4-5

Enlisted Personnel
Recruit training at San Diego in 1934, 11-21; the heavy cruiser Houston (CA-30) was given preference when athletes were assigned to various warships in the mid-1930s, 24-25; living and working routine for men on board the heavy cruiser Portland (CA-33) in the mid-1930s, 26-45, 52-57; liberty in various Pacific ports in the mid-1930s, 43-51; enjoyed reading Our Navy magazine in the 1930s, 51-52; living accommodations at Coco Solo Fleet Air Base in Panama in the late 1930s, 57-58; because of the slow rate of advancement for enlisted men in the 1930s, it took King a considerable time to become a petty officer while stationed in Panama, 65-68; some of the enlisted men in the Portland were quite well educated, 68; while in Panama in the late 1930s, sailors found liberty both in the town of Colon and on the fleet base at Coco Solo, 84-85; in the late 1930s, enlisted men with families sought to avoid overseas duty with the Asiatic Fleet, 100; in the late 1930s, the records of Navy enlisted men, including continuous service certificates, were maintained by yeomen, 103-105; the staff personnel office for Commander Base Force arranged inter-ship transfers for men in 1940, 112-115; men who served in the Asiatic Fleet in the 1930s and early 1940s often had colorful personalities, 118-121; enlisted men who retired

from Asiatic Fleet duty often stayed on in the Far East as "bamboo Americans," 120, 123; enlisted men of the Asiatic Fleet were prohibited from marrying foreigners prior to World War II, 135-136; oriental attractions for sailors on liberty around 1940, 142-144; advancement to chief petty officer at the beginning of World War II did not follow the prewar routine, 206; enlisted personnel sometimes got flight pay while on the staff of the Chief of Naval Air Training circa 1950, 275-276; role of the personnel office on board the carrier Midway (CVB-41) in the early 1950s, 279-288, 300-305

Fake, Lieutenant Commander Frank C., USN
　　Naval aviator who crashed a glider while stationed at Coco Solo, Panama, in the late 1930s, 61-62

Falcon, USS (ASR-2)
　　Submarine rescue ship that towed targets in the vicinity of Panama in the late 1930s while under the command of colorful Lieutenant (j.g.) Richard E. Hawes, 86-87

Families of Servicemen
　　In the late 1930s, enlisted men with families sought to avoid overseas duty with the Asiatic Fleet, 100; enlisted men of the Asiatic Fleet were prohibited from marrying foreigners prior to World War II, 135-136; King had difficulty arranging to be with his wife when their first child was born with a curved spine in 1946, 256, 261; enlisted family quarters on Ford Island in Pearl Harbor provided great creature comforts for occupants in the late 1940s, 266-267; in the early 1950s, King's pay as a warrant officer working in the Pentagon was so low that he had to have a part-time job to support his family, 312-313

Fechteler, Admiral William M., USN (USNA, 1916)
　　Working style as Chief of Naval Operations in the early 1950s, 314-316, 319

Fighting Squadron Two (VF-2)
　　King served as stenographer during debriefings of squadron pilots on board the carrier Hornet (CV-12) during World War II, 218, 241

Fishing
　　President Franklin D. Roosevelt embarked in the heavy cruiser Houston (CA-30) for a fishing trip in the Galapagos in 1935, 37-39; while serving as Chief of Naval Air Training in the late 1940s, Vice Admiral John W. Reeves liked to go fishing often near Pensacola, Florida, 269-271

Fitness Reports
　　Admiral Robert C. Carney was unusually brief in writing a fitness report on Lieutenant Herbert Carroll of the CNO's office in the early 1950s, 317

Flowers, Yeoman First Class, USN
　While serving in the yacht Sequoia (AG-23) in the 1930s, advanced a coxswain to first class petty officer on the say-so of President Franklin D. Roosevelt, 236-238

Food
　Role of mess cooks in preparing meals on board the heavy cruiser Portland (CA-33) in the mid-1930s, 27-30; Chinese cooked fine meals while serving in the USS Augusta (CA-31) in 1940, 122; U.S. sailors on liberty in China in 1940-41 sometimes ate chicken of dubious origin, 142-143; members of the ABDA Afloat staff ate enjoyable Dutch food in Surabaya, Java, in early 1942, 195; hungry chief petty officers devoured a basket of hamburgers on a cross-country train in 1943, 209-210; Japanese prisoners on board the carrier Hornet (CV-12) in World War II ate hotcake sandwiches, 222; King was so preoccupied during one combat action that he didn't even realize he was eating a steak sandwich, 226-227

France
　A warrant officer from the carrier Midway (CVB-41) had difficulties with a customs official in Cannes in the early 1950s, 295-296

Franklin D. Roosevelt, USS (CVA-42)
　Not as well built as sister ship Midway (CVA-41), illustrated by engineering problems in mid-1950s, 326-327; not as clean or as good an operating ship as the Midway, 327-328; voyage from the Pacific to the Atlantic around Cape Horn in 1956, 331-333

Galapagos Islands
　President Franklin D. Roosevelt embarked in the heavy cruiser Houston (CA-30) for a fishing trip in the Galapagos in 1935, 37-39

Gambling
　A group of U.S. Navy men had an all-night poker game on board the Dutch passenger ship Zandam at Java in early 1942, 196-197; a gambler in the crew of the carrier Hornet (CV-12) in World War II was probably thrown over the side, 224; a sailor on board the USS Midway (CVB-41) staged a successful robbery from the participants in a crap game in the early 1950s, 376-380

Ginder, Commander Samuel P., USN (USNA, 1916)
　Paid for the babysitting of his young son while assigned as executive officer of Coco Solo Fleet Air Base in the late 1930s, 62

Gliders
　Lieutenant Commander Frank C. Fake crashed a glider while attempting to land at Coco Solo Fleet Air Base in Panama in the late 1930s, 61-62

Gold Star, USS (AG-12)
   King mishandled a message regarding this Guam station ship prior to a visit she made to Hong Kong around 1940, 125-127

Grand Banks Patrol
   Several U.S. destroyers endured miserable weather while looking for German submarines in the Atlantic in 1939, 97, 109-110

Guam
   Radioman First Class George Tweed was advanced to chief radioman after the carrier Hornet (CV-12) recovered him from Guam in 1944, 234-236, 238

Guantanamo Bay, Cuba
   Source of rum for warrant officers in the carrier Midway (CVB-41) in the early 1950s, 306

Gunnery--Naval
   Target practice with the 8-inch and 5-inch guns on board the heavy cruiser Portland (CA-33) in the mid-1930s, 31-33; antiaircraft practice with the 5-inch guns of the cruiser Houston (CA-30) in 1941, 156-157; intense antiaircraft fire by U.S. warships in the Central Pacific in 1944, 227-228

Guns
   Operation of the 8-inch and 5-inch guns on board the heavy cruiser Portland (CA-33) in the mid-1930s, 31-33; procedure for operating the 5-inch guns on board the cruiser Houston (CA-30) in 1941, 156-157

Habitability
   Navy recruits at San Diego in 1934 fell to the deck until they got used to sleeping in hammocks, 12-13; sailors slept in bunks on board the heavy cruiser Portland (CA-33) in the mid-1930s, 55-56; bedbugs were a problem in the barracks for enlisted personnel at Fleet Air Base Coco Solo in Panama in the late 1930s, 57-58; enlisted family quarters on Ford Island in Pearl Harbor provided great creature comforts for occupants in the late 1940s, 266-267

Halmahera
   The destroyer Peary (DD-226) beached here for temporary repairs in December 1941 before going to Ambon and then on to Australia, 190-191

Hart, Admiral Thomas C., USN (USNA, 1897)
   Demonstrated a great deal of competence while serving as Commander in Chief U.S. Asiatic Fleet, 1939-42, 128-130, 165-166; met with British Vice Admiral Tom S. V. Phillips at Manila in December 1941, 167-168; the remnants of the U.S. Asiatic Fleet staff set up shop under Admiral Thomas

C. Hart as ABDA Afloat in Surabaya, Java, early in 1942, 193-195

Hawaii
Enlisted quarters on Ford Island in Pearl Harbor provided great creature comforts for occupants in the late 1940s, 266-267

Hawes, Lieutenant (junior grade) Richard E., USN
Colorful skipper of the submarine rescue ship Falcon (ASR-2) when she towed targets in the vicinity of Panama in the late 1930s, 86-87

Hayward, Captain John T., USN (USNA, 1930)
Offered to take King in the crew of the carrier Franklin D. Roosevelt (CVA-42) when he got command in 1956, 313-314; demonstrated air of confidence and polish while commanding the Franklin D. Roosevelt, 329-330, 332

Hirst, Ensign William B., Jr., USNR
Served as a communication watch officer on the Asiatic Fleet staff before being killed on board the destroyer Peary (DD-226) in 1942, 126-127, 191-192

Ho, Chief Commissary Steward Jimmy, USN
Served in the Asiatic Fleet flagships in 1940, later joined the U.S. Navy and ran the mess of the Secretary of the Navy in Washington, D.C., 122-123

Homosexuals
In the mid-1930s, sailors in the heavy cruiser Portland (CA-33) discussed two establishments in San Francisco as being havens for homosexuals, 50-51; case of a mess cook in the chiefs' mess of the USS Hornet (CV-12) in World War II, 382-383; case at Coco Solo Fleet Air Base in Panama in the late 1930s, 383-384

Hornet, USS (CV-12)
Some crew members from the previous Hornet (CV-8) were in the new one when she was commissioned in 1943, 210-212; Captain Miles R. Browning was dedicated and hard-driving as the first commanding officer, 212, 219-220, 394-397; periodic preparation of personnel lists was a challenge when the ship was first in service, 213-215; combat operations in 1943-44, 215-218, 225-228, 238-240, 242-244; flight deck mishaps in 1943-44, 216-218; Rear Admiral Joseph J. Clark was a colorful task group commander embarked in the ship in 1944, 220-223, 233-236; burials at sea, 224-225; Captain Browning relieved of command in 1944, 229-231; hangar deck accidents, 231-232; general quarters alerts, 245-246; case of a homosexual mess cook in the chiefs' mess, 382-383

Hoskins, Captain John M., USN (USNA, 1921)
As the first commanding officer of the carrier Princeton (CV-37) in 1945-46, proved difficult for King to get

along with, 250-255, 261-264; rumored to have a continuing vendetta against King when ordered to ComAirPac in the late 1940s, 265-266

Houston, USS (CA-30)
Heavy cruiser that got preference when athletes were assigned to various warships in the mid-1930s, 24-25; embarked President Franklin D. Roosevelt for a fishing trip to the Galapagos Islands in 1935, 37; comparisons with the USS Augusta (CA-31), which was Asiatic Fleet flagship until the Houston took over in 1941, 154-155; Captain Jesse B. Oldendorf had the loyalty of the crew while commanding the ship in 1941, 165

Hunte, Lieutenant (junior grade) Louis H., USN (USNA, 1927)
Naval aviator who made guard mail runs in an O2U while assigned to Panama in the late 1930s, 60

Hudson
Lockheed bombers that mistakenly attacked the U.S. destroyer Peary (DD-226) as she approached Celebes in December 1941, 188-189, 191

Identification Cards
Gray card issued to King in 1957 at the time of his retirement from active duty, 334-335

Indianapolis, USS (CA-35)
Heavy cruiser that was considered quite attractive in appearance when she went into commission in the early 1930s, 25-26

Ingram, Commander Carlyle, USN (USNA, 1934)
As executive officer of the carrier Midway (CVB-41) in the early 1950s, was involved in investigating a shipboard robbery, 380

Ink, Dwight
Government official for whom King worked at the Atomic Energy Commission in the 1960s and for the Price Commission in the 1970s, 345-347

Inspections
Personnel and seabag inspections conducted frequently at recruit training at San Diego in 1934, 20; mess cooks in the heavy cruiser Portland (CA-33) in the mid-1930s were given frequent inspections for venereal disease, 52; Vice Admiral John Dale Price noticed pinup pictures of girls during inspections of aviation commands in the early 1950s, 276; King prepared the personnel office of the carrier Midway (CVB-41) for an administrative inspection in the early 1950s, 305-306

Intelligence
In 1941 the Japanese collected information about members of the Asiatic Fleet staff ashore in Manila, 168-169

Investigations
   King served as reporter for a court of inquiry following
   the crash of a Pan American plane in Panama in the late
   1930s, 63-64; men from the Office of Naval Intelligence
   came aboard the USS Midway (CVB-41) after a shipboard
   robbery in the early 1950s, 378-380; ONI capture of an
   enlisted man who was stealing from shipmates in the
   Midway in the early 1950s, 381-382

Japanese
   Hassled Americans in Shanghai, China, in the period
   shortly before World War II, 146-148, 150-151; gathered
   intelligence about members of the Asiatic Fleet staff in
   Manila in 1941, 168-169; Japanese soldiers put on an
   impressive show when they marched in Tsingtao, China,
   shortly before World War II, 169-170; a Japanese warship
   did not identify the destroyer Peary (DD-226) as she fled
   south from the Philippines in December 1941, 184-185; an
   Emily seaplane made an unsuccessful attack against the
   Peary, 186; survivors of sunk Japanese ships spent a
   brief time on board the carrier Hornet (CV-12) in 1944,
   221-223; some jumped overboard during refueling, 223

Java
   The remnants of the U.S. Asiatic Fleet staff set up shop
   under Admiral Thomas C. Hart as ABDA Afloat in Surabaya
   early in 1942, 193-195; comfortable living conditions
   ashore for staff members, 195; a group of U.S. Navy men
   had an all-night poker game on board the Dutch passenger
   ship Zandam at Tjilatjap in early 1942, 196-197; King
   made his own plans as to what he would do if the Japanese
   invaded Java, 204-205

King, Chief Warrant Officer Cecil S., Jr., USN (Ret.)
   Boyhood years and education in Texas in the 1920s and
   1930s, 1-7; parents of, 1-3, 5-10, 21, 199-200, 349-350,
   365-368; brothers of, 1, 5-6, 134-135, 137-138, 142-143,
   181-183, 202-203, 350, 368; recruited into the Navy in
   1934, 7-10; recruit training at San Diego in 1934, 11-21;
   duty as a junior enlisted man in the heavy cruiser
   Portland (CA-33) in 1934-35, 25-57, 354-356, 360; became
   a rated yeoman while serving at Coco Solo Fleet Air Base
   in Panama from 1935 to 1938, 57-87; reenlisted in the
   Navy in 1938 after a brief period of civilian life, 88-
   90; served in the new destroyer Davis (DD-395) from 1938
   to 1940, 90-99, 102-112, 356-357; was married to
   Catherine Jackman, 1939-43, after meeting her as the
   result of a bet, 93-95, 100-101, 210; served briefly in
   the USS Warrington (DD-383) in 1940, 99-101; transfer to
   the Asiatic Fleet in 1940, 112-117; service on the staff
   of Commander in Chief Asiatic Fleet, 1940-42, 118-173;
   long, involved escape from the Japanese after the outset
   of hostilities in World War II, 173-194, 362, 372-373;
   served as part of staff of Commander ABDA Afloat in Java
   in early 1942, 194-195; was evacuated to Australia for

some easy shore duty in 1942, 195-205; had a series of temporary assignments in mid-1943, 205-210; duty as a chief yeoman in the new carrier Hornet (CV-12), 1943-44, 210-246, 382-383, 394-397; Emily Westall became King's second wife in 1945, 210-212, 251, 256, 261; brief service at Naval Air Station Minneapolis in early 1945, 247-249; service in the aircraft carrier Princeton (CV-37) in 1945-46, 250-264; children of, 251, 261; service on the ComAirPac staff in the late 1940s, 264-267; duty in various Atlantic Fleet aviation commands in the late 1940s, 267-277; promotion to warrant officer in 1950, 277-278; service in the carrier Midway (CVB-41), 1950-52, 279-306, 374-382; brief service at Anacostia Naval Station in 1952, 306-308; duty in the office of the Chief of Naval Operations, 1952-56, 308-325; service in the carrier Franklin D. Roosevelt (CVA-42), 1956-57, 325-333; painful retirement from active duty in 1957, 333-336; post-retirement work for the Atomic Energy Commission, 335-347; work as a volunteer for the American Cancer Society in the 1970s and 1980s, 347, 349, 363-364

King, Emily Westall
Met King at Norfolk and married him in 1945, 210-212; needed help in 1946 when first child had a birth defect, 251, 256, 261; helped sell cookware in the mid-1950s to make ends meet financially, 312-313; encouraged husband to retire from active duty in 1957, 334; work as a volunteer for the American Cancer Society in the 1970s, 347

King, Rear Admiral Ernest J., USN (USNA, 1901)
Was nearly killed in early 1937 when the seaplane in which he was riding crashed in Acapulco, Mexico, 80-82; prescribed some unusual uniform combinations while embarked in the USS Wright (AV-1) in the late 1930s, 82-83

Leave and Liberty
Navy recruits on liberty in San Diego in 1934 liked to pretend that they had drunk more than they actually had, 14-15; dance halls were popular with sailors, 16-17; Long Beach, California, had a number of attractions for sailors on liberty in the mid-1930s, 43-44; sailors from the heavy cruiser Portland (CA-33) went on liberty in Hawaii in the mid-1930s, 47-48; San Francisco was viewed by sailors as a glamorous liberty port in the mid-1930s, 50-51; Navy men had to wear civilian clothes when on liberty in Panama at 11:00 P.M. in the late 1930s, 58-59; while on liberty in Panama in the late 1930s, sailors found liberty both in the town of Colon and on the fleet base at Coco Solo, 84-85; King met his future wife as the result of a foolish bet while he was on liberty in Bermuda in 1939, 93-94; King and his brother nearly tangled with crew members of the cruiser Cincinnati (CL-6) while on liberty in Manila in 1941, 137-138; oriental attractions for sailors on liberty around 1940,

142-144; the flag lieutenant for Commander in Chief Asiatic Fleet cautioned new members of the staff to avoid contacts with Japanese while on liberty, 150-151; rickshaw drivers attached themselves to American sailors who went ashore in Shanghai, China, 151-152; the Asiatic Fleet band played for dances when sailors went on liberty in Tsingtao, China, around 1940, 158-159; U.S. Navy men were very popular with the citizens of Perth, Australia, in early 1942, 198; a group of chief petty officers took over a San Francisco hotel for a three-day liberty in the spring of 1943, 207-208; a warrant officer from the carrier Midway (CVB-41) had difficulties with a customs official in Cannes, France, in the early 1950s, 295-296; King established a basket-leave program in the Midway in the early 1950s, 303-304; chaplains on board the Midway (CVB-41) were likely to be sympathetic to requests for emergency leave, 304-305; the pleasure of talking with fellow Navy men while on liberty in the 1930s, 354, 359

Le Breton, Captain David M., USN (USNA, 1904)
As commanding officer of the heavy cruiser Portland (CA-33) in the mid-1930s, maintained an active correspondence with Broadway greats Alfred Lunt and Lynn Fontanne, 32; role in target practice incident on board the ship while in command, 32-33; fired the Portland's guns at a glacier in Alaska, 48

Lewis, Lieutenant Richard P., USN
Mustang officer with whom King did not get along well when both served in the carrier Princeton (CV-37) in 1945-46, 251-255, 263-264

Litch, Rear Admiral Ernest W., USN (USNA, 1920)
Flag officer who was inconvenienced along with his family by an overzealous Marine guard at the Corpus Christi Naval Air Station in the late 1940s, 268-269

Long Beach, California
Offered a number of attractions for sailors on liberty in the mid-1930s, 43-44

Macon, USS (ZRS-5)
Dirigible that operated with the fleet in the Pacific before crashing off Point Sur, California, in February 1935, 46-47

Mahlmann, Chief Boatswain's Mate Ernest R., USN
Became something of a legend in the Navy as the "Pantless Gunner of Panay" for his efforts in defending the USS Panay (PR-5) when she was attacked by the Japanese at Nanking, China, in December 1937, 79-80

Mail
A chaplain at recruit training in San Diego in 1934 directed King to write home to his parents because he had been lax about doing so, 17

Maintenance
    The Douglas P2D patrol plane required carpenter's mates for maintenance at Coco Solo, Panama, in the late 1930s, 59

Malta
    The airstrip was difficult for landings in the early 1950s, 294

Manila, Philippines
    King and his brother nearly tangled with crew members of the cruiser Cincinnati (CL-6) while on liberty in Manila in 1941, 137-138; in June 1941, the Asiatic Fleet staff moved ashore to the Marsman Building in Manila and encountered the Japanese frequently, 168-169; the city suffered only limited Japanese attacks when war began in December 1941, 175-176; declared an open city on Christmas of 1941, 178-180; condition of war-torn city in 1946, 259-260

Marine Corps, U.S.
    A puckish Marine allegedly painted a humorous legend on the stern of the transport Chaumont (AP-5) around 1940, 115-116; Colonel William Clement was the highly regarded senior Marine on the Asiatic Fleet staff at the outset of World War II, 163-164; an overzealous gate guard hassled Rear Admiral Ernest W. Litch about leaving Corpus Christi Naval Air Station in the late 1940s, 268-269

Marshall, Captain William J., USN (USNA, 1925)
    Had a loud telephone voice while serving as senior aide to the Chief of Naval Operations in the early 1950s, 318

Massachusetts, ex-USS (BB-2)
    Decommissioned battleship whose wrecked hulk provided a good site for fishing near Pensacola, Florida, in the late 1940s, 270

McCain, Vice Admiral John S., USN (USNA, 1906)
    While serving as commanding officer of Coco Solo Fleet Air Base in Panama in the late 1930s, chewed out King for a prank involving false news reports, 69-72; recounted the prank when he ran into King at Manus, New Guinea, in 1944, 73-74; McCain was a colorful character with a lot of class, 72, 74-75; King has written to McCain's grandson, a U.S. senator, 374

McCain, Rear Admiral John S., Jr., USN (USNA, 1931)
    While serving as Chief of Information in the early 1960s, struck King as having a quieter nature than this father, who was also an admiral, 374-375

McCone, John A.
    Former businessmen who was an energetic chairman of the Atomic Energy Commission from 1958 to 1961, 339-344

McKillip, Lieutenant John C. S., USN (USNA, 1926)
While serving at Fleet Air Base Coco Solo in Panama in the 1930s, was involved in trying to get to the bottom of a prank perpetrated by enlisted men, 69-72; aided King in his attempts to get advanced in rating, 77

Medical Problems
Recruits suffered from sunburn at boot camp in San Diego in 1934, 13; venereal disease was rare on board the heavy cruiser Portland (CA-33) in the mid-1930s, 52-54; a fireman suffered heat prostration and died on board the carrier Hornet (CV-12) in World War II, 225; King had difficulty arranging to be with his wife when their first child was born with a curved spine in 1946, 256, 261; in the early 1950s Vice Admiral John Dale Price decided not to go through with an operation intended to remove a malignant growth behind his ear, 276-277

Mendenhall, Ensign Gerald W., USN
Mustang officer who helped King get a transfer from Naval Air Station Minneapolis in early 1945, 248-249

Mediterranean Sea
Operations of the carrier Midway (CVB-41) as part of the Sixth Fleet in the early 1950s, 292-294

Mexico
An experimental XP3D seaplane crashed in Acapulco in early 1937 with Rear Admiral Ernest J. King on board, 81-82

Midway, USS (CVB-41)
Operation of the ship's personnel office in the early 1950s, 279-288, 300-305; atmosphere on board ship, 288-290; role of the warrant officers as specialists in the early 1950s, 290-292; operations in the Mediterranean, 292-294; a warrant officer from the ship had difficulties with a customs official in Cannes, France, in the early 1950s, 295-296; customs officials in Norfolk seemed shrewd about who had what items, 296-297; handling of captain's mast cases on board in the early 1950s, 300-303; initiation of basket-leave procedures, 303-304; chaplains were likely to be sympathetic to requests for emergency leave, 304-305; successful administrative inspection in the personnel office, 305-306; outshone sister ship Franklin D. Roosevelt (CVA-42) in a number of categories, 326-328; a crew member staged a successful robbery from the participants of a shipboard crap game in the early 1950s, 376-380; a chief master at arms compelled an enlisted man to get rid of a number of pistols stored in his locker in the early 1950s, 380-381; capture of a sailor who was stealing money from shipmates in the early 1950s, 381-382

Minneapolis (Minnesota) Naval Air Station
Served as a stopover point for aircraft passing through in early 1945, 247-249

Moorer, Lieutenant Thomas H., USN (USNA, 1933)
PBY pilot who may have made a contact report on the destroyer Peary (DD-226) as she approached Celebes in December 1941, 187-190, 372-374

Murphy, Lieutenant Mike, USN
Limited duty officer who took a limited view of his duties while supervising the administration of the office of the Chief of Naval Operations in the early 1950s, 309-310

Music
Chief Sid Zeramby was the colorful leader of the Asiatic Fleet band around 1940, 158-159

Naval Intelligence, Office of
Men from the Office of Naval Intelligence went aboard the USS Midway (CVB-41) to investigate after a shipboard robbery in the early 1950s, 378-380; ONI capture of an enlisted man who was stealing from shipmates in the Midway in the early 1950s, 381-382

New Jersey, USS (BB-62)
Opened up with intense antiaircraft fire against Japanese planes one night in 1944, 227-228

News Media
In 1939 a reporter for a Boston newspaper promoted a romance between King and a girl he had met on liberty in Bermuda, 95-97

Nilon, Lieutenant Leo W., USN (USNA, 1927)
As flag lieutenant for Commander in Chief Asiatic Fleet shortly before World War II, cautioned new members of the staff to avoid contacts with Japanese while on liberty, 150-151

O2U Corsair
Vought observation plane with handcrank starter, used for guard mail runs by a utility squadron based at Coco Solo, Panama, in the late 1930s, 60

Oldendorf, Captain Jesse B., USN (USNA, 1909)
Had the loyalty of his crew while in command of the cruiser Houston (CA-30) in 1941, 165

Our Navy Magazine
Popular with enlisted men on board ship in the mid-1930s, 51-52

P2D
Old Douglas patrol plane that required carpenter's mates

for maintenance at Coco Solo, Panama, in the late 1930s, 59

Panama
The climate of the country was such that personnel at Fleet Air Base Coco Solo were on tropical working hours in the late 1930s, 57-58; Navy men had to wear civilian clothes when on liberty in Panama at 11:00 P.M. in the late 1930s, 58-59; O2U Corsair was used for guard mail runs from Coco Solo to Balboa in the late 1930s, 60; King served as reporter for a court of inquiry following the crash of a Pan American plane in the late 1930s, 63-64; while on liberty in Panama in the late 1930s, sailors found liberty both in the town of Colon and on the fleet base at Coco Solo, 84-85; the submarine rescue ship Falson (ASR-2) towed targets in the vicinity of Panama in the late 1930s while under the command of colorful Lieutenant (j.g.) Richard E. Hawes, 86-87

Pan American Airways
King served as reporter for a court of inquiry following the crash of a Pan American plane in Panama in the late 1930s, 63-64

Panay, USS (PR-5)
The sinking of this gunboat by the Japanese at Nanking, China, in December 1937 served notice on the rest of the Navy that war was approaching in the Far East, 79-80

Pay and Allowances
Pay for Navy junior enlisted men in the mid-1930s was low but sufficient, 17, 43; former members of the U.S. Asiatic Fleet staff in Java in January 1942 were paid in Dutch currency, 196-197; enlisted personnel sometimes got flight pay while on the staff of the Chief of Naval Air Training circa 1950, 275-276; in the early 1950s, King's pay as a warrant officer working in the Pentagon was so low that he had to have a part-time job to support his family, 312-313

Pearl Harbor, Hawaii
Enlisted family quarters on Ford Island provided great creature comforts for occupants in the late 1940s, 266-267

Peary, USS (DD-226)
Four-stack destroyer that fled southward from Corregidor in the Philippines on 26 December 1941 to evacuate Navy men to the Dutch East Indies, 182-188, 362, 372-373; attacked by Lockheed Hudsons while approaching Celebes, 188-189; beached for temporary repairs at Halmahera before going to Ambon and then on to Australia, 190-192; sunk at Port Darwin, Australia, in February 1942, 192, 203

Personnel
  See Enlisted Personnel

Philippines
  King and his brother nearly tangled with crew members of the cruiser Cincinnati (CL-6) while on liberty in Manila in 1941, 137-138; the Asiatic Fleet gunnery officer was wounded when the Japanese attacked Cavite Navy Yard on 10 December 1941, 163; in June 1941, the Asiatic Fleet staff moved ashore to the Marsman Building in Manila and encountered the Japanese frequently, 168-169; U.S. soldiers began arriving in late 1941 but did not inspire a great deal of confidence, 170-171; Manila suffered only limited Japanese attacks when war began in December 1941, 175-176; Manila was declared an open city on Christmas of 1941, 178-180; Asiatic Fleet staff members were evacuated to Corregidor on 26 December, 181-182; the carrier Princeton (CV-37) took the body of President Manuel Quezon back to the Philippines in mid-1946, 256-257, 261; condition of war-torn Manila in 1946, 259-260

Philippine Sea, Battle of
  The USS Hornet (CV-12) was one of a number of aircraft carriers that fought in this dramatic battle off the Marianas in June 1944, 238-240

Phillips, Vice Admiral Sir Tom S. V., RN
  British flag officer who conferred about strategy with Admiral Thomas Hart and General Douglas MacArthur in Manila in December 1941, 167-168

Photography
  A panoramic camera allowed a chief petty officer to play a trick in a recruit training company photo at San Diego in 1934, 19

Pilots
  Chief Boatswain Albert E. Baker was pilot of an experimental XP3D seaplane that crashed in Acapulco, Mexico, in early 1937 with Rear Admiral Ernest J. King on board, 81-82; King served as stenographer during debriefings of squadron pilots on board the carrier Hornet (CV-12) during World War II, 218, 241; a dead Hornet pilot was pushed over the side in his plane, 224-225; Commander Frederick L. Ashworth provided King with rides home to Asheville, North Carolina, during proficiency flying time in the early 1950s, 298

Portland, USS (CA-33)
  Heavy cruiser that was considered quite attractive in appearance when she went into commission in the early 1930s, 25-26; living and working routine for enlisted men on board in the mid-1930s, 26-30, 45, 55-56, 354-356, 360; operation of the 8-inch and 5-inch guns during target practice, 31-33; work of the captain's office in handling correspondence, 33-36, 46-47; an officer in the

ship was put in hack because of his liquor problem, 36; went to the Galapagos Islands in 1935 for a fishing trip in which President Franklin D. Roosevelt visited the ship, 37-39; scraping of the ship's bottom while in dry dock at Bremerton, Washington, 39-41; liberty opportunities for the crew in various ports in the mid-1930s, 43-51; venereal disease was rare, 52-54; discipline was not a big problem, 54-55; some of the enlisted men in the Portland were quite well educated, 68; comparison with Asiatic Fleet flagship Augusta (CA-31), 154-155

Price, Vice Admiral John Dale, USN (USNA, 1916)
Highly respected while serving as Commander Air Force Pacific Fleet in the late 1940s, 264-265; service as Chief of Naval Air Training in the early 1950s, 275-277

Princeton, USS (CV-37)
New aircraft carrier that went into commission in late 1945 at Philadelphia under Captain John M. Hoskins, 250-256, 261-264; took the body of President Manuel Quezon back to the Philippines in mid-1946, 256-257; shakedown cruise following commissioning, 257-259

Prisoners of War
Survivors of sunk Japanese ships spent a brief time on board the carrier Hornet (CV-12) in 1944, 221-223; some jumped overboard during a transfer attempt, 223

Promotion of Officers
King became a warrant ship's clerk in 1950 following 16 years of service as an enlisted man, 277-278

PT Boats
Evacuated Navy men from Manila when the city was being attacked by the Japanese in December 1941, 180-181

Puget Sound Navy Yard, Bremerton, Washington
The crew of the heavy cruiser Portland (CA-33) scraped barnacles from her bottom while she was in dry dock here in the mid-1930s, 39-41; relations between sailors and yard workers, 48-49; scant liberty opportunities in Bremerton in the 1930s, 49-50

Quezon, Manuel
Former Philippine President whose body was returned to Manila by the carrier Princeton (CV-37) in mid-1946, 256-257

Queneaux, Seaman First Class K. E., USN
USS Peary (DD-226) crew member who was killed when the ship was attacked by Lockheed Hudsons in December 1941, 188, 190; buried ashore, 225

Railroads
King and other chief petty officers had an interesting

time while riding a train across the United States in mid-1943, 208-210

Recruit Training
Being sunburned and falling out of hammocks were two of the difficulties recruits had to face at boot camp in San Diego in 1934, 11-14; fatherly Chief Petty Officer Adams was in charge of King's boot camp company, 12, 18-19; a chaplain at recruit training in 1934 directed King to write home to his parents because he had been lax about doing so, 17; the curriculum in 1934 was more practical than academic, 19-21; sailors expressed varying preferences for their first sea duty, 22

Recruiting
Cecil King, Sr., was turned down by a Navy recruiter in Texas early in World War II because he was overage and had false teeth, 6; recruiters in Corpus Christi and Houston, Texas, got Cecil King, Jr., into the Navy in 1934 by selling security and travel, 7-10

Reeves, Vice Admiral John W., Jr., USN (USNA, 1911)
While serving as Chief of Naval Air Training in the late 1940s, liked to go fishing often near Pensacola, Florida, 269-271; demanding officer with a strong temper, 271-272; issued a good deal of paperwork in the late 1940s to make the Navy's case against the Air Force, 272-275

Refueling
While taking on oil at sea in World War II, the carrier Hornet (CV-12) tried to transfer Japanese prisoners to the oiler, but some jumped overboard, 223

Registered Publications
The U.S. Navy's registered publications issuing office in Perth, Australia, moved to Melbourne in the spring of 1942, 200-203

Relief, USS (AH-1)
Sailors who rode this hospital ship from San Diego to Long Beach in 1934 were awed by the sight of a dead aviator in the ship's morgue, 23-24

Retirement
King found it painful to leave active duty when the time came in 1957, 333-336

Robinson, Lieutenant Commander James M., USN (USNA, 1925)
Asiatic Fleet gunnery officer who was wounded when the Japanese attacked Cavite Navy Yard on 10 December 1941, 163

Roosevelt, Franklin D.
President for whom the heavy cruiser Houston (CA-30) was a favorite in the 1930s, 24, 37; demonstrated his political skills during a visit to the heavy cruiser

Portland (CA-33) in 1935, 38-39; while serving in the yacht Sequoia (AG-23) in the 1930s, a yeoman advanced a coxswain to first class petty officer on the say-so of President Roosevelt, 236-238

Rosenblatt, Lieutenant Herman S., USNR
Involved in the advancement to chief petty officer of Radioman George Tweed after the carrier Hornet (CV-12) recovered Tweed off Guam in 1944, 235-236, 238

San Diego, California
Site of recruit training for new Navy men in 1934, 11-14; provided a number of opportunities for young sailors on liberty in 1934, 14-15; dance halls were popular with sailors on liberty, 16-17; local merchants got sailors involved in time payment plans for merchandise in 1934, 18-19

San Francisco, California
Viewed by sailors as a glamorous liberty port in the mid-1930s, 50-51; a group of chief petty officers took over the Turk Hotel for a three-day liberty in the spring of 1943, 207-208

Seaborg, Glenn T.
Highly methodical individual who served as chairman of the Atomic Energy Commission from 1961 to 1971, 343-345

Security
In 1941 members of the Asiatic Fleet staff were not formally given security clearances but got access to material by virtue of their jobs, 161

Sequoia, USS (AG-23)
In the 1930s, a yeoman advanced a coxswain in this yacht's crew to first class petty officer on the say-so of President Franklin D. Roosevelt, 236-238

Service Records
In the late 1930s, the records of Navy enlisted men, including continuous service certificates, were maintained by yeomen, 103-105

Shanghai, China
U.S. sailors had social contacts mostly with White Russians in 1940-41, 144-145; Americans were hassled by Japanese in the period shortly before World War II, 146-148, 150-151; King and a shipmate found liquor to be readily available at low prices in 1940-41, 148-149; rickshaw drivers attached themselves to American sailors who went ashore in Shanghai, 151-152

Sikorsky, Igor I.
Aircraft designer who testified at a Navy court of inquiry in Panama following the crash of a Pan American plane in the late 1930s, 64

Slocum, Captain Harry B., USN (USNA, 1919)
Was humorless and businesslike while serving as operations officer for the Asiatic Fleet, 1940-42, 125; bawled out King for not sending a prewar message in time but later saved him when Asiatic Fleet staff members were being evacuated at the outset of World War II, 127-128, 173, 179; trusted King to prepare daily movement reports on fleet ships in 1941, 159-160; helped establish ABDA Afloat staff in Java in January 1942, 194; while serving in the Bureau of Personnel in the spring of 1943, helped King with a set of orders, 206

Smoking
On board the heavy cruiser Portland (CA-33) in the mid-1930s, smoking by enlisted men was not only condoned but expected, 30-31; on board the carrier Hornet (CV-12) in World War II, Rear Admiral Joseph Clark smoked at movies on board the Hornet, even when others were prohibited, 234

Sturgeon, USS (SS-187)
Submarine that evacuated a number of former Asiatic Fleet staff members from the Dutch East Indies to Australia in early 1942, 128, 197-198

Surabaya, Java
The remnants of the U.S. Asiatic Fleet staff set up shop under Admiral Thomas C. Hart as ABDA Afloat here early in 1942, 193-195; comfortable living conditions ashore for staff members, 195

Swimming
King became overly ambitious during swim call from the heavy cruiser Portland (CA-33) while on a trip to the Galapagos Islands in 1935, 37-38

Szymanski, Boatswain's Mate F. J. USN
Disciplined King while serving in the heavy cruiser Portland (CA-33) in the mid-1930s, 54

Target Practice
The submarine rescue ship Falcon (ASR-2) towed targets in the vicinity of Panama in the late 1930s while under the command of colorful Lieutenant (j.g.) Richard E. Hawes, 86-87; antiaircraft practice with the 5-inch guns of the cruiser Houston (CA-30) in 1941, 156-157

Tattoos
King had a pig and rooster tattooed on his feet in the late 1930s in Panama because of a superstition that it would save him from drowning, 152-153; a chief photographer took a picture of King's tattooed feet on board the carrier Hornet (CV-12) in June 1944, 240

Terry, Lieutenant Paul A., USN
   Hard-working individual who served as flag lieutenant to the Chief of Naval Air Training in the late 1940s, 273-274

Thach, Captain John S., USN (USNA, 1927)
   While serving at Pensacola in the late 1940s, helped develop propaganda to make the Navy's case against the Air Force, 273

Tjilatjap, Java
   A group of U.S. Navy men had an all-night poker game on board the Dutch passenger ship Zandam here in early 1942, 196-197

Training
   Boot camp at San Diego provided a demanding regimen for Navy recruits in 1934, 11-14; the curriculum in 1934 was more practical than academic, 19-21; target practice with the 8-inch and 5-inch guns on board the heavy cruiser Portland (CA-33) in the mid-1930s, 31-33; training manuals were used by enlisted men studying for specific ratings in the late 1930s, 67

Tsingtao, China
   Exotic attractions for U.S. sailors on liberty in this city in 1940-41, 142-143; the Asiatic Fleet band played for dances when sailors went on liberty in Tsingtao around 1940, 158-159; Japanese soldiers put on an impressive show when they marched in Tsingtao shortly before World War II, 169-170

Tweed, Radioman First Class George R., USN
   Advanced to chief radioman after the carrier Hornet (CV-12) recovered him from Guam in 1944, 234-236, 238

Uniforms--Naval
   Recruits wore white uniforms with leggings at boot camp in San Diego in 1934, 13; Rear Admiral Ernest J. King prescribed some unusual uniform combinations while embarked in the USS Wright (AV-1) in the late 1930s, 82-83; enlisted men in the U.S. Asiatic Fleet around 1940 bought tailor-made uniforms decorated with embroidery, 141

Utility Squadron One (VJ-1)
   When an aviator in this squadron was killed in the late 1930s, Captain John S. McCain of Coco Solo Fleet Air Base handled the situation with compassion and understanding, 74-75; Chief Boatswain Albert E. Baker of VJ-1 was pilot of an experimental XP3D seaplane that crashed in Acapulco, Mexico, in early 1937 with Rear Admiral Ernest J. King on board, 81-82

Varian, Lieutenant Donald C., USN (USNA, 1925)
   As executive officer of the destroyer Warrington (DD-383)

in the spring of 1940, expressed misgivings over the way in which King requested a transfer to the Asiatic Fleet, 112-115

Venereal Disease
Was not much discussed as part of the curriculum of recruit training at San Diego in 1934, 20-21; rare on board the heavy cruiser Portland (CA-33) in the mid-1930s, 52-54

VF-2
See Fighting Squadron Two

Warrant Officers
Comparison of status and responsibility of warrant officers with the role of chief petty officers around 1950, 278-282; role of the warrant officers as specialists on board the carrier Midway (CVB-41) in the early 1950s, 290-292; in the early 1950s, King's pay as a warrant officer working in the Pentagon was so low that he had to have a part-time job to support his family, 312-313

Warrington, USS (DD-383)
Destroyer with hard-driving officers during King's brief tenure in the crew in the spring of 1940, 99-101; executive officer D. C. Varian was unhappy with the manner in which King requested transfer from the Warrington to the Asiatic Fleet in 1940, 112-115

Wassell, Lieutenant Commander Corydon M., MC, USNR
Navy doctor who treated injured men at Tjilatjap, Java, in January 1942, 197

WAVES
A young woman naval officer was embarrassed when heckled by enlisted men at San Francisco in the spring of 1943, 205-206

Women
A young woman naval officer was embarrassed when heckled by enlisted men at San Francisco in the spring of 1943, 205-206

Wright, USS (AV-1)
Was serving as flagship for Rear Admiral Ernest J. King, Commander Aircraft Base Force, in early 1937 when the seaplane in which he was riding crashed in Acapulco, Mexico, 80-82; Admiral King prescribed some unusual uniform combinations while embarked in the Wright in the late 1930s, 82-83

Wren, Chief Yeoman, USN
Retired to the chiefs' quarters while serving in the USS Davis (DD-395) in the late 1930s and left the running of the ship's office to King, 103-104

VJ-1
   <u>See</u> Utility Squadron One

XP3D
   Experimental seaplane that crashed in Acapulco, Mexico, in early 1937 with Rear Admiral Ernest J. King on board, 81-82

<u>Zandam</u>
   A group of U.S. Navy men had an all-night poker game on board this Dutch passenger ship at Java in early 1942, 196-197

Zeramby, Chief Musician Sid, USN
   As the colorful leader of the Asiatic Fleet band around 1940, worked on interesting arrangements for various pieces of music, 158-159

www.ingramcontent.com/pod-product-compliance
Lightning Source LLC
Chambersburg PA
CBHW080624170426
43209CB00007B/1508